D1116475

# JAYHAWK

# JAYHAWK

Love, Loss, Liberation and Terror over the Pacific

JAY A. STOUT WITH GEORGE L. COOPER

**CASEMATE**
*Philadelphia & Oxford*

Published in the United States of America and Great Britain in 2020 by
CASEMATE PUBLISHERS
1950 Lawrence Road, Havertown, PA 19083, USA
and
The Old Music Hall, 106–108 Cowley Road, Oxford OX4 1JE, UK

Hardcover Edition: ISBN 978-1-61200-883-7
Digital Edition: ISBN 978-1-61200-884-4

A CIP record for this book is available from the British Library

Printed and bound in the United States of America by Sheridan

Typeset by Versatile PreMedia Service (P) Ltd

For a complete list of Casemate titles, please contact:

CASEMATE PUBLISHERS (US)
Telephone (610) 853-9131
Fax (610) 853-9146
Email: casemate@casematepublishers.com
www.casematepublishers.com

CASEMATE PUBLISHERS (UK)
Telephone (01865) 241249
Email: casemate-uk@casematepublishers.co.uk
www.casematepublishers.co.uk

# Contents

# Preface

Most of them were dead. My previous book, *Air Apaches,* focused on the mightily armed B-25 crews of the 345th Bomb Group and the low-level air war they fought against the Japanese. The very few gentlemen that I interviewed for it served during the latter part of World War II. I was unable to get accounts of the group's early fighting from anyone still extant.

I wasn't even certain there were any left alive. That is, I assumed virtually everyone who had fought the early, bloody air battles over Rabaul and other iconic targets in the southwest Pacific had "gone West." More bluntly, I thought they were all dead. And my elementary school math skills supported that thinking. With very few exceptions, the pilots assigned to a combat unit in 1943 were 21, or older. That would have made them 96—at the youngest—when I wrote *Air Apaches* in 2018.

But not long after the book was published, I received a message from Laurie Putthoff whose father, George Cooper, flew with the 345th's 499th Bomb Squadron, the "Bats Outta Hell." Laurie had ordered the book for George. "I'm sure Dad would love to talk to you if you have the time. He just turned 99 in February and is a little hard of hearing, but still sharp and remembers many of his 74 missions. Maybe you could give him a call some time?"

I did and am grateful for it. George L. Cooper joined the 345th in South Carolina when it was formed in 1942, and subsequently flew in many of the group's early and most desperate air battles. Directly from him I learned more about what it was like to fly heavily armed B-25s at astonishingly low altitudes into the teeth of fierce Japanese air defenses. But George's story—and that of his family—is more than air combat. And it is a story that is real and that tells, more richly than most, the whole of what the World War II experience was about.

Indeed, my recently developed relationship with this man is one that I treasure, and one which obviously produced this book. And it is a book that I believe is unique and special for many reasons. Firstly, it is a story about family and love—aspects that are seldom discussed in other accounts of air combat.

And it covers George's years growing up in the Philippines, an experience that was shared by few if any other wartime pilots. Moreover, the greatest part of George's air combat took place in the southwest Pacific, a theater of war that in terms of coverage has always taken a back seat to the fighting in Europe and elsewhere.

George is now 100 years old. Very few people can share with us what the Philippines of the late 1920s—a period which is very much in George's memory—looked and felt and smelled like. And it is likely that no one else can give a detailed, firsthand account of the arrival of the great flying boat, the *China Clipper*, over Manila Bay on that sultry November day in 1935. And almost certainly, there is no one left who shares a similar combat career—one that started in New Guinea and ended in Japan.

With all these reasons as background, I hope that you enjoy reading this book as much as I reveled in writing it. And I additionally hope that you agree it is both a distinctive and intimate story that can only be told by a man who—by many measures—is the very last of his time.

# Acknowledgements

Much gratitude goes to Colonel Cooper—George—and his family for all the support they have provided during the year it has taken to put this book together. I'm grateful not only for their enthusiasm and energy, but also for their willingness to share photos, letters, notes and other writings from members of the family who are now gone. George's daughter Laurie Putthoff has been especially helpful in ensuring that I got familial details correct and made good suggestions relevant to the rest of the manuscript.

Likewise, I'm grateful to the team at Casemate Publishers who recognized the value of this book. This was a story that was too good to lose, and I'm glad it will be shared with a broad audience.

And of course, I acknowledge and am thankful for the support of my own family because … well, they're my family and they haven't poisoned me in my sleep. Yet. And I love our dogs.

# Prologue

George Cooper had never seen anything like the magnificently deadly panorama into which he was hurtling as he cleared the ridge and skimmed his B-25 down the backside of the jungle-clad mountain. High above, dozens of fighters turned and tossed and tumbled about each other in deadly, close-quarter gunfights. Losers fell in flames—smoke trails marked their paths.

Below and ahead, George saw other B-25s racing low and fast over the Japanese-held town of Rabaul; their dark forms cast dark shadows as they sped only 50 feet or so above the ground. Behind them, the bright white forms of small parachutes speckled the scene. Suspended below them were fragmentation bombs—too small to see from such a distance until they exploded in bright, white–orange flashes.

The B-25s fired their guns. Tracers arced down into buildings, supply stores, boats, and aircraft. Tracers also sprayed up from the ground as the Japanese defenders fired their antiaircraft guns after the American attackers. One or more of them found their mark; George winced as a B-25 tumbled to the ground and disappeared in a blinding flash of fuel and bombs.

Larger caliber antiaircraft guns added to the terror. Their big, explosive shells burst brightly and then blotched the sky with ugly black smears. In the harbor, Japanese warships added to the chaos with their guns, both large and small.

George checked that the bomb bay doors were open as he and his crew prepared to drop their deadly load. In his hand, he felt the control yoke tremble ever so slightly as the doors vibrated in the airstream. Ahead, he identified the enemy position onto which he intended to drop his bombs.

At the same time, a flight of Japanese fighters plummeted down onto George's squadron. Behind him, he heard and felt *Jayhawk*'s top turret guns fire after the enemy aircraft. One of the fighters flashed in front of the formation and a B-25 from the adjacent flight turned hard after it before stopping directly above George and his flight. The other aircraft's bomb bay doors opened as it readied to make its attack. George cursed its pilot over the radio and hauled his aircraft hard into a bank.

An instant later, bombs started rippling down from the other B-25.

## CHAPTER I

# "Kiss Your Mother Good-Bye"

It was a muggy Manila day in March 1940 when George Cooper waved down from the deck of the *Laura Maersk*. His mother and father, arm-in-arm in the hot sun, waved back from where they stood on the smooth, worn timbers of the pier. Beyond them, the hurly-burly of men and ships and machinery that characterized life on the city's docks continued unperturbed by the Coopers and their farewell.

George's father let go of his mother's arm and started toward the ship's gangway. George checked his pockets reflexively; perhaps he had forgotten his wallet or passport or some other important document. At the top of the gangway, his father turned and strode steadily toward him. "George," his father said as he stopped in front of him, "I think you should go back down and kiss your mother goodbye."

A few minutes later, George held his mother's tear-streaked face, then pulled her close as she buried her head in his shoulder. It was at that moment that he shed forever his callow young man's idea of what was masculine and what was not. Never again would he be embarrassed at showing tenderness and love to those he held dearest.

Behind him, the ship's horn blasted and the shouts of the crew intensified. He kissed his mother one more time, hugged her tight, let go and said goodbye a final time.

\*\*\*

George's father, Lawrence A. Cooper, was a spirited and charismatic man who had been born on the other side of the world in Peabody, Kansas, in 1882. It was the twilight of the Wild West, a time during which the last of the buffalo and the Indians who depended on them were pushed onto tiny reservations that were the worst bits of a rich and vast geography. As a youngster,

Lawrence played in prairie grass that grew as tall as a man, and raced horses at breakneck speeds over the plains that spread flat and seemingly endlessly below the Flint Hills.

Ranching and farming required hard work—work that was sometimes dangerous. He endured cuts and bruises but recalled that his sister Gertrude suffered worst. While playing in the barn, a hay hook fell and sliced her scalp which poured forth prodigious quantities of blood. Another day, working in the field with a corn knife, Lawrence accidentally severed her forefinger at the first knuckle. Indeed, injuries and illnesses were a regular part of life.

Still, the family prospered. However, in 1902 they left the farm in the care of a relative and moved to Lawrence, Kansas, where they opened a rooming house in a brick building that still stands. And Lawrence—always a precocious student—attended Kansas University where he excelled at journalism. Many years before, his mother had watched the school's first buildings rise out of the ground and vowed to herself that one day her children would study there. Lawrence realized his mother's dream, graduated in 1907, and arrived in the Philippines in June of that year as part of a wave of American teachers eager to spread the gospel of education as it was practiced in the United States.

But he was not a naïve rube on an altruistic lark. Rather, he had taught in a one-room schoolhouse before going to college, had spent time as a reporter in revolutionary Mexico, and had taken a steamship around the world. Moreover, he was proficient in seven languages. In return for his experience and talent he was promised a salary of 2,800 pesos, or about 1,400 dollars per year.

The Philippines was being molded into something it had never been. Once a multiplicity of diverse tribes and cultures spread across thousands of islands, the archipelago had been conquered and colonized by Spain beginning in the 16th century. And more recently, the Philippines had been ceded to the United States in 1898 following the Spanish–American War. America was keen to remake its new prize into, if not its own image, then an educated and modern nation with a similar form of government, and with sympathetic ideas and ideals.

Nevertheless, those efforts started slowly as the Filipinos, having only just been freed from centuries of sometimes harsh Spanish rule, quite understandably chafed against trading one colonial master for another. The Filipino revolutionary forces that once fought to expel the Spanish now turned against the Americans. However, it soon became apparent that they could not win, and they finally surrendered in 1902, although scattered insurgencies lasted into the next decade.

Despite the fighting—and sometimes tragic cruelties—the United States genuinely sought to improve the lives of the Filipino people, and education was made a priority. Schools were built wherever American soldiers were garrisoned, and the soldiers themselves often served as teachers. Whereas the Spanish had concentrated on educating the elite—and with an emphasis on religion—the Americans made primary education compulsory, and spiritual convictions were generally left outside the classroom. Hundreds of teachers began arriving from the United States beginning in 1901, and schools were soon being raised in the remotest corners of the islands.

The Americans were keen not only to spread their own sensibilities, but also to give the Filipinos a sense of nationhood and a common language. At that time, although Spanish was the language of the government and the elite, more than a hundred other languages and dialects were also spoken. Naturally, the Americans taught in English and it soon displaced Spanish and became widespread throughout the archipelago. Aside from basic subjects, importance was also attached to teaching the vocational arts, as well as health and hygiene; declines in the death rate from diseases such as cholera and dysentery were coincident with the arrival of the Americans.

Bringing education to the Filipinos required an almost missionary zeal. It was a type of enthusiasm embodied by Lawrence Cooper who quickly showed himself to be an excellent teacher with an innate capacity for organization and leadership. He was quickly promoted to superintendent of schools for one of the more remote districts, Ilocos Norte, located in the northwest part of Luzon Island. There, his responsibilities included not only the administration of established schools, but also the creation of new ones.

His recollection of a ten-day, horseback circuit through his district during a typhoon underscored his guts and grit. On his way to visit one of his schools, he stopped at the edge of a coastal stream that the storm's heavy rainfall had turned into a ferocious torrent during the few hours since he had crossed it from the other side. Wild water from the river crashed violently into head-high waves blown in from the sea.

Fearful of being trapped in the typhoon with no food or shelter, he nudged his horse into the water. "A few more steps and the mare was swimming," he recalled. "The breakers were rolling in from the sea with increasing violence. A big one reached us and immersed us completely. I and my horse were swept upstream several yards by the breaker. As it spent itself, it rolled back carrying us toward the sea. For a few moments I was in desperate panic. My mare had her nose under the water and I feared that both of us would be carried out to sea."

Lawrence slid from the horse's back and swam alongside her. "We made some progress forward until another breaker again caught us," he said. "We were again hurled upstream. Freed of my weight on her back, the mare kept her head out of the water this time and I clung desperately to her, holding to the saddle by her side." Man and horse, battered in turn by current and waves, struggled together until finding footing on the far bank.

Later, Lawrence and his loyal horse struggled along a narrow, muddy, mountain track, still caught in the teeth of the typhoon. "On a slippery curve, the earth under my horse's feet started to slide," he said. "My heart jumped into my mouth. My precious mare was about to pitch headlong down the steep mountainside. Fortune again was with us. Some small pine trees grew where the mare was slipping. It checked her long enough so that, with my pulling on her forelock and bridle, she was able to regain her footing on the trail."

He did not slog through the hinterlands for the experience of adventure and hardship. Rather his goal was to help bring learning to the Filipinos. During a break in the storm he encountered villagers who had hurried to their fields to plant rice seedlings. The headman said to Lawrence that he supposed such work was done with machinery in America. "Many years ago, we were poor like you," Lawrence observed. "We did all our work without many tools. We worked and tried to find better and easier ways and our efforts produced wealth so that we could do more and more." His statement made an impression. "The man begged us to place a teacher there so that our ways might be learned by their children. This I promised to do next school year."

A few years later, Lawrence's eye was caught by a 16-year-old Filipina teacher, Prisca Edrozo. A mestiza of Spanish–Filipino heritage, she came from a well-to-do, landholding family in Vintar, a town in Ilocos Norte. There, her father had been the mayor before he died of heatstroke soon after Prisca was born. Prisca was not only pretty, bright and engaging, but comported herself with a poise and confidence beyond her years. When her small school needed a principal, Lawrence promoted her to the position. When she turned 18 in 1913, he began to court her. The courtship was a whirlwind affair and the two were married that same year.

There followed several years during which Lawrence grew the number of schools and teachers in his district, and also during which he and Prisca grew their family. A girl, Helen, was born in 1915, and a boy, Marion, came in 1917. It was soon after Marion was born that Lawrence—having spent more than a decade as a teacher and superintendent in the Philippines—began to reconsider the life that he wanted for Prisca and his children. World War I brought with it a period of tumult and confusion, but also one of opportunity.

George's maternal grandmother, Indalecia Agcaoili Edrozo, was from a landed family in the town of Vintar, in Ilocos Norte on the island of Luzon. (George Cooper)

Although opportunity was not in short supply in the Philippines, Lawrence was curious about the prospects he might be able to exploit back in Kansas—he had been away for more than a decade. To that end, he, Prisca, the children and two servants traveled home to Peabody.

Perhaps he had been away too long. For whatever reason, Lawrence found nothing at home compelling enough to convince him to stay. He made forays out of Kansas, including a few months as a bolter for the Bethlehem Shipping Works at Sparrows Point, Maryland. But nothing that he found anywhere generated any enthusiasm. Moreover, Prisca was homesick and worse, the flu pandemic that took the lives of so many millions during that time also claimed one of the Filipino servants. He was buried in Peabody. Disheartened, Lawrence and his family returned to the Philippines during the summer of 1919. Lawrence took a position as a high school principal at Malolos, north of Manila.

"I was conceived in Kansas before the folks headed back to the Philippines," said George Cooper, the next son. "Many months after returning, my mother started having contractions in the shower and I was almost born there and then." He came on February 5, 1920, into a house his mother recalled as "barn-like," that was situated immediately behind the high school.

Although he was quite successful—and even loved—in his various capacities as an educator, Lawrence was not immune to the caprices of big bureaucracies and the ethical and moral shortcomings of those who sometimes ran them. He recorded that he, "was dismissed from the bureau of education for waging war against a drunk and degenerate superintendent of schools." It was a hard and cruel blow to a proud man who had done so much in such a short time for the furtherance of education in the Philippines.

Lawrence's reputation and character were such that he was shortly reinstated, however he soon turned his head to business rather than education. He was gregarious and likeable by nature and approached people easily. Moreover, his mastery of several languages—he was quite fluent in Spanish—made him an especially good fit for the multi-national commerce that was centered in the capital city of Manila. He also knew the Philippines and its people. These attributes in combination got him hired by the Goodyear tire company.

The family soon moved to a new home on Leveriza Street in the Manila neighborhood of Malate. This house—and the household staff the family was able to afford—reflected Lawrence's business successes as Goodyear's provincial representative. Indeed, young George's immediate needs were met by a servant, an "amah," named Cilay. "Mother always had someone 'from the province [the countryside]' to serve as a house girl or house boy, to watch us children, and to take care of various household chores such as cleaning, laundry, cooking, yard work and driving," said George. "In the Philippines, there were distinctions by economic class; it was not dignified for the well-to-do to perform manual labor. After all, labor was cheap and there were people who wanted and needed the work."

However, George's father Lawrence was not particularly mindful of class distinctions and sometimes mowed the lawn himself for exercise and diversion. Such a thing was very unusual and Prisca often admonished him: "Lawrence, what will the neighbors think?"

The neighborhood reflected Manila's international character and included English, Irish, Spanish, American and German residents—among others. George's earliest memories included an aged Spanish man, a Mr. Paloma, "who plied me with candy. As a boy of four or five, candy was a strong inducement for me to visit the elderly man. He delighted in my joy at receiving his sweet gifts."

And as young boys do, George pestered his older sister and her friends. He recalled an instance when the girls sat "on the lawn, envisioning being

Baby George Cooper with older siblings Marion and Helen. Philippines, 1920.

romanced by the period heart throb, Rudolph Valentino, and singing 'The Sheik of Araby.'" George mimicked and mocked them and was quickly chased off.

It was an idyllic time to be affluent in Manila. Lawrence's business successes continued to grow; he took a new position with Goodyear's competitor, the B. F. Goodrich Company, as the head of its branch in the Philippines. The family moved once more, this time to a larger house on Wilson Street in the newly built neighborhood of San Juan Heights. It occupied almost three acres and enjoyed expansive views of Manila and the bay. Stone was quarried from the site to build a wall, and a hand-wrought iron gate guarded the entrance. Bigger and newer than their house on Leveriza Street, the new home better accommodated the growing family, and the servants lived in another house on the property.

A beautiful little girl, Alice, was born during this time in 1921. But no family was immune from tragedy, and an ugly one was visited upon the Coopers. Happy and healthy Alice was stricken by what was probably pneumonia when she was still an infant. The disease didn't care that the Coopers were happy and clever and well-off. Baby Alice's lungs were overwhelmed

Lawrence and Prisca Cooper were frequent guests at Manila society events. (George Cooper)

and she passed away a short time later. For a time, the Cooper house was a very sad place.

As part of his grieving, Lawrence penned a poem that honored Prisca, his wife. It read in part, "Did we not stand hand-clasped, sob-wracked, Watching the Angel of Death, Snatch the last fruit of her dear womb ...?"

Not soon after, a fine baby boy, Lester, was born to the grieving couple in 1922.

"My father's salary propelled us into a community of prosperous Americans," said George. "We were members of the Wack Golf and Country Club, and the Baguio Country Club [both still extant]. Mother and Dad were on standing invitation lists for important functions, including socials at the Malacañang Palace for the American Governor-General." Across the street from the Coopers lived Claro Recto, the famed Filipino lawmaker and nationalist. His young second wife, Aurora, was a frequent visitor. "She often came over to seek comfort and advice from Mother," said George, "sometimes after some hurt from her husband. Mr. Recto presented a somewhat stern visage. He called our house one morning, very upset because one of our monkeys had gotten into his house and eaten his breakfast. I ran out to the monkey cage in disbelief

Prisca and Lawrence Cooper, Philippines, circa 1915. (USAAF)

and, sure enough, the young male monkey was gone. He returned a couple of hours later looking quite self-satisfied."

The family vacationed regularly, including trips to the Taal Volcano Resort, and Baguio. "The road to Baguio from the plains and into the mountains was a single lane. It was very narrow and was cut into the side of a gorge through which a fast mountain stream rushed," said George. "There was a waystation every few miles that was large enough for cars to pull over and stop, or to pass each other. At each waystation was an operator who called ahead to see if any cars were coming in the opposite direction. The steepness of the grade necessitated frequent and prolonged downshifting to second or first gear. Cars often overheated and arrived at the waystations almost hidden by plumes of steam, and in desperate need of water for their radiators. It was a great adventure."

Especially anticipated were visits to Prisca's mother's home in Vintar where they reunited with cousins and other relatives. "Grandma Edrozo always made certain that we children were provided the means to have a good time, providing horses to ride, or organizing a picnic or a dinner," said George. "When our family was all there together, we were certain to be treated to a feast which included roasting a pig on an open pit of coals."

George Cooper, age 12. (George Cooper)

Among the series of cars that Lawrence purchased was a Studebaker President 8. "It was a beautiful, long, seven-passenger car," said George, "with dual spare tires in fender wheel wells, side parking lights, a rear-mounted trunk, two, fold-down seats in front of the spacious rear seat, and interior lights which brought expressions of awe from our friends. Our chauffeur kept the car spotless and polished. Mother made certain that the windows were always clean before we drove anywhere."

Notwithstanding the fact that he grew up in a large house surrounded by household staff, George remained unspoiled, although appreciative of his situation. "We weren't given a lot of material things as children, but we enjoyed the freedoms that financial security brings to a family." Still, if he wanted to buy something, he had to earn his own money. He and his friends collected and sold glass bottles to a Chinese bottle collector—the botella man. "When I was younger, my father made a deal to pay a centavo—about half a penny—for every dead fly I brought to him. But we had screens on all the windows so there wasn't a lot of money to be made. So, I went out to the trash pile to swat flies. After a while, I think he probably figured out what was going on."

George Cooper, center and behind, is flanked by his older sister, Helen, and older brother Marion. Younger brother, Lester, is in front. Circa 1933. (George Cooper) ·

Another time he spied a raincoat in the Montgomery Ward catalog and, thinking it very snappy, decided to make one for himself by repurposing one of his father's disused coats. "I found some old rubber tire tubes which I cut into patches, and sewed them onto the coat in shingle fashion," he recalled. "It turned out to be quite heavy when finished and to eyes other than mine, probably ludicrous. I thought that it was a great success and was eager to try it out in the first rain. My mother, however, forbade me wearing it outside the home."

George was a boy who did boy things. A fan of the Tarzan series, he fancied himself as nimble in the trees as his jungle hero. "I climbed a large tree in the backyard," he said, "and made a jump for one of the branches that spread further out. I caught the branch but my legs kept going and spun up toward the sky." George lost his grip, fell earthward and slammed into the ground. "The first thing I saw when I regained consciousness was my mother's face, hovering over me. The servants had found me on the ground and carried me to my bed."

Although the Cooper children were generally healthy, illnesses sometimes sent them to the hospital. When George was in grade school he was hospitalized with a case of dysentery. On one particular day his mother and her friend visited at his bedside. "In their conversation," George remembered, "I heard the word, 'circumcision.'" George announced with authority that he knew the meaning of the word and both women turned their attention to him, curious; it wasn't typical for a small boy to be familiar with genital surgery. With no small amount of pride George declared, "Magellan circumcised the world!"

The two women laughed until tears came.

While he loved his parents and they reciprocated, no child was perfect and that included George. As a young teenager, he once spoke impertinently to Prisca when she denied him permission to do something. She slapped him sharply before the words finished leaving his mouth. "I was humiliated," he said, "and never again spoke disrespectfully, not because I feared being slapped, but in the realization that to ever again behave in that manner, I would lose her trust. It was important to all of us children that our parents be proud of us, and we were fortunate that they very often expressed that pride."

He and his brothers and the other neighborhood boys—particularly, George Wightman, the son of Scottish missionaries—spent most of their time outside and played typical games of the day—marbles, and capture-the-flag. They played a variation of kick-the-can that included tree climbing. "Fights with wooden swords and shields," said George, "often ended with bruises and tears. But fort fights during which we wore pots for helmets and threw rocks at each other, usually didn't get anyone hurt so long as the fort was built strong enough and the helmet covered your head."

"George Wightman, my brother Lester, and I formed a sort of neighborhood triumvirate during much of the time we were growing up," said George. Together, the three boys rode their bikes—often on multi-day camping trips—and also hiked the nearby hills, and fished and swam in the streams that cut through them. A favorite destination, far afield, was the Montalban Dam across the Marikina River. "We loved to camp by the stream," said George, "where we spent hours swimming in the nude, and where we looked for large freshwater lobsters. In the evening, swarms of bats streamed out of caves in the mountains. There were so many that it looked like a dark cloud passing by."

Many of their adventures were with Boy Scout Troop Number 1. George headed the Gray Wolf Patrol which included his younger brother, Lester. Several of the scout masters were from local military garrisons, and one of the jamborees was held at the island fortress of Corregidor, which at that time was little known outside the Philippines.

George, Lester and George Wightman built a boat. And not just a slapdash, rickety boy's idea of a boat. "The construction required a keel

George's friend, George Wightman, center of top photo, and left side of bottom photo, often went bike camping with George and his brother Lester. (George Cooper)

George, at right, was an active Boy Scout. (George Cooper)

and prow which we hacked and chiseled out of wood," George said. "We decided on clinker, or lapboard, construction; the boards were bent around the bulkheads and secured with brass screws. The seams were caulked with oakum and sealed with tar, and a retractable center board was fitted to the keel." A covered foredeck served as a small cabin, and a sailmaker was paid for a large mainsail.

The evening prior to the boat's maiden voyage, the boys told their parents they intended to sail it to Manila Bay. "It was remarkable how trusting they were," George said. "We had no life vests and none of us had ever sailed a boat of any kind in a river or the ocean." On the big day, the boys paid for a truck to haul the boat to a nearby tributary, and then paddled down the placid San Juan River and into the larger Pasig. "Our small vessel rocked lightly over the swells from passing barges," said George. "We floated past Malacañang Palace, under the Jones Bridge and the Santa Cruz Bridge, and then into the more congested estuary where the Pasig emptied into Manila bay. The change from the relative security of the river to the wide open bay unnerved us a bit. And then, as our little boat swept up the crest of the first large swell and plunged down the other side, we wondered if we had gotten ourselves into trouble."

As it developed, the boys were able to turn their little boat around, and splash back into the Pasig. It quickly became clear that their sailing skills—and their oarsmanship—were no match for the current. It was nightfall before they were able to get the boat ashore at a point from which they could find a phone and call their parents. The boat was hauled home with a truck the following day.

Although the boys preferred outside activities, their parents insisted they develop their musical potential. Helen studied and excelled at piano. "We three boys took violin lessons under Professor Herman, a German of the old aristocracy," said George. "He showed us scars he had received from fencing duels. He admired Adolf Hitler as someone who would restore Germany to greatness. We had no idea of the persecution of Jews at the time. Our parents sometimes had us entertain guests with our music. Marion was by far the best of us violinists and he could evoke real emotion with his playing."

Another baby joined the family in 1933. Dorothy Ann was healthy and adored her brothers. She tottered after them, often to their annoyance. "I don't know how it got started, but she used to call us 'Brother,'" said George.

George, George Wightman and brother Lester with the boat they built and sailed down a local tributary into the San Juan River, the Pasig River and finally into Manila Bay. Little sister Dorothy did not go with them. (George Cooper)

"She'd call out, 'Brother George,' or 'Brother Lester.' It was kind of endearing."
Dorothy was also gifted. She showed a talent for music—especially piano—that
was recognized from a young age as being very special.

Both George and his older brother Marion were taken with the idea of
becoming pilots, and eagerly devoured the pulp aviation magazines of the
day which touted the exploits of famous World War I pilots. Nichols Field,
an Army airbase was nearby. "Big Keystone [B-3A] bombers often flew low
over our home," said George. "These were slow, twin-engine biplanes that
cruised at only 100 miles per hour. The gunner in the front machine-gun
position was quite visible and when I waved, I often received a wave in
return."

George first realized his dream to fly in 1934—he was 14. In the company
of a neighbor family, he went to a local airport. "There was a lone aircraft,"
he recalled, "a World War I-era Jenny parked by a small building. We were
the only visitors. A young man dressed in a leather jacket and leather helmet,
and with his goggles raised to his forehead, came out to meet us."

George with baby sister Dorothy, 1933. (George Cooper)

As a boy, George used to wave to the low-flying crews of B-3A Keystone bombers. He usually received a wave in return. (U.S. Army)

The pilot offered rides for a dollar. "I had saved money from small jobs," George said, "and was only too eager to spend it for such an opportunity. He told me to climb into the front cockpit and secure myself with the seat harness. After checking that I was strapped in, he stepped into the rear cockpit, set the controls for an engine start and then got out and spun the propeller once, twice, three times. The engine coughed, fired and roared to life. He pulled the wheel chocks, got back into the rear cockpit and taxied out to the runway."

George was airborne seconds later. "The aircraft lifted and a whole new world opened up to me. It was amazing to see an entire relief map of Manila and its suburbs—Manila Bay, the Pasig River and San Juan. I could not distinguish people, but I could see what few cars there were, and many carromatas [pony-drawn carts] crawling across what looked like a multicolored carpet. So, this is what the world looked like from above. I knew then that I was going to be a pilot!"

Another event the following year reinforced his desire to fly. At that time Pan American Airways was eager to exploit the Pacific travel and transport market with its fantastic flying boats—the famous "Clippers." The newest of these, the Martin M-130, was chosen to serve the route from San Francisco to Manila. It was the largest transport aircraft of its day and could fly more than 3,000 miles non-stop at 130 miles per hour. And it could accommodate 30 passengers in unrivaled and spacious luxury.

The inaugural flight was scheduled to arrive at Manila on the afternoon of November 29, 1935. It was an event that put the city abuzz. George remembered that "on the day it was announced to arrive, we all went to the breakwater wall at Manila Bay. A murmur of excitement went through the crowd when the plane first appeared, a small object in the sky." That small object—an M-130 named *China Clipper*—actually weighed 26 tons and had a wingspan of 120 feet.

The gathered crowd, which had grown to several thousand, grew excited as the big ship grew closer. The governor–general recorded in his diary, "Like a great silver bird. Tremendous excitement—women rather hysterical."[1] George's account included no mention of hysterical women. "The plane became clearly visible. It circled over the city and gracefully descended before touching lightly on the water and finally settling to a stop."

It was a watershed event in aviation history that made the world smaller by a certain degree. Indeed, the clippers pioneered routes and developed long-range flying practices that later proved invaluable during the all-consuming war that would wrack the Pacific only a few short years later. But still, such operations

George was at Manila Bay when the famed Martin M-130 *China Clipper* made its inaugural flight to the Philippines. (San Diego Air & Space Museum)

were—and would remain—dangerous. The navigator for the *China Clipper* that day, Fred Noonan, was lost alongside Amelia Earhart two years later in 1937. The captain, Edwin Musick, was killed the following year when his aircraft exploded in flight not far from Pago Pago.[2]

It is likely that George did not appreciate much of this as he watched the big ship settle onto the gentle surface of Manila Bay. But regardless, the sight of the *China Clipper* fortified his passion to fly.

However, he still had to finish school. He attended Central School located on Taft Avenue where classes started at 7:30 and finished at noon to avoid the worst of the tropical heat. "Our high school classes had about 25 students and I normally ranked within the top five," George recalled. "We were taught traditional subjects—math, history, science and such—and we always had homework. I believe that I was a good student as I liked school and looked forward to learning; I never tried to cheat, and I disliked those that did."

That being said, he was a typical teenage boy and was once sent to the principal's office after being caught throwing a paper wad at another boy. "I didn't have much of a reputation as a troublemaker. She just looked at me

The Lawrence Cooper family, circa 1936. George is standing on the right. (George Cooper)

with what I thought was a twinkle in her eye and said that I'd better sit down and keep her company until the start of the next period."

"There was little dating," George said. "Parties were always chaperoned and sexual advances didn't happen as most girls were still very guarded around boys and would not think of ruining their reputations. And most of us boys respected them. Of course, there were always two or three who claimed to have made sexual conquests, but for the most part sex was not a priority. I recall going on only a couple of dates—one with the daughter of a Spanish family, the Burgos, who lived down the road. I borrowed the family car and took her to the Wack Wack Golf and Country Club to swim and have lunch. The other date was with a schoolmate. We met on the Luneta which was a park that fronted Manila Bay. We had ice cream and climbed the rock seawall."

While George and his friends studied and threw paper wads and hiked and played and dabbled in dating, the wider world tilted inexorably toward a great conflagration. News of the Spanish Civil War, the Italian seizure of Ethiopia, Hitler's occupation of the Ruhr and other territories, was followed closely

Manila's Central School graduating class of 1938. Cooper is last row, far right. Tony Saiz, fourth from right, top row, was accused by the Japanese of being a spy. His hands were cut off and he was decapitated. Jimmy Young, far left, second row from top, was killed during the Bataan Death March. Betty Gewald, front, dark dress, tall, died in captivity at Santo Tomas. Most of Cooper's classmates were interned by the Japanese. (George Cooper)

by the international community in Manila. "Politics and world events didn't consume all of my attention, or that of my friends," said George, "because we were teenagers. But the radio and newspapers did keep us aware of what was happening."

Most unsettling, primarily because of its proximity to the Philippines, were events in China. "The Japanese invasion of China was covered extensively." George said, "It was featured in the Pathé newsreels which were always shown at the movie theaters—along with a cartoon—ahead of the feature film. The newsreels showed the Japanese bombing Chinese cities, the Rape of Nanking and other atrocities."

Indeed, the threat Japan posed to the Philippines and other parts of Asia was well understood for the menace it was. George's father Lawrence decried the fact that scrap iron and other material was allowed to be sold from the United States to Japan where it was made into weapons, "to wage war on

China." For this and other reasons, George recalled that, "President Roosevelt was not very popular in our household."

In fact, Americans and citizens of other nations were evacuated from China to and through Manila. "Our Boy Scout troop was sometimes sent to the docks to help with refugees being brought from China," said George. "On one occasion, as the passengers were debarking, an earthquake hit Manila. The large steel structures of the warehouses rumbled and roared—it sounded as if bombs were exploding. Many of the evacuees started to scream, thinking that the Japanese had attacked Manila."

Following his high school graduation, George worked at several different jobs to save money. He wanted to go to the United States to attend Kansas University. "My grandmother had watched it being built and vowed that her children would study there," George said. "When we were young, my father regaled us with stories of his time there, and often led us in the school chant: 'Rock chalk, Jayhawk, K.U.!' My older sister Helen left the Philippines in

George's little sister Dorothy with his dog, Spot, and a kitten. (George Cooper)

1933 to study there, and so did my older brother Marion a few years later. And that had been my intention as well until the war came along."

"My father had been able to pay for Helen's schooling, but he couldn't do the same for us boys," said George. In fact, although the family never wanted for the essentials, the Great Depression was global in scope and it impacted the Coopers. Goodrich struggled and Lawrence left after six years to become the president of the Northern Luzon Transportation Company. After several years there, he formed a cooperative that dealt primarily in food and household goods, but that venture flagged and he took a job as a manager for an import/export business, F. H. Stevens & Company. The heady business days of the 1920s during which he had enjoyed so much success were a distant memory as the 1930s came to an end.

"So then," George said, "my father, through his business contacts, found me a position as an apprentice seaman aboard the *Laura Maersk*, a Danish

George Cooper, center, with his mother, father, younger brother, Lester, and little sister Dorothy. His father would be interned by the Japanese in the infamous Santo Tomas internment camp, while his mother and sister would be left on their own in their house. Brother Lester served in the Merchant Marine. (George Cooper)

freighter bound for the United States. In exchange for whatever work I did, I would get free passage to the United States."

\*\*\*

At the top of the gangplank, George turned and waved goodbye to his tearful mother and solemn father. It would be more than five years, and nearly an entire savage war before he would return to Manila to search for them.

## CHAPTER 2

# "Several Scantily Dressed White Women"

The *Laura Maersk*, at 484-feet long and more than 9,000 tons, was a large and modern ship. Built in 1939, it was part of the famous, Denmark-based Maersk commercial shipping fleet.[1] The crew was friendly to George, despite the fact that his seagoing experience was limited to the day when the Pasig River dumped him, his brother Lester and George Wightman—and their homemade sailboat—into Manila Bay. "The Danish sailors were nice," he said, "and almost everyone spoke English, so I had no trouble communicating. I was quickly adopted by two young men close to my own age. Hans Holger was educated and intelligent and liked to take charge. It was obvious that he would rise to become a ship's captain."

"Eric was more fun-loving and was the sort who took one day at a time," George recalled. "He wasn't particularly committed to making a life at sea. When I talked of my father's family in Kansas and their farm, he asked if I could get them to hire him—he wanted to go to the States and become an American citizen."

"My father had used the connections he had from the import and export business to get me assigned to the ship as a cadet so that I could be trained as an officer. It was an unpaid position but it came with certain privileges—access to the officers wardroom, better berthing and such. But I had no plans for a career at sea, and I needed more money, so I talked with the captain and he let me serve as a basic seaman instead. I worked all over the ship and learned a lot in short order."

Indeed, George was given the opportunity to stand watch at the helm of the big ship. "I was told to hold a certain course, but I struggled initially. I swung the wheel around and tried to correct the swing of the compass as the ship rose up on the waves and was pushed leeward by the wind. The helmsman taught me not to chase the compass, but rather to hold the helm steady and to let the ship correct itself, and then make small course changes when required."

Other duties were more mundane and included chipping paint, washing dishes, and scrubbing the deck. On one of his first days George was told to dump the kitchen scraps overboard. It was a classic prank played on new crew members. Most paid little attention to the prevailing wind and didn't understand that they should move to the leeward side. Consequently, when they tossed the slop over the rail it was immediately blown back onto them.

George's new friends watched with bemused expectation, certain he would fall for the trick. "It seemed odd that there were so many of them watching me get rid of the trash," he said. "I thought that perhaps they were watching to make sure I didn't fall overboard." It was luck rather than wisdom that compelled him to drag the can to the leeward side of the ship. There, he tipped it down toward the water and watched the scraps fall into the wake. The wind whipped a few bits back to the deck, but it was hardly the wave of garbage that his friends expected. His clothes unsullied, and still ignorant of the practical joke he had escaped, George was confused at the disappointed faces he saw when he turned around.

"I got paid about five dollars a month," George said. "It wasn't much, but there wasn't any good place to spend it aboard the ship." However, that wasn't the case in Hong Kong where George enjoyed his first liberty call. "We arrived as the sun was setting," he said. "The Chinese junks with their distinctive sails looked like colorful dragonflies. It reminded me of a rainbow kaleidoscope as the oranges and reds and pinks of the setting sun gave way to the blues and blacks of the night sky, and to the twinkling lights of the streets and houses on the broad hill that was Hong Kong."

Crewmen scurried to get ashore the following morning. Hans and Erik were among them; they had both been to Hong Kong and were eager to show George its many delights. "They took me under their wing and we hurried aboard a launch that was lowered onto the water. There was lots of laughing and singing. We sang 'Roll out the Barrel,' which was a popular polka song at the time. As we moved across the water, it seemed to have a peculiar fluorescence, and there were swarms of jellyfish that floated like balloons trailing very fine ropes."

Ashore, they clambered into a rickshaw. Hans shouted at the small Chinese man who immediately trotted them into the heart of the city. Being young men—and sailors—it was only natural that their first stop was a whorehouse. "We stopped at a door in a row of apartment houses," George said. When the three of them stepped inside, he squinted into the dimly lit room. He was struck by the stink of cigarettes and perfume and sweat and sadness. "There were several scantily dressed white women lounging about," he said. "One of them asked us in English if we were looking to have a good time. She was heavily made up and looked very coarse."

George was not at all against having a good time, but he was suddenly quite certain that he didn't want to have it in that place with those women. He felt a combination of pity, embarrassment and anxiety. "I wasn't experienced at that sort of thing. I had never had sex, and I recalled all the admonitions I had received about venereal diseases and illicit women."

"I told Hans that I didn't want to stay," said George. "He looked disappointed but I sensed that he was also a bit relieved that he did not have to prove his manhood to me. We got back into the rickshaw and he gave the man directions to a bar. We spent the rest of the day and into the evening drinking beer and listening to music. We talked to a woman most of the time. She was a White Russian who had come to Hong Kong to escape the communist purges. Each time we took a swallow of beer she topped our glasses."

It was late when the three young men found their way back to the *Laura Maersk*. George was flush-faced and his pulse raced. A headache pounded his skull. "I hadn't had very much to drink," he said, "because I didn't want to spend all my money on beer. And what I did drink was spread over several hours."

That night had been the first time he had consumed alcohol of any sort. He would experience similar reactions during later drinking episodes. It is likely that he was alcohol intolerant, a condition caused by the body's inability to metabolize it. Also known as Asian flush, it is more common among that race; George likely inherited the condition from Prisca.

Nevertheless, he recovered quickly and enjoyed the next couple of days in Hong Kong. As was common, local merchants were allowed aboard the ship to peddle their goods. "Chinese tailors were noted for their workmanship with British wool," said George. "I thought that I ought to have a nice, fitted suit and I had myself measured. The suit was finished and brought aboard the next day—and for an excellent price. Other peddlers also came aboard and I bought a nicely carved box for my Aunt Gertrude who was still in Kansas. It cost 50 cents." Aunt Gertrude was the sister whose forefinger was accidently lopped off by George's father, Lawrence, when they both were children.

Following the stop at Hong Kong, the ship sailed for Shanghai where it anchored for a few days before sailing for Japan. It arrived at the port city of Yokohama on April 9, 1940. "The Germans invaded Denmark the next day," said George. "The Japanese were allied with Germany and impounded our ship. They didn't actually board it, and the crew was allowed to come and go, but the ship was not permitted to leave the pier."

George was stuck. After a few days it was clear to him that the *Laura Maersk* was not sailing for the United States any time soon. "Somehow, I found my way into the city," he said, "and telegraphed my parents to withdraw all my savings from the bank and wire it to me." While he waited, George made friends with a Japanese girl who worked on the docks. "She was about my age and taught me simple words and phrases. I think she liked me, and she sang to me what she said was her favorite song, 'You Are My Sunshine.'"

But the sociability of George's new friend was not the behavior he experienced when he went into the city. "The Japanese I encountered were not outwardly hostile," he said, "but neither were they very welcoming. They sometimes turned away from me and were very curt when they had to do business with me at places like the bank and telegraph office. I think this was, in part, due to the tensions between our two countries. And they had been heavily criticized by much of the world for the atrocities they were committing in China."

George finally booked passage to Seattle aboard a Japanese ship, *Hie Maru*. He said goodbye to Hans and Erik and his other friends before leaving with the few belongings he had. Aboard *Hie Maru*, he found that he wasn't the only American. "There were others leaving Japan—several families," he said. "Many of them were leaving for good, sensitive to the possibility of a war."

While some of the passengers aboard the *Hie Maru* considered the possibility of a metaphorical storm between Japan and the United States, a very real storm whipped the ocean on which they sailed. "The waves were massive," George recalled, "and towered above the ship's masts. The ship climbed the waves very steeply—so high that the screws came out of the water. When that happened, the entire ship shuddered and vibrated. And then, it plunged down the backs of the waves and into the troughs, before starting up again. And during the times that it was possible to serve food, the plates slammed back and forth against the rails that were put in place on the tables to stop them. It was an astonishing experience for a novice seaman like myself."

*Hie Maru* unloaded cargo and debarked passengers in Vancouver, Canada, before arriving in Seattle on April 27, 1940. "When I went through customs," said George, "I stepped up to the counter with a girl that I had met on the ship. The customs officer told me that I could sign for both myself and my wife. I was a little embarrassed, but she thought it was funny."

"It was Saturday and the banks and post office were closed," George said. "I knew there was supposed to be a letter waiting from my mother and father, and a money order for 50 dollars. But right then I had nothing but 50 cents and nowhere to go and nothing to eat. So, I spent the rest of the weekend walking around town, and staying on a bench in the train station. But I was able to get something to eat because a loaf of bread and a pint of milk together cost less than 25 cents. So, I didn't really go hungry."

George had never been to America, but he managed well enough during his first couple of days. Of all the new things he encountered, the most jarring was the culture. "I had never seen Americans do manual labor—it just wasn't something that happened in the Philippines. But in the States, or at least in Seattle, it was normal. I wondered how I would do if it turned out that I couldn't find any sort of work other than manual labor."

On the Monday, George went to the post office and picked up the letter from his parents. Of George's adventures and experiences, his father wrote, "It is the old, old story of a young man making his contacts with the world, good and bad." On the other hand, his mother was angry at Germany and how the Nazis had upset her son's plans. "The Germans have gotten us tangled up in their mix-ups in some way." But she showed confidence in him: "You are a man now, son, introduced to the wicked world. I am sure that you will be able to take care of yourself and do what is always best. Love and kisses, Mama."

## CHAPTER 3

# "May God Protect and Help You"

George squatted like an infielder at the end of the conveyor belt. As the newly manufactured drill press approached, he wrapped his arms around it, stood, swiveled, took several steps to a pallet, bent at his knees and set it into place. He took a breath or two, moved back to the belt and waited for the next item. The factory—the Central Specialty Company—was located in Ypsilanti, Michigan, and made tools for big distributors such as Sears Roebuck.[1] "That day, the job was manual labor," said George. "And in a very short time it taught me a good deal about hard work and character."

After leaving Seattle by train at the start of May 1940, George went to Ypsilanti via Peabody, Kansas—his father's hometown. Even though he had never met his many aunts and uncles and cousins, his arrival at Peabody was like a homecoming; he was finally able to put faces to the names he had heard all his life. "They really welcomed me," George said. "Aunt Gertrude gave me a room of my own filled with furniture that once belonged to my father's parents. She fed me all I could eat and more—her fried chicken and bread rolls were wonderful. My cousins paraded me all around town and beyond as if I were a celebrity. And I helped my father's brother, Uncle Lester, on the farm. He taught me how to do various sorts of chores, including milking the cows. I learned how to squirt milk at the cats—they sat up on their haunches, paws flailing and mouths open to catch the milk."

George's bucolic break ended in early July when he left Peabody on a bus for Ypsilanti. A friend from the Philippines had secured him a job at the Central Specialty Company. "I had never worked so hard in my life. Some of the tools weighed more than 100 pounds—not much less than me. After my first day of work, I went home, lay on my bed and went to sleep. I was exhausted to the point I wasn't even hungry."

As it turned out, George's day on the receiving end of the conveyor belt was intended only as an indoctrination to the shipping floor. He was put into the office where he prepared invoices and shipping documents. "My starting pay was 18 dollars a week," he noted. "I was able to rent an attic room in the house of an elderly woman for two dollars a week, and I bathed out of a small, galvanized steel tub. I ate supper at a boarding house for seven dollars a week. So, I was able to start saving money right away."

By that time, the summer of 1940, virtually all of Europe was under the Nazi boot and only Great Britain still stood defiant. "I followed news of the war in Europe very closely," George said. "I wanted to fight. I wanted to fight not only for the freedom of the countries that the Germans had invaded, but also for the adventure." Still, the United States was not yet at war, and George remained committed to saving enough money to study at Kansas University.

George did good work and was awarded a pay raise. He found that he had the time and means to socialize—the company bowling league gave him something to do, and so did girls. A young woman at work took him home to meet her parents, but the relationship didn't go far. "And then one night," he said, "I was bowling by myself when a fellow and a girl sat down at the lane where I was bowling. The girl was pretty—a petite brunette. I told them that I was almost finished, and then I concentrated on bowling well so that I might impress her. But I needn't have bothered as she didn't even look at me."

George next saw the pretty girl at a party hosted by a married couple he knew. "Her name was Betty Smith, and she was renting one of their rooms. The hostess—who was rather flirtatious—kept sitting in my lap, and putting her arms around me and such. This didn't impress Betty at all. In fact, she was interested in my brother Marion who was visiting at the time; she had no idea he was already married."

George was given another opportunity to make an impression on Betty. "Sometime later, the lady who had hosted the party invited me to a dance, as her husband wasn't much of a dancer. As it turned out, she got sick and I invited Betty to go with me instead. This was the start of a relationship that soon consumed me. It was not love at first sight, but I found something that gradually filled me with the desire to make her a permanent part of my life. We went to parties, rode bikes and picnicked. We had ice cream together and when it got cold later that year we went ice skating on Ford's Pond. She invited me to go with her to visit her family in Hales Corners, a suburb of Milwaukee, Wisconsin."

"I thought she was wonderful. And as a practical matter she was very employable. She was an excellent secretary and was working for an eye doctor who also used her to help him during various medical procedures. I felt that she and I would make a great team. Although I planned to work while I studied at Kansas, I figured that she could also get a good job to help get us through the time when I was earning my degree.

In fact, Betty had had a difficult life to that point. Born in Tacoma, Washington, as Ruth Jean O'Dell, her father had left her mother when she was an infant. Because she shared the same first name with her mother, she was called Betty after another relative. After a short time, her mother remarried a man, Louis Smith, who took them to his family's dairy farm in Wisconsin.

Life for Betty and her two half-brothers and three half-sisters continued contentedly until her mother died of complications from asthma just as Betty was about to enter high school. Louis was overwhelmed, and struggled to make a living while simultaneously raising six children. He quickly married a neighbor.

Betty's new stepmother was an insecure woman who tried to erase all traces of Louis' former wife—Betty's mother. She compelled Betty to drop out of school and stay home to cook and clean for the family, as well as the

Ruth "Betty" Cooper captured George's heart and never let it go. (George Cooper)

farm's hired hands. Betty's shock and misery at losing her mother and being abruptly forced from childhood into a form of servitude, was compounded when an insensitive relative revealed that Louis—the only father she had known—was not her actual father. Betty was not alone in her despair; one of her half-brothers committed suicide a few years later.

Ultimately, a wealthy great aunt, Carrie Tucker, saw that Betty's life was being ruined and that her potential could never be realized. She brought Betty to Ypsilanti and pulled strings to get her enrolled into Cleary Business College, despite the fact that she had never attended high school. There, Betty excelled at secretarial skills. She developed to be not only pretty and quietly witty, she was smart, practical and accomplished.

She stayed with Aunt Carrie for a while, and the two of them were joined by her son Preston Tucker and his wife Vera. Preston Tucker was an icon in the automotive world and would make substantial contributions in armaments and assault boats during the coming war effort. Postwar, he would dazzle the driving public with his innovative Tucker '48, a remarkable automobile which was ultimately doomed by jealousy-driven lawsuits and a certain degree of naivety on his part. The lawsuits failed and Tucker's reputation was restored but his subsequent efforts to manufacture automobiles came to nothing. For her part, Betty recalled that Tucker "liked to drive very fast."

***

Although George likely didn't see it, a small article appeared in newspapers across the country on March 31, 1941. It indicated that an old friend was being pressed into service for the United States. And the article made it apparent that the friend had somehow escaped the Japanese. It read: "Meanwhile, the U.S. Maritime Commission in Washington yesterday announced that it has seized six Danish ships and has assigned five of them to the American President Lines for its Far East trade, and one to the Oceanic Steamship Company for its Australia–New Zealand service."[2] Among the six ships that had been put into American service was the *Laura Maersk*.

***

By the spring of 1941, America was hurrying to get onto a war footing and George was doing invoice and shipping work at a plant that made parts for the Douglas A-20 bomber. His salary of $200 per month was nearly three times what he had been paid when he first started work. Still, he was anxious to do something—anything—to help fight the Nazis. "A friend and I fastened on the idea of going to Canada to be trained as fighter pilots for the Royal Canadian Air Force. We figured that would be the quickest way to get into the fight in Europe. We agreed to meet early one morning and then cross into Windsor, Canada." As it developed, George arrived on time at the agreed upon rendezvous point but his friend did not. After waiting a couple of hours, he went home.

He decided on a different course of action. At that point, with the United States rushing toward war, the Army Air Corps was anxious to get men into service. "I found out about the aviation cadet program," George recalled. "To be selected, you had to take a test which was equivalent to the entrance examination for the military academy at West Point, and you had to pass a rigid physical exam. I took evening courses that summer at Wayne University in Detroit. They were designed to prepare students for the examination. We received instruction in mathematics, chemistry, history, vocabulary and English. Because I had no car, I hitchhiked from Ypsilanti to Detroit after work. This was at the tail end of the Great Depression and people went out of their way to help each other. I seldom had trouble getting a ride."

Notwithstanding his desire to get overseas to fight, George continued to court Betty Smith. "I wanted her to be a part of whatever I was about to do," he said. "I borrowed a car one evening and took her out to Ford's Lake where I found a quiet place and parked. After a short time, I screwed up my courage and asked her to marry me. I felt a great rush of heat and my heart pounded with excitement and uncertainty. It seemed a long time before she answered. And her answer wasn't exactly what I hoped for."

Indeed, George had imagined a Hollywood movie scene with Betty throwing her arms around him and exclaiming, "Yes, yes, yes!" "Her reply was not that," he said. "Although she didn't say no, she didn't say yes, either. She was very practical and wanted some time to consider my proposal."

George stayed in touch with his parents as he prepared for his future. That he and his brothers were good sons was underlined in a letter from Prisca who was very pleased that they all had extended her wishes for a wonderful Mother's Day. "You don't know how happy it makes your mother to have such thoughtful and loving sons like all you three boys. It makes me so homesick for all of you that I have to cry it out." Sister Dorothy wrote to George in her child's hand about her new pet, "You will be surprised to know it is the cutest little black and brown pig and she knows how to stand on her hind legs!"

Lawrence wrote to George at the end of May 1941, and it was apparent that he was keeping a close eye on the fighting in Europe. He opined that the United States should send as many bombers and fighters as it could to England. With those, he believed that the English could hold off the Germans and perhaps turn the war against them. His prescience was remarkable when he wrote, "If the U.S. fails in this, you will be in the war by this time next year."

Another letter from a friend still in the Philippines underscored the fact that the United States understood the potential for Japanese aggression there. Fred Holmes wrote to George that, "The situation back here is supposed to be quite serious, but according to my opinion, there is nothing to worry about. The Japanese wouldn't dare attack; they are having enough trouble with the Chinese army. However," he noted, "we received another boatload of soldiers from the U.S. a few days ago. The USAT *Washington* came in with about 4,000 head of khaki-covered individuals."

George applied to the aviation cadet program during the early fall of 1941. He and a large group of other candidates were directed to undergo a physical examination. "We all stripped naked and a doctor went down the line checking our heart and lungs. He pressed his hand against our testicles and told us to cough so that he could check for hernias. And he had us bend over so that he could examine our anuses for evidence of piles. Happily, we got to take the other tests—eyes and ears and such—with our clothes on. When it was all finished, only about 20 of us had passed."

During this period, George took some time off to go back to Peabody, Kansas. "My Aunt Gertrude had a tree in her yard that needed to be removed, along with some other work. So, I spent a few days down there to help her out. When I returned, Betty told me that she had missed me, and that she wanted us to be married. I think that she was touched by the fact that I went down to Kansas to help Aunt Gertrude. She also said that I wasn't like most other men. She never explained what she meant by that, and I didn't press her; I was just happy that we were engaged."

George was sent with more than a hundred other prospective aviation cadets to Selfridge Field, just north of Detroit. "It was a very cold day, and the wind coming off Lake St. Clair was biting. As it happened, the classes I took at Wayne University paid off. Whereas more than half of the men who took the test failed it, I passed. I was told that I would be called up for pilot training just as soon as the next aviation cadet class started." George made the decision to definitely postpone his plans to study at Kansas University.

The Japanese sneak attack on Pearl Harbor hastened his call to duty. "I was at the movie theater when there was an announcement that I was to go

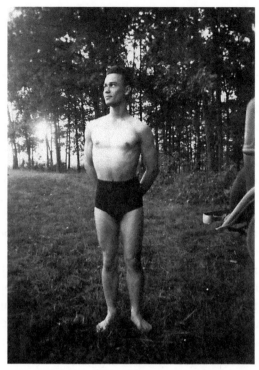

George was a fit young man, physically well-qualified for service with the USAAF. (George Cooper)

home immediately. When I got home there was a telegram ordering me to duty. At the turn of the new year, January 1942, I was ordered to report to Kelly Field, Texas, for pilot training."

On the other side of the world, George's sister Dorothy was an eyewitness to the attacks the Japanese launched against Manila at nearly the same time as they struck Pearl Harbor. "We saw the Jap planes bombing different places in Manila—our house sat up on a hill and we could see the entire city and the bay. The planes looked like flies as they buzzed around and then dived and dropped their bombs."

\*\*\*

The next few weeks went by in a flurry as George readied himself and his affairs for military service. His activity reflected that of most of the nation. Now that the United States was truly at war, people went about their business with a special urgency. Where Betty was concerned, George had no particular worries. "She continued to work with the ophthalmologist and we agreed that we would get married when the situation permitted. It was sort of a moot point anyway as aviation cadets were not allowed to be married."

The attack on Pearl Harbor alarmed George, just as it did most Americans. However, the simultaneous attacks on the Philippines caused him even greater concern. "I was worried that my family or friends might be injured or killed by the bombing, but I really didn't consider that the Japanese would be able to defeat MacArthur in the Philippines. No one did. He was considered to be our greatest general, and the United States had been busy fortifying the Philippines for at least a year."

In Manila, George's father Lawrence felt similarly, as Dorothy recalled: "We listened to Roosevelt address the nation after Pearl Harbor. People were saying that we should try to leave, but my father said 'no.' He said that MacArthur and Wainwright would handle the Japs. He had a confidence in MacArthur that was obviously misplaced."

Indeed, Lawrence continued to be confident for at least the first couple of weeks after the fighting started. "I went to my place of business every day and tried to carry on as usual," he said. "As the Japanese planes flew leisurely over Manila and its environs dropping bombs, our antiquated antiaircraft guns popped at them to no avail. The fire was dangerous only to the people of Manila on whom it might fall. The Japanese confined their bombing to military objectives and the only time that bombs fell near was when they were bombing shipping in the Pasig River within the city."

Like most of the city's citizens, Lawrence anticipated an overwhelming American response. Surely help was on the way. "Every day I looked for some of our fighting planes of the latest models to come swiftly in from somewhere to shoot down the Japanese bombers or send them scurrying back to Japan. Day after day, they failed to come."

The shocking reality that help was not on its way—and that Japan would soon rule the Philippines—hit Lawrence like a brickbat. "One day when returning home from the office, I stopped on the road to pick up some young American soldiers who were walking with their guns in hand. They thanked me feelingly for the ride but were otherwise silent until I dropped them where they wished to get out. Then, one of them said: "May God protect and help you."

"For the first time," Lawrence said, "I realized that these soldier boys knew that help was not coming and that we had no force in the Philippines that was able to stop the Japanese invasion." Lawrence pondered this revelation during the remainder of his drive home. Manila under Japanese occupation was not a reality that he relished considering.

Knowing that Manila was indefensible with the forces he had, and desirous of protecting its history, its beauty and its people, MacArthur declared it an open city on December 26, 1941. American units inside the city abandoned their garrisons, and the equipment and stores they could not take with them were put ablaze or given away. "Gasoline stores in Manila were set on fire," said Lawrence, "and the city was illuminated all night by the flames. Red Cross and military food supplies were opened to the public and all comers were invited to carry away whatever they were able to."

"I thought of the press accounts of the Japanese occupations of Chinese cities—looting, rape and murder," said Lawrence. "I remembered the words of the young soldier, 'May God protect and help you.' There was no more hope for rescue."

The Japanese entered the city on January 2, 1942. That entrance was peaceable for the most part, and during the next few days Japanese units paraded through Manila's main streets. Filipino officials stood by stiffly and waved the small Japanese flags that had been thrust into their hands.

Lawrence filled the gas tank of his car in order to be ready if he decided to flee with Prisca and Dorothy. He also stocked extra food, having been able to get rice, and two, 100-pound sacks of cracked wheat from a Red Cross storehouse. "We buried some of our food supplies under the house," he said, "and hid some of our valuables in the rafters, hoping they would escape the eyes of any Japanese soldiers who might come to our house."

Lawrence, Prisca and Dorothy waited fearfully for what might happen next. During the early evening of January 3, 1942, they were in the front yard when a car stopped at the gate. In it were Japanese soldiers. "They got out and came up our driveway," Lawrence said, "and I went out to meet them. They were a Japanese lieutenant and two soldiers. The lieutenant could speak some English and he politely said, 'Good evening, will you loan me your car for a while? I will bring it back tomorrow.'"

Lawrence took only a moment to consider the enemy officer's request. He was in no position to resist, and doing so would only put himself, his wife and his daughter in danger. "So, I got the key to the car for him. It was very evident that he was not at all familiar with cars as he was unable to start it." For the last time, Lawrence started his prized Studebaker President. Then he stepped out to make room for the enemy officer. "He tried to back out of the yard to reach the road but did not know how to shift the gears."

The Japanese officer got out of the car and Lawrence slid into the driver's seat. He backed the car into the street and then pulled it forward before stopping it and stepping out again. The lieutenant crawled awkwardly behind the steering wheel one more time. "He then took over with faltering success," Lawrence said. "That was the last I ever saw of the car. At that, we were all very thankful that our first encounter with the Japanese soldiers had not been one of violence."

They continued to wait, anxious at what the Japanese would do with, or to them. "On January 8, we saw some Japanese in a station wagon stop at our neighbor's house. They took our neighbors, Mr. and Mrs. Carman. We had been visiting over the fence with them daily and it was disheartening, to say the least, to see them taken away."

The enemy men in the station wagon visited the Cooper house next. Lawrence recognized a Japanese businessman who had worked in Manila before the war. The man, "advised me in a very friendly tone of voice to prepare to go with them soon, some other day. He advised me to carry a cot, a change of clothing and food for three days. 'After three days, you will come back,' he said." The man made no mention of taking Prisca or Dorothy. "I made the preparations to go at once," Lawrence said, "but days went by and no one came for me."

Lawrence was understandably anxious as he waited. Although the Coopers had not experienced any harm beyond a stolen automobile, stories of Japanese atrocities were already making the rounds. It was difficult for him to consider those stories while knowing that he was essentially helpless to do anything to protect Prisca and Dorothy.

His waiting ended in mid-January. "The Japanese took over one of the leading newspapers," he said. "In it, the Japanese printed their orders and instructions to the people of the Philippines. An order appeared which directed all Americans to report to Japanese headquarters on January 15, 1942, for enrollment." Lawrence complied with the order and two days later a truck came to the home and took him to the University of Santo Tomas in Manila. Prisca and Dorothy were left on their own.

Founded in 1611, 25 years before Harvard, Santo Tomas came into being with the permission of King Phillip III of Spain, and grew to become one of the most highly regarded universities in Asia. The Japanese shut it down during January 1942 and converted it into an internment camp for enemy non-combatants, to include men, women and children. Most of the population was American, but there was also a large contingent of British citizens and a smattering of other nationalities.

It was not meant to be as harsh or regimented as a POW camp and Lawrence's observations reflected that. "Those who were picked up early suffered great hardships," he said. "Some were seized in the streets and had no opportunity to get any clothing or supplies or make any disposition of their belongings. They were held for several days in Villamor Hall with no food supplies nor sleeping accommodations."

"But by the time I got there," he recalled, "it was fairly well organized. Through the efforts of the internees themselves, and with help from friends and relatives outside the camp, the place was fitted with toilets and showers. They were far from adequate, but they made the situation endurable. The kitchen and cooking for the entire camp was organized, and a hospital was set up with doctors and nurses and a few supplies. Dentists also volunteered, and there were barbers and people to repair shoes and garments, and a place to manufacture soap."

Indeed, a can-do spirit pervaded the entire place; internees pitched in according to their professions and abilities. "Plumbers, electricians, carpenters and mechanics all contributed their services," said Lawrence. "It became a great cooperative community of some 4,000 people—men women and children. In addition, groups were allowed to go out from day-to-day to buy food and other camp supplies. And relatives and friends were permitted to bring food and other supplies to the camp gate twice a week—although they were not allowed to see the internees." It seemed to Lawrence that aside from being separated from Prisca and Dorothy, his time at Santo Tomas might not be so bad after all.

The Japanese continued to bother Prisca and Dorothy for a time. "They poked around our house and property to see what else of value there might be that they could steal," said Dorothy. "My mother talked them out of taking the piano. Even at that age I was an expert pianist and she had me play the Japanese national anthem for them. It had been blasted at us ever since they had marched into Manila, and I couldn't help but have it memorized—I had learned it by ear. Anyway, I played it beautifully and the Japanese officers all stood around and smiled and nodded. When my mother explained to them that the piano actually belonged to me, they decided to let us keep it.

## CHAPTER 4

# "We Had a Beauty Contest Yesterday"

George leaned forward to see the airfield at Cimarron sliding under the nose of his open cockpit PT-19 trainer. He smiled to himself at the stunt he had planned—an inverted pass over the landing area and flight line. He twisted around in his seat to make certain there was no conflicting traffic in the vicinity, lifted the little aircraft's nose just slightly, and then pushed the control stick to the left, stepping on just enough rudder to maintain coordinated flight. The aircraft obeyed him and the horizon rolled upside down.

Clunk! There was a jolt and George's seat slipped on its rail before catching at the next stop. The sudden, jarring movement startled him and he gripped the sides of the cockpit, afraid that his safety harness might fail, and that he might fall out. Inverted, he craned his head upward and spotted his seat cushion fluttering down toward the airfield. An instant later, he recovered his wits, snatched the controls and swung the aircraft back upright. Catching his breath, he made a diving turn away and hoped that no one had seen him.

\*\*\*

George had arrived at Kelly Field in San Antonio, Texas, a couple of months earlier on January 22, 1942. If Kelly wasn't a madhouse, it could at least have been described as chaotic. The United States Army Air Forces, the USAAF, was racing toward a recently stated goal of producing 70,000 new pilots annually. It was a gargantuan task as, at that point, the service counted less than 50,000 pilots in its ranks.[1] Producing almost double that number of pilots—every year—seemed almost impossible. Regardless, George and his classmates, Class 42-H, were quickly sucked into the vortex of pseudo-pandemonium that was the rapidly expanding USAAF pilot training machine.

Aviation Cadet George Cooper at the start of his flight training. (USAAF)

"There are a lot of rules to learn," George wrote to Betty on the day he arrived. "After a meal we have to arrange our dishes and utensils but one way. In eating, we sit four inches from the edge of the chair, eat with but one hand, and talk only when asking for something."

Soon after arriving, he and the other young men were shorn of their hair, issued winter uniforms and introduced to military drill—marching. "Schooling started immediately," he said, "with indoctrination in military culture, instructions on the proper way to salute, the meanings of different bugle calls, and classes on how to wear the uniform and its insignia. They also taught us the importance of military courtesies and the need for cleanliness in the barracks, and good personal hygiene." The cadets also reviewed various academic disciplines—particularly mathematics—as they related to flying.

This was the preflight phase of training—a combination military charm school, classroom, and processing center—and George's cohort was among the last scheduled to finish the curriculum in five weeks. Subsequent classes were required to complete an expanded nine-week course. Reports from the field indicated that the pilots being produced by the training command were adequate as aviators but were often lacking in their conduct as officers and leaders.

After completing preflight, George and his classmates were shuttled from Kelly Field during February 1942, to Cimarron, just north of Oklahoma City. Cimarron was a primary flight training installation where civilian contract pilots provided ab initio training to new cadets. Civilian instructors were used because there simply weren't enough military instructors. It was believed, and proved, that civilian pilots could provide adequate instruction during this "winnowing-out" phase. The few USAAF pilots that were assigned to primary flight training duty were used mostly to perform check flights.

As had been the case at Kelly, the newly arrived cadets were additionally "trained" by the class ahead of them, 42-G, which was halfway through the syllabus at Cimarron. George and his classmates were derided by the upperclassmen as "dodos"—flightless birds—and were otherwise denigrated. "When an upperclassman spoke to us," said George, "we had to come to attention and answer in a respectful manner, always prefacing our answers with 'Sir.' The upperclassmen liked to trap us in games that we could not win. For example, they might ask someone if he was a 'hot' pilot. If he said no, he was ordered to go stand next to the coal-fired heater where he roasted. If he said yes, he was sent outside in the cold where he froze. That sort of thing went on until the upperclassman got tired of it."

The mess hall was the site of additional hectoring. "A favorite command," George remembered, "was to 'eat on the beam.' This was an order to eat while looking up at the ceiling beams and it was disastrous if you were eating soup. And some upperclassmen tried our patience by speaking to us as we were about to take a bite of food. When they did so, we were required to place our utensils on our plates and come to attention. It sometimes happened that you had little time to eat and you went hungry."

The hazing was sometimes good-natured and added comic relief. "I had to face one of the boys and recite Fuzzy Wuzzy without laughing," he wrote home to Betty. He failed. "I was told to wipe that smile off, throw it down, call it a cad and stomp on it. If you don't think it hard to keep a straight face, just try it."

Borrowed from the military academy at West Point, these hazing practices were intended to test how the individual cadets handled pressure and difficult situations. An inadvertent and beneficial side effect was the leadership development of the cadets. Regardless of whether they were the bullies, or those being harassed, they were exposed to the ways that different individuals reacted to different situations.

Aviation cadets were young, and horseplay was fun. George Cooper is second from left. (USAAF)

Inevitably, as the USAAF grew by orders of magnitude, the practice occasionally got out of control. For instance, impromptu, late night, sleep-depriving "physical training" sessions were sometimes conducted which unnecessarily left the cadets fatigued on the following day. And the hazing could be small-minded and stupid, as was an incident that George described to Betty: "We had a beauty contest yesterday. We had to bring out our girls' pictures and have them judged. You took first place, darling."

He recalled the situation of a classmate named Pruitt, from Detroit. "His family was quite well-to-do and politically connected. Pruitt wrote about the hazing to his father who then wrote to his congressman, asking him to intercede. The congressman made some phone calls and the next thing we knew, Pruitt was paraded through all the barracks in nothing but a makeshift diaper. As he came through our barracks there were tears of anger streaming down his face."

This sort of unfettered hazing was stopped later during the war. As it was unmonitored, it sometimes created real harm unnecessarily, and no doubt

George on the flight line at Cimarron Field, Oklahoma. (George Cooper)

caused the release or failure of cadets who otherwise would have made excellent pilots and officers. For his part, George endured the bullying and stayed focused on his goal of becoming a pilot. "I went along with all the harassment directed at me," he said, "and as a consequence I was eventually relieved of that sort of torture."

But during his time at Cimarron the hounding was still rampant everywhere, including the sky. "It was customary for the flight instructors to be rough on the students, cussing them when they made mistakes and berating them with demeaning phrases and words," George said. However, as he did in the barracks and the mess hall and everywhere else, George put up with the abuse and did well with his flying.

"I was definitely not a natural pilot," George said. "Initially, it was a bit disorienting to me, and I didn't always understand what my instructor wanted. I was surprised on one flight early on, during March," said George. "I didn't think it had gone that well and my instructor, Mr. Marrs, gave me a hard time through the entire flight. Then, he made me land and taxi to the edge of the field where he climbed out and walked away. I just sat there looking at him. He turned and took a few steps back toward the airplane and shouted, 'What the hell are you waiting for? Take her up!' That was my first solo flight." It was an exciting achievement and George recalled that he, "felt exhilaration and yet a certain apprehension at being alone." Nevertheless, the flight went well and he landed without incident.

As he progressed through his training, George kept a close watch on developments in the Philippines. There was no good news, whatsoever. Organized American resistance to the Japanese invaders was nearing collapse and there was no hope for a reversal. In fact, Allied forces were retreating everywhere in the Pacific.

Of his father and mother and sister, George could only guess at their situation. His father Lawrence was shuttered away at the Santo Tomas Internment Camp, and his mother Prisca and sister Dorothy were on their own. Yet, he knew none of this and could do little other than pray for their safety, even as he worked his way through flight training.

George's progress through the primary phase was good and he liked the little PT-19. Made by Fairchild, it was a low-wing monoplane powered by a

Aviation Cadet George L. Cooper during the primary phase of flight training at Cimarron Field, in Oklahoma in early 1942. (USAAF)

200-horsepower inline engine. It was a good design although it did present maintainability issues as the plywood material that made up much of the wings tended to deteriorate in harsh weather. Nevertheless, it was a popular aircraft and had a reputation for virtually viceless handling characteristics. That being said, George did ground-loop his aircraft on one occasion. His classmates heckled him with good-natured jeering, and for a time he was known as, "Ground Loop Coop."

The student sat in the forward cockpit while the instructor sat in the rear and shouted at him though a Gosport, or voice tube. The PT-19 had a higher wing loading and greater performance than its biplane contemporaries, and better approximated the types of aircraft to which the students would graduate. "It was a good little airplane," George said, "and I loved doing the aerobatics—the loops, chandelles and barrel rolls, and such. Aside from the ground loop and my failed attempt to fly inverted across the airfield, I really had no trouble."

But that wasn't the case with many of his classmates. Quite a few failed or were "washed out." It was not uncommon for up to a third or more of the aviation cadets in a given class to be eliminated during this phase of training. Most

George Cooper about to climb aboard a Fairchild PT-19 primary training aircraft at Cimarron Field, Oklahoma. (USAAF)

failed due to their lack of flying aptitude, but academics—including mechanical fundamentals, meteorology, the theory of flight, etc.—also took their toll.

Aircraft accidents, although they didn't happen daily, were also a factor. "One of my classmates," George said, "was practicing a spin and was thrown out of the cockpit when he shoved the stick forward to start his recovery; he had forgotten to strap himself into the aircraft. Fortunately, he was wearing his parachute." The disconsolate student, suspended under his parachute, could do little other than watch his aircraft career toward and into the earth.

The commanding officer at Cimarron lectured the cadets against marrying while in military service as it would be unfair and cruel to leave a new bride in the States only to be killed in combat overseas. "We may have to live apart for a long time," George wrote to Betty, "and I may not even come back. I am leaving it up to you. You know I will always love you. I will not have any other woman for my wife, and I do not ever want you to feel that I would be selfish enough to ask you to do something that might make you very unhappy later."

George finished the primary phase of flight training at the end of March 1942. "A big graduation party was planned for Friday, April 3, for those of us who had been successful. I invited Betty to come down to Oklahoma City

George L. Cooper, front, and others sit with his civilian flight instructor, R. E. Marrs, at right. (Via George Cooper)

to join me. I told her that if she wanted to get married, she should bring down the wedding ring I had given her at the same time she had accepted my engagement ring." It was apparent that the admonitions against marrying had made little impact on George.

"She arrived on the day of the party and took a room downtown at the Skirvin Hotel. A military bus picked her up along with a number of other women who were also guests of one or another of the cadets. After the party," George said, "I went back to Betty's hotel room with her. She showed me the wedding ring. I didn't go back to the base that night."

At that point, aviation cadets were not only discouraged from marrying, they actually were forbidden to do so. Although it was a regulation that was widely violated, and one to which senior officers often turned a blind eye, it was still grounds for expulsion from the program. The service wanted the cadets to be fully focused on their training. Needy wives and the babies that frequently accompanied them were problematic distractions.

George didn't care—his love for Betty was like nothing he had known. "I couldn't wait to get married," he said. "We got up the next morning, April 4, 1942, and then stepped outside the hotel and hailed a cab. It was Saturday morning and I asked the driver where we could get a marriage license."

"Of course, everything was closed," George said. "But this driver took a strong liking to us—and he knew people. He made some phone calls and drove us around to different places until we had all the requisite documents. Once that was done, he found a preacher to marry us and took us to a Baptist Church. There, we met my good friend Hal Herrick who had just washed out and was waiting to go to navigator training. Anyway, this taxi driver and Hal both stood up for Betty and me, and we were married that day. When I asked him how much I owed him for the day, the taxi driver told me to keep my money—his service was a gift."

Filled with passion and love and wonderment, George was emotionally overwhelmed. "The realization that I had pledged to take care of that beautiful girl through sickness and in health, for richer or poorer, until death ... brought out a deep feeling not only of responsibility, but also of pride. The following day was Easter and it was the happiest day of my life. To my mind, there was no question about my surviving the war. We were going to be together forever." Betty returned to Ypsilanti the next day and George—a newly minted breaker of official USAAF regulations—returned to the airfield.

He didn't stay there long. He was sent back to San Antonio, this time to Randolph Field, the "West Point of the Air," where he started the basic phase of flight training. Whereas the base at Cimarron had been a hastily erected affair with little feel of permanence or importance, Randolph was a long-established showcase of the Army Air Forces, purpose-designed from scratch as the service's center of flight training, and consistently constructed in the Spanish Colonial Revival style. It was, in fact, a beautiful place that accommodated the cadets comfortably. The food was good and served in a well-appointed mess, and rather than multi-bed, squad bay barracks arrangements, the cadets slept in two-man rooms. "My roommate was John Moore," remembered George. "I'd never seen someone with so much hair—he was covered like a wooly mammoth! We got along great together."

But compared to Cimarron, life was more structured at Randolph with greater emphasis on military spit-and-polish, and regular formations and parades. The training served to make George and his classmates not only better officers and leaders, but it also reinforced the reason they were there—service to country. "The solemnity of the very first ceremony when we formed for retreat at the end of the day made a real impression on me," said George. "The bugle notes echoed clear and timeless as the flag was slowly lowered. I felt a tingling in my entire body. This was my country for which I would soon be fighting, and possibly dying."

"Each morning, reveille was sounded at 0600," said George. "We had to get dressed, make our beds and get outside for formation within five minutes. It couldn't be done without taking shortcuts, and I slept in my underwear on top of my blanket. When reveille sounded, all I had to do was pull my blanket taut, slip on my clothes and make a dash for formation. While we were assembled in formation, senior cadets inspected our quarters and searched for evidence of dust or anything else that might smudge their white gloves. Offenders were given demerits."

After being "awarded" a certain number of demerits—for any number of different offenses—a cadet was made to walk them off by marching up and down the aircraft parking ramp a certain number of times while carrying a rifle. If the demerits or a specific gaffe were flight related, he was compelled to wear his parachute. No aviation cadet, including George, escaped this form of discipline regardless of whether or not it was warranted.

The flying for the basic phase at Randolph during that period was performed at the controls of the North American BT-14. Like the PT-19, it was a low-wing monoplane, but its 420-horsepower radial engine was twice as powerful as the PT-19's inline engine, and it had an enclosed cockpit. The training in the basic phase built upon what the cadets had learned during the primary phase, and it additionally introduced new aspects, to include night and instrument flying, and navigation.

George Cooper, right, and his fellow aviation cadets stand in front of a BT-14 trainer aircraft at Randolph Field, Texas, during May 1942. (USAAF)

Night flying made the biggest impression on George—it was new and sometimes unnerving. "The ground was black and dotted with lights from the city and surrounding area," he said. "The sky was also black and it was dotted with stars. There often was no clear horizon and the ground merged with the sky in such a way that caused vertigo." Vertigo caused disorientation and an inability to determine up from down from sideways from not. "One boy in our class crashed soon after takeoff and was killed," George said, "almost certainly due to vertigo."

The nighttime traffic pattern at the airfield could be especially dangerous. "We had to be particularly alert for other aircraft," recalled George. "After takeoff we each proceeded to our assigned sectors to do our required maneuvers. This minimized the potential for collisions but there were no such safeguards in place when we returned to land. We had to listen to the radio and keep a close watch for other aircraft entering the pattern at the same time." Indeed, nighttime training proved to be one of the most dangerous segments of the syllabus.

George and Betty, like millions of newly married couples across the nation, were adjusting to life apart. Betty declared in a letter, "I must see you soon—it's terribly lonesome without you. I get so tight inside, it hurts. And then I want to do something drastic, like throwing something and smashing it to bits." Reminders of her new husband—who was beyond her reach—were everywhere. "Whenever I hear that Air Corps song on the radio, I either feel very happy, or tears come into my eyes—it depends on the mood I'm in."

George's time at Randolph was essentially unremarkable as he encountered few problems and completed his time in the BT-14 on schedule. He was subsequently sent 100 miles southeast to Foster Army Airfield, near Victoria, Texas, on July 3, 1942, for the advanced phase of flight training. The mood was different at Foster as compared to Cimarron or Randolph. The training was far nearer the end than the beginning, and virtually everyone who would wash out had already done so. The cadets were treated with more respect and they acted more like officers. And the flying they did more closely resembled the flying they would do in combat.

That flying was done at the controls of the North American T-6 which was an evolution of the BT-14 that George had flown during the basic phase. Just as the BT-14 had been more powerful and advanced than the PT-19, the T-6 was more powerful and advanced than the BT-14. Another low-wing monoplane, it had retractable landing gear, an enclosed cockpit and was provisioned to carry machine guns. Its radial engine generated more than 600 horsepower. It was, in fact, an almost-fighter that fit the advanced trainer role perfectly, and served as such across the globe for another 50 years.

Still, after enjoying the thoughtfully arranged comforts of Randolph, George found Foster lacking. Like Cimarron, it was a new and hastily constructed installation. It sat low on the coastal plain and was situated only about 40 miles from the Gulf of Mexico. It was beset with heat and insects. "The sun is terrifically hot," he wrote to Betty, "but it isn't the heat or mosquitos that make it so bad here. It's the food. Last night for supper we had potatoes, spaghetti and pickles."

Aside from continued instruction in navigation and instrument flying, the advanced syllabus included formation flying and aerial gunnery. The aerial gunnery flights were flown for about a week from an outlying airfield on nearby Matagorda Island. During this training the cadets fired their .30-caliber machine guns at a target sleeve towed by an instructor pilot. "We were aggressive," said George, "and oftentimes pressed our attacks until we were very close and almost directly behind the instructor towing the target. More than one time I heard the instructor scream at a cadet who got too close, 'God dammit, get off my tail!'"

Like many of his classmates, George struggled with aerial gunnery. "Honey, I am tired of this," he wrote to Betty. "No matter how well I come in on the target, it seems that I can't hit it. I had tracers in my belt and it seemed like I got in rather close. I felt sure that I had hit it. I thought that this would be my best day. Well, I have one more try at aerial gunnery tomorrow."

In truth, aerial gunnery was an incredibly demanding discipline which very few men ever mastered. It required a pilot to keep his aircraft in balanced flight while evaluating the target's flight path, airspeed and range. That done, the pilot pulled the nose of his aircraft ahead of the target, determined the proper aim point and fired his guns. If he had done everything perfectly, his bullets and the target arrived at the same three-dimensional point in space simultaneously. Most of the time it was not done perfectly and only a very tiny fraction of the vast quantities of bullets fired in training and combat ever found their mark.

One aspect of training that George particularly enjoyed was "rat racing." It was essentially dogfighting without guns. "The instructor flew as the 'enemy' aircraft," he remembered, "and we did our best to get behind him and latch onto his tail. This required hard turns and dives and variations of loops and barrel rolls and other aerobatics. On one of these flights I heard a ripping sound as I pulled out of a dive. When I got back to level flight, I was unnerved by the sound of what seemed like air rushing through my airplane. It flew reasonably well, but after I landed and climbed out of the cockpit, I found that half of the aluminum skin on one side of the fuselage was torn away."

The flying at Foster further fired George's desire to be assigned to a fighter unit. That desire was elevated even more when the cadets were visited by Boyd "Buzz" Wagner during August 1942. Wagner, flying P-40s, had fought the Japanese as they invaded the Philippines. He became the nation's first ace and was credited with downing eight Japanese aircraft before being pulled from combat and sent back to the States so that he could share his experiences with those headed overseas.

Wagner's recounting of his exploits over the Philippines struck close to home for George. "He told us of the superior performance of the Japanese Zero fighter aircraft and explained the tactics that he and others used to counter their maneuverability," said George. Wagner's proven performance—and the wartime expediencies with which the USAAF was struggling—had propelled him from the rank of first lieutenant to lieutenant colonel in less than eight months. During peacetime he might never have reached that rank during a 20-year career. He was only three years older than George.[2]

That same month, a notice was posted which declared that the service had changed its stance on marriage and that those cadets who had hidden their marriages no longer needed to do so. It seemed that love had triumphed over USAAF regulations. "Betty joined me just before graduation," George said. "We rented a room for a short time and then, at the ceremony during which we were awarded our wings and commissioned as second lieutenants, Betty pinned my wings to my uniform." The boy who had waved so enthusiastically at Keystone bomber crews—many years and most of a world away—had finally realized his dream.

Together with Betty, George prepared to travel to his first assignment as an officer and a pilot. He had hoped, as had most of his classmates, to be assigned to a fighter group. And he was, as were most of his classmates, disappointed. "We were told that out of the 200 pilots that made up our class, 10 percent were to be assigned to fly P-38s. Most of the rest of us—70 percent—were to be sent back to the training command as instructors. The remainder were to be trained as B-25 pilots. They drew lots for the P-38 assignments and I lost out. Since I wanted to go to combat, and because I had no interest in being an instructor, I was able to get one of the B-25 slots."

"I was surprised at how many of my peers wanted to stay in the States to be instructors," George said. "Although I understood that it was important that there be enough instructors to train all the students coming behind me, that wasn't the reason I had joined the service. It was almost beside the point. I didn't want to teach. I wanted to fight."

"I didn't fully realize it at the time, but in retrospect it seemed as if Providence—God—was guiding me in the direction I really wanted to go. That direction was to the Pacific, and then to the Philippines. And ultimately, back to my parents and to the home where I had grown up."

CHAPTER 5

# "I Didn't Go Any Closer"

George looked through the window from where he sat at the desk and watched the B-25—its landing gear and flaps extended—turn from base leg onto final. Columbia Army Air Base, in South Carolina, was the USAAF's main training center for the B-25, and George was the 309th Bomb Group's officer of the day. He had been passing his time as aviators do, by watching other aviators.

The aircraft he watched slowed to landing speed and then slowed some more. And then it slowed too much. George stood up out of his chair and willed the other pilot to add power and to push the nose of the aircraft down. George's will wasn't enough. The B-25's nose pitched up into a stall, fell off on a wing, and then hit the ground and cartwheeled down the runway. He dashed for the door before the bomber—or what was left of it—even stopped moving.

George sprinted directly toward the crumpled, smoking wreck only a few hundred yards away. Ambulances and fire trucks raced past him, sirens wailing. A minute or two later, his lungs sucking for more air, he slowed to a hurried walk. Already, the rescue crews were pulling a crewman from the destroyed B-25. They placed him gently onto a litter before carrying him past George to a waiting ambulance. "The body was soaked in blood from head to toe," he remembered. "I didn't go any closer. It was the first wreck I had seen—the first dead bodies I had seen. The entire crew was dead."

***

After being winged and commissioned at Foster Field, George returned to Ypsilanti by train with Betty during September 1942. "As much as I would have liked to have visited with friends and maybe shown off my uniform and new wings, I just didn't have enough time off—I didn't get to see as many people as I would have liked." George had orders to train on the B-25 at Columbia,

South Carolina. "To save a couple of traveling days, Betty's cousin, Preston Tucker, offered to buy me an airline ticket to Columbia," George said, "but I was able to catch a ride on an Army plane and got there in plenty of time."

The 309th Bomb Group was responsible for training new B-25 pilots. "I had never even seen a B-25 until I got to Columbia," George said. "Most of us hadn't. It was a multi-engine aircraft of course, but the training command hadn't produced nearly enough multi-engine pilots at that point, so most of us who showed up for training were would-be fighter pilots. Some of the boys were disappointed but I was kind of excited. It was a real combat aircraft. In fact, it was already famous as the bomber that Jimmy Doolittle had used to bomb Japan after taking off from an aircraft carrier. Aside from that, I liked the idea that I'd be leading a crew."

Designed and manufactured by the North American Aircraft Corporation, the same company that produced the famed P-51 Mustang, the B-25 carried a crew of six—pilot, copilot, bombardier-navigator, flight engineer, gunner and radioman. It was powered by two, Wright Cyclone R-2600 Twin Wasp, air-cooled, radial engines that produced 1,700 horsepower apiece. Those engines were mounted to wings with outer sections that had a small degree of droop, or anhedral. This distinctive arrangement gave the aircraft an appearance that—from head-on—was distinct and ominous. The empennage, or tail, was characterized by two vertical stabilizers, or fins, mounted to each side of the horizontal stabilizer. The fuselage was deep for the aircraft's size, and the glass-paneled, or greenhouse, nose gave it an open-ended appearance.

Built as a medium bomber and intended to operate at altitudes of 10,000 to 15,000 feet, it had a top speed of about 280 miles per hour at that height, and could carry a bomb payload approaching two tons. It was sturdily built and weighed in at nearly ten tons before being loaded with fuel, guns, bombs, ammunition and crew. It was also readily adaptable and was modified many times through its service career which had only started the year before.

"We were given a few weeks of ground school," said George. "We spent quite a bit of time in the classroom where we learned about the aircraft's different systems. It was quite a step up in complexity from the T-6 that we had most recently flown. Outside the classroom we received familiarization training on the guns. At that time, the B-25 had a top and bottom turret, each with two .50-caliber machine guns. There was also a single gun in the nose that the bombardier was supposed to man. There were no guns in the tail of that particular model, although later models did carry them."

The B-25 was a very workmanlike aircraft—and it flew like it. "On my first flight," said George, "I was surprised at how much force it took to move the flight controls. It wasn't exactly a plane that you had to horse around, but it required a strong hand. However, after a while it became second nature and I never really thought about it until later in the war when I was training new pilots. Sometimes I'd have to take the controls from them and really lean into the yoke, or put in a boot full of rudder because they were too gentle with it." But if the B-25 was a tough airplane to move around the sky, it was also tough to break—a facet of the design that George and others would come to appreciate during the coming years.

"So early in the war," George said, "there were a lot of us who were new to what we were doing—we didn't have any real experience, and sometimes the training was lacking because most of our instructors had only barely more training than we did. And it wasn't just the pilots, but also the mechanics and the support personnel and just about everyone else." George was right. It was a dangerous time. Indeed, through the war, more aircraft and men were lost to accidents than to combat. A pilot might make any number of mistakes that could kill him and his crew. So might a mechanic. And so might a logistician if the wrong part was put into an aircraft.

"Anyway, we had a great many accidents," said George. "A lot of people were getting killed, and rumors started going around that the B-25 was a bad design—a bad aircraft. People started putting in for transfers, trying to get away from the B-25. It got so bad that the group commander called us all together for a meeting and told us that no one was getting orders anywhere, and that the B-25 was a fine aircraft—safer than most. He made the point that if it was flown and maintained well, it would do everything we asked of it. And he was right."

Certainly, most of his peers were conscientious pilots, but George went beyond what was typical in order to gain familiarity and expertise with the B-25. "Our training included emergency procedures and instrument flying under a canvas hood, or 'bag,' that was pulled up and over the pilot and the instrument panel so that he could read his instruments, but not see outside. Consequently, he had to rely entirely upon the instruments for flight and navigation."

"I wasn't required to do it," said George, "but on my own I practiced emergency procedures while under the canvas hood. For instance, I practiced the loss of an engine at the same time as I was making an instrument landing. This helped to increase my confidence not only in myself, but also in the B-25."

"On one flight I wanted to practice—at a safe altitude—the loss of an engine while in the takeoff configuration. Several crews had been killed when that had happened. I warned my men what I was going to do and joked that if things went wrong, I would tell them when to bail out. I had a new, young flight engineer with me and he seemed particularly nervous."

"I stabilized the aircraft in level flight at about 4,000 feet," George said, "and then I slowed and configured it just as I would for takeoff with the flaps partly down and the landing gear extended. Then, I pulled the power to the right engine to simulate its failure and pushed the power to maximum on the left engine to keep us flying. This required me to push full left rudder with my foot to keep the aircraft upright and flying in the right direction."

"Then I reached down toward the floor between my seat and the copilot's. I grabbed the rudder trim control and started twisting it to lessen some of the pressure against the left rudder. Because of my short stature—I was about five feet, six inches—I really had to stretch, and as I did so my foot let off the rudder pedal just a bit. The aircraft immediately whipped itself upside down and started a split-S dive which of course got everyone's attention. My young flight engineer was terrified. He had his parachute on and shouted, 'Now!?! Should we bail out now?!?'"

George brushed off the frightened young man, reduced the power on the left engine to idle, pulled the aircraft out of its dive, and then shoved the power back up on both engines. He then raised the landing gear and put the aircraft into a slight climb. "My copilot and I agreed," George stated the obvious, "that it was important for him to back me up on the controls—especially during an emergency."

"One other maneuver I practiced was a dead stick landing—landing without any engine power at all. It was unlikely that I'd ever have to do such a thing during actual operations, but it was still a possibility, particularly if we returned from a mission with very little fuel remaining. Essentially, I practiced all these sorts of emergencies because I wanted to know my aircraft as well as I possibly could."

It wasn't until well into his training that George asked Betty to join him at Columbia. "We were told that we could move off base, but housing was tight." Indeed, such was the case all over the nation—anywhere the military put a big base, or wherever large industrial concerns were turning out war material. Aside from the 16 million men who were put into uniform, millions of civilians moved to where the war work was. The country played a massive, lodging shell game. Where one family's son left to serve in uniform, another family's daughter might take work at the local factory and move into his bedroom. When a man and his wife moved out of their extended family's upstairs apartment, a pair of military couples might double up in the same space.

George and Betty had to make similar arrangements. "At first we had a very nice situation in a fully furnished large house with a housekeeper—the family was away. We shared that house with another lieutenant and his wife. It was nice because Betty had an instant friend. But the family came back and we had to find a new place to stay."

"We moved in with an older southern couple, Arthur and Elizabeth Davis, and their daughter, Caroline. Elizabeth had Persian cats and was a powerful personality, whereas poor Arthur was just along for the ride. She fancied herself as our away-from-home mother, and really took Betty under her wing. She gave her a steamy novel about a slave girl who was given to an Arab sheikh—I didn't get to read it. But we really came to like both Elizabeth and Arthur. And Caroline was a wonderful girl and very pretty. She had lots of attention from the boys on the base and went on to become an Army nurse."

Columbia and the south in general presented Betty with a bit of a shock. "She got on the bus not long after having arrived," said George, "and went to the back and sat down. The driver stopped the bus and walked to where she sat. He explained to her that she wasn't allowed to sit there. It was for colored people, only."

A new B-25 group, the 345th, was formed at Columbia on November 11, 1942. Staffing of the group's headquarters and its four squadrons, the 498th, 499th, 500th and 501st began immediately. "I was one of the first seven pilots assigned to the 499th Bomb Squadron," George said. "And I was assigned as an aircraft commander rather than a copilot—I was to be in full command of a crew. At that point aircraft commander assignments were made on the basis of who was commissioned when. The more senior officers were designated as aircraft commanders and the junior pilots were made copilots."

This practice of making assignments based on seniority—so long as an individual was capable of performing his duties—was typical of the military. It rewarded time in service and eliminated the need for commanders and their staffs to evaluate the young pilots on the subjective qualities of leadership, flying skills, presence, bearing and other officer-like characteristics. No matter how carefully they might have made their assessments, there would have been grousing and friction if junior pilots were chosen over more senior counterparts.

"The commander of the 345th was Colonel Jarred Crabb," said George. "He was an excellent pilot and an outstanding leader. He chose to fly with me a couple of different times, and sat in the copilot's position both times. It presented a few difficulties because I was shorter than average, and he was even shorter than me. When we flew together he used all the extra seat cushions so

The 345th Bomb Group to which George belonged operated the B-25D-5. (USAAF)

that he could comfortably reach the controls. In the event that I had to get on the controls to help him, I had to stretch out quite a bit."

George didn't think as much of his squadron commander as he did of Colonel Crabb. "Our first squadron CO [Commanding Officer] was Buell Bankston. He and his crew were killed when he took off on a flight to Houston to see his wife and newborn child. He called over the radio after he got airborne to report that he was climbing through 8,000 feet and was still in thick clouds. We never heard from him again as he crashed, killing himself and his crew."

"Edison Walters took over for Bankston," George said. "He was a West Point graduate and a by-the-book disciplinarian with a stiff leadership style that didn't really work well in a flying squadron. He was a 'yes sir, no sir' sort of officer which rubbed many of us the wrong way. Worse, he wasn't a very good pilot. Socially, he was a bit awkward and uncomfortable, and I think he tried to cover up his shortcomings with all that military nonsense. To be fair, he was still young and the challenges he faced were considerable."

"When Walters was put in charge of the squadron, he started wearing command pilot wings," said George. "Those denoted a very experienced pilot that had at least 3,000 hours of flight time. Of course, he had only been flying for a couple of years and had nowhere near that number of hours. I was with Colonel Crabb when he spotted Walters wearing those wings. The colonel asked him what in the world he thought he was doing and Walters explained that since he was in command of the squadron, he deserved to wear command pilot wings. Colonel Crabb told him to take them off right there. I tried very hard and not very successfully to keep from laughing and it did nothing to ingratiate me with Walters."

As the 345th received new personnel and aircraft, the focus of training shifted from individual crews flying individual flights, to training that emphasized small formation operations. That training was followed by squadron-sized missions, and then missions that brought all four of the 345th's squadrons together. "We did everything pretty much by the book," said George, "which was written by people who had never flown those types of operations in combat. In fact, there was no one who had any combat experience. We just used the books and learned as we went, making adjustments along the way."

Bombing practice was done at nearby Lake Murray, while gunnery practice was performed just offshore of Myrtle Beach. Full-scale training missions saw the 345th hit "enemy" targets all over the southeast United States. "Things didn't always go smoothly, but we learned something new every time we flew," said George. "After a while we really started to come together as a team. I think that was in large part due to Jarred Crabb, the group's commanding officer. He was a steady, smart and commonsensical gentleman and leader—and a great pilot. Our improvement was also due to the fact that everyone was committed to the notion of teamwork to get the job done. Everyone knew they had to do their job right, regardless of whether they were pilots, gunners, mechanics or cooks."

George's own crew came together during this period. "The pilots really had no choice as to who was assigned to their crews—it was mostly an administrative exercise, and we took the men we were given. The oldest man in my crew was Harvey Green, from Minneapolis. He was in his mid-30s which seemed quite old to the rest of us; he wasn't in any risk of being drafted, but he wanted to serve. He was the radioman and was very good at his job. And he was responsible for manning the guns in the lower turret. He was very calm, almost unflappable."

"Henry 'Bud' Jepson was another good one," said George. "He was from Texas and was my flight engineer—he made sure everything was working properly while we were airborne, and he manned the top turret guns. He was an excellent shot. I could count on him in every situation."

"Bill Parke was my copilot, and a good friend. In fact, Betty and Bill's wife, Billie, were also good friends. Bill was a bit taller than me at almost six feet and was a good pilot in his own right. He had a great personality for the job—responsive and steady. Although we were both new to the B-25, he never resented being assigned as my copilot rather than having his own crew. He was very supportive."

"Ralph Stevens was from Texas and was our bombardier-navigator," George recalled. "He was a tall, lanky fellow, good at his job, and liked to have a good time. Sometimes, he was just a little too enthusiastic with his fun-making—especially when he'd had a drink or seven. But he was a really good man."

"Alston Bivins, from Shelby, North Carolina, was my gunner," said George. "He was responsible for making sure that our guns and the associated equipment were in good working order. He typically manned the .30-caliber waist guns and helped other men with their duties as required."

"The man on the ground who made sure our aircraft was always in top shape was our crew chief, John Lipp. He was from South Dakota and was a classic Swede—quiet, efficient, hardworking and accommodating. That was later evidenced in the performance of our aircraft. During all of my combat missions with the 345th, I never had to abort due to maintenance problems. We couldn't have asked for a better crew chief."

The 345th's men moved to Walterboro, South Carolina, during early March 1943 to complete their training. "Walterboro wasn't as finished as Columbia was," said George. "We established ourselves almost from scratch as if we had arrived in a combat theater. We set up a headquarters building, an operations shop, a mess hall, a motor pool and other necessary functions. The troops were quartered in tents."

"Our wives accompanied us to Walterboro and we found places to live out in town for the few weeks we were there. There wasn't much to do, but Betty and the other girls arranged informal little social gatherings. It was a nice time and we all got a bit closer which made it both easier and more difficult once we went into combat.

"One of our final exercises," remembered George, "tested our ability to get airborne as quickly as possible in the event an enemy air raid was inbound. When the siren started to wail, we dashed out to our aircraft which the ground crew had already made ready, and then we took off. Everyone hustled to be the first to take off."

The size and the complexity of the practice missions continued to increase until the group was declared ready for combat during April 1943. Just where the men were to be sent had been an open question since the 345th's formation. "We assumed that we were going to be assigned somewhere in England or North Africa," said George. "Maps of both places had been posted in the various operations and training spaces, and many of the lectures we received were focused on combat flying over Europe, and on German tactics and equipment. All of that was reinforced when we were issued cold weather gear."

"And then, the idea got loose that we might be headed for the Aleutians," George said. "No one wanted that. Even then, it was recognized as a backwater where not much was happening. And the flying conditions in that part of the world were miserable." Although the men considered that they might be sent to the Pacific to fight against the Japanese, most of the war news was coming out of Europe and most believed it was their likely destination.

It was during this time that George's squadron, the 499th, settled on a nickname. "It didn't come up in a meeting or anything, but someone suggested the name, 'Bats Outta Hell,'" George said. "Most of us thought it was pretty good. It was fierce enough, and it rolled off the tongue alright. I don't remember anyone making any objections or any other suggestions, and so it became our nickname without much fuss."

*** 

American and Filipino forces on the Bataan Peninsula, out of food, equipment and ammunition—and vastly outgunned—surrendered to the Japanese on April 9. George had enjoyed Boy Scout outings there a decade or so earlier. He didn't hear it, but one of his high school friends, Norman Reyes, made the famous "Bataan Has Fallen" radio broadcast. Although the Japanese had forbidden civilians to have radio sets, it is certain that the news almost immediately reached Lawrence in Santo Tomas, and Prisca and Dorothy in the family's San Juan home. Some of the most powerful parts are excerpted:

> Bataan has fallen. The Philippine–American troops on this war-ravaged and bloodstained peninsula have laid down their arms. With heads bloody but unbowed, they have yielded to the superior force and numbers of the enemy …
> Besieged on land and blockaded by sea, cut off from all sources of help in the Philippines and in America, the intrepid fighters have done all that human endurance could bear …
> Bataan has fallen, but the spirit that made it stand—a beacon to all the liberty-loving peoples of the world—cannot fall![1]

***

While the 345th, still based at Walterboro, made final preparations for an overseas deployment, the crews were sent south to the B-25 depot at Hunter Army Airfield near Savannah, Georgia. There, they were assigned factory-fresh B-25D-5s. "They took me and the crew out to the aircraft, handed me the key to the crew hatch, and had us crawl all over and through it," said George. "It smelled just like a brand-new car! We had to do an acceptance inspection in order to make sure that the aircraft had all the equipment it was supposed to have, and that everything was in place. It actually took us quite a bit of time to go through all the checklists."

When the acceptance process was finished, George—whose personal net worth was less than 1,000 dollars—signed a receipt for a quarter-million dollars' worth of B-25. The aircraft was subsequently released to his care, and he and his crew proudly flew it back to Walterboro. Among the many things that still needed to be done to get the aircraft ready for combat, naming it was one. As the aircraft commander, it was George's prerogative to give it a name, and he had known for a while which one he wanted.

"*Jayhawk*," he said. "It was the mascot for Kansas University. Although I had grown up in the Philippines, I was steeped in Jayhawk lore, and it was where I intended to study after the war. The name not only pleased me, but I know that it would have excited my father and his family due to their connections to the school."

As the 345th readied for movement overseas, the men who had wives sent them home. "Betty and I didn't really dwell on what might happen, or what might not. She already knew that what I was doing was dangerous; she knew men who had been killed while we were training. And she was smart enough to know that many more would be killed when we were in combat. Certainly, we were sad at the notion of being separated and in love, but there were no histrionics. We took care of all our practical arrangements and said goodbye."

Betty left in company with Bill Parke's wife, Billie. They traveled to Pennsylvania where Betty visited with Billie's family for a few days before leaving for Wisconsin. There, at Hales Corners near Milwaukee, she moved in with her stepfather and his wife and their children.

George said nothing to Betty, but there was a part of him that felt guilty. The truth was that even though he loved her with every bit of his heart and soul, he was still excited to be going into combat. There were many reasons behind that excitement, and they were as timeless as the history of warfare. No doubt, he was anxious to put into practice the money and energy that the government had spent to train him, but there was also a sense of adventure. And it was the purest sort of adventure—the sort that might kill him. And

Betty used George's hat to try to hide her pregnancy from the camera just before he left for combat duty in the spring of 1943. (George Cooper)

too, he was keen to know how he would perform under fire. He wanted to prove to himself, as much as to anyone else, that George Cooper was a man, and that he could do whatever was asked of him and more.

\*\*\*

As Betty made her way back to Wisconsin, she prayed that George would survive to meet the child she carried in her womb.

## CHAPTER 6

# "I Sat There for Some Time"

The B-25's engines were loud, but the loudness was deep and smooth. It should have been reassuring to George but was little more than background noise as he considered the two cloud decks in front of him. The gray layer below *Jayhawk* sloped gradually upward, while the smooth ceiling of clouds above him slanted down toward the other. They converged in a solid mass several miles ahead.

Soon after the 345th received orders to start for Australia in early April 1943, the crews from the different squadrons flew their aircraft back down to Hunter Army Airfield to receive a thorough inspection and any needed modifications. *Jayhawk* performed poorly for George, as he wrote in a letter to Betty: "My left engine was cutting out so badly that I feared that any minute I would have to feather the prop and come in on one engine. It was not necessary, however, and we got in safely."

This action of feathering a propeller was to change the pitch, or alignment, of the blades so that their edges were turned into the airstream, or direction of travel. Thus configured, they offered very little air resistance. If an engine failed and the propeller was not feathered, the blades created a tremendous degree of drag, which forced the remaining engine to work all the much more, heightening the odds that it might also fail.

George shared his frustration with *Jayhawk*'s reliability in his letter to Betty. "We worked all the next day changing the spark plugs and checking the engines. Some people would say that I was having rather rotten luck, but with all the trouble I have had with the plane, I am lucky that I'm still alive."

Once the depot finished its work on the 345th's aircraft, the crews started for the west coast. On April 12, anxious to get on his way, George checked the weather and filed a flight plan with base operations before meeting Bill

Parke and the rest of the crew at the aircraft. They gave *Jayhawk* one more going-over before loading their bags and taking off.

Now, approaching Macon, the weather—and the two layers of clouds—showed dark and threatening. The forecast had warned of thunderstorms along George's route, but the weathermen had assured him that he would be able to see and avoid them. They were wrong. He knew that once he penetrated the wall in front of him, he would be flying blind.

Still, he had no reason to change course. He might alter his heading a few degrees left or right, but where the thunderstorms were or were not was unknown. Consequently, his current heading was as good as any. A short time later, *Jayhawk* punched into the smothering gray, and George and Parke transitioned to their flight instruments.

The first burble of turbulence rocked *Jayhawk* only a minute or two later. Fat raindrops—just a few at first—splatted onto the windscreen and pulsed in sporadic bursts against the fuselage and wings. George gripped the control yoke more firmly and focused on the attitude gyro to ensure he kept *Jayhawk* on course and upright. Already the needle on the altimeter was jumping as wind shears snatched the aircraft upward and just as suddenly flung it back toward earth.

A sudden, furious thrumming reverberated through the aircraft as the rain, now mixed with hail, increased in volume many times over. Turbulence smashed the aircraft up and down and sideways. Through the windows, the crew could see *Jayhawk*'s wings flapping almost as if they were part of a living thing.

The aircraft's structure shrieked and creaked. Whatever wasn't fastened down was suspended in midair one moment, and then hurled back down the next. Dirt and dust and fine metal shavings from the aircraft's recent manufacture floated into the crew's eyes and ears and nostrils—as did ashes and cigarette butts from the ashtrays. Ralph Stevens had neglected to strap himself to his seat and his head was bashed against the dome light. Now it was cracked and smeared with blood. And Stevens was crumpled on the floor.

The instruments on the panel in front of George shook so violently they were almost impossible to read. While it was a cardinal rule to never turn around in a thunderstorm as the far side was generally closer than the point of entry, George wasn't certain that this particular storm had a far side. He did know that *Jayhawk* might be shaken apart if it was forced to endure much more.

Aware that storm fronts in that part of the country ran from southwest to northeast, George hauled the aircraft around in a descending left turn to the south. At the same time, he leaned to either side to check the aircraft's wings.

Noting that they appeared intact, he turned his attention inside. Despite the beating *Jayhawk* was taking, all was as it should have been.

The fury of the storm lessened as the aircraft lost altitude toward the south. George slowed the rate of descent as he and Parke peered through the windscreen for any sign of the ground. It wasn't until they felt their way down through 1,000 feet that they broke free of the clouds. George took a moment to regain his bearings before turning left again, back toward Savannah.

An hour later, they were on the ground. George taxied *Jayhawk* to the flight line, completed his post-landing checklist and shut the engines down. He looked at Parke and drew a long sigh. He had never been so frightened and he felt physically akimbo. Exhausted, he dropped his gaze to his legs. They shook against each other involuntarily and violently. "I sat there for some time before leaving the airplane," he said.

George wasn't the only aircraft commander to run into trouble on this first leg of the 345th's deployment to the far side of the globe. Indeed, the 500th Bomb Squadron's Lester Shepherd and his crew crashed and perished not far from Savannah. The 345th would lose many more men as it moved toward Australia.

While readying to start west again the following day, Henry Jepson, the flight engineer, discovered that *Jayhawk*'s engines were nearly out of oil. Had George and his crew not been forced back by the storm, the engines would have likely failed some time during the flight. Further inspection showed that the engine cylinders were badly scored. They might have been damaged by dust or other contaminants, but they could have been delivered defective from the manufacturer. In fact, Wright was being investigated by the Truman Commission during that very time for fraud associated with shoddy quality control.[1]

Regardless of the reasons behind their near-failure, *Jayhawk*'s engines were topped off with oil. It was determined that the aircraft was safe enough to fly to the maintenance depot at Macon, about an hour from Savannah. At Macon, the maintenance experts decided that both engines should be changed. However, work went slowly and five days later George complained to Betty that, "They are having trouble getting it into running condition. If I had only known how long I would have been here, I would have had you fly down. I miss you, and it will be hard to get along without you for so long."

On April 21, he wrote to Betty from the Adolphus Hotel in Dallas. Finally, *Jayhawk* seemed to be performing as it always should have. "The plane is in excellent condition as far as I can determine. I should not be writing you according to Army regulations, but I know you will not mention my stay here to anyone. This hotel seems to get quite a lot of traffic," he wrote. And he was impressed with Dallas which he described as, "quite a large city and rather nice."

George and his crew arrived at McClellan Field, near Sacramento, California, a couple of days later. "We flew on automatic pilot most of the way," he wrote. "Parke wrote a letter and read while I slept. Most of Texas and Arizona was barren country with little sign of life. California is a pretty place. The mountains are still snowcapped, and the valleys are all shades of beautiful green."

Most of the 345th's crews were already at McClellan by the time George and his crew arrived aboard *Jayhawk*. The 345th was pausing at McClellan while 600-gallon fuel tanks were mounted into the bomb bays of the aircraft. These tanks were necessary for the next leg of the deployment—the long overwater flight to Hawaii.

George was quite taken with Sacramento; he liked its size and the wide variety of things to do. The 345th's leadership, probably wisely, made certain that the men were not too taken with the city or its citizens by making them report to base at 0900 and 1300 each day.

George reported to Betty that he and Bill Parke went horseback riding and, "met several girls on the bridle path. I thought they were just kids and told Parke so when he wanted to stop and talk with them." As it developed, the girls were all of age and proved to be pleasant company. "We asked them to go riding with us the next day," George wrote, "and to bring a picnic lunch. We had a rather enjoyable time." He did note that none of them rode so well as Betty.

George's squadron mate and friend, Norman Hyder, took his aircraft airborne on April 26 for a test flight after it had been serviced for controllability problems. Hyder put the B-25 through a series of hard turns during which, as George described, the aircraft lost a control pulley and went into a spin. Hyder pulled desperately on the control yoke and brought the B-25 back to level flight only a few feet above the ground. A few minutes later he wrestled the aircraft down to the ground in a controlled crash. Although Hyder and his crew survived, the aircraft never flew again. As a result of the accident, all of the group's aircraft were grounded for a few days until their control systems were checked.

The jumping-off point for Australia at that point in the war was Hamilton Army Air Base, north of San Francisco. The 345th's crews flew there from McClellan during the last few days of April 1943. It was a prewar airfield and had a feel of permanence, unlike many of the installations that had been hurriedly constructed in response to the growing global conflict.

George arrived on April 30 and noted that it was a "lovely base." On the cusp of leaving the United States, he took time to write a very pointed letter to Betty about what paperwork she must prepare and have at hand in the event that he was killed. "Don't poo-poo what I am asking you," he said, "because you know that it is a very good possibility that I may die. I hate to put it that way, but I only want to emphasize the importance of it."

The crews readied to fly to Hickam Field, Hawaii, as single aircraft rather than in formations. Flying in formation consumed too much fuel as it required the wingmen to constantly adjust and readjust their power settings. As it was, even with the extra tanks that had been installed at McClellan, the fuel margin for the flight to Hawaii would be perilously thin.

"My crew was up early," George said, remembering May 3, 1943. "After we ate breakfast I stopped by base operations and was told to stand by; they would alert us when the winds were considered to be favorable. They were exercising a good deal of caution as just the week prior, three aircraft ran into unexpected headwinds and had to put down in the sea."

The meteorologists were cautious for a reason. Men might die should they make a mistake. And they might die if they didn't make a mistake. Although the weather men received reports from ships and aircraft, information was still sketchy and the science of forecasting was immature. So then, although the aircrews were nervous about the crossing, the meteorologists were nervous about predicting the conditions that would clear them for departure.

"Since the gunners weren't necessary for the flight," said George, "we left Bevins behind. The group's gunners went on separate transport aircraft. So did many of the bombardier-navigators. For instance, Ralph Stevens was more of a bombardier than a navigator, and was replaced on my crew by a navigator on loan from the Air Transport Command, or ATC. It was standard practice as the ATC men were trained in celestial navigation. They were supposed to be able to pinpoint our position throughout the entire flight—day or night."

George and the crew fretted away the hours as they waited to be cleared for takeoff. They talked, read or cat-napped to pass the time. "At around 1800 we were alerted to get ready, and we assembled at base operations to await our release. But it wasn't until midnight that we were finally cleared to go."

"Before we took off," said George, "I asked Bill Parke if he wanted to fly in shifts—one pilot flying while the other pilot napped. We had been awake for about 18 hours at that point and we were about to take off on a 12- or 13-hour flight. Neither of us had ever done anything like that before. In truth, not even a tiny fraction of all the pilots in the world had ever flown such a long flight."

"We took off into a pitch black, moonless night and passed over San Francisco as we climbed to 8,000 feet. The city was blacked out because of scares from Japanese submarines. I set the engine manifold pressures and RPMs for long-range cruise which gave us an airspeed of only about 175 miles per hour.

After about an hour, with *Jayhawk* established on the proper course at the correct altitude, George set the autopilot and handed control over to Parke. He then went quickly to sleep. "Sometime later," he said, "I snapped awake. It took me an instant to figure out where I was. I looked over at Bill and he was dead to the world. And the navigator, Relle Wolfe, was out as were Jepson and Greene, the radioman. We had literally been asleep at the controls."

The aircraft had drifted only a few degrees off course and lost only a couple hundred feet of altitude. George got everyone awake and put *Jayhawk* back on track. "After that, I told Bill that I'd do the flying—I was much too excited to fall back asleep."

The B-25 droned through the black toward Hawaii without encountering any weather of consequence. From time-to-time the ATC navigator, Wolfe, pointed his instruments through the Plexiglas astrodome to check their progress against the remaining fuel. George scanned the engine instruments regularly, checking for any sign that the engines were preparing to betray him. They gave no indication of doing so, and their syrupy low growl was a comfort.

"The rising sun was a welcome sight," he recalled. "High above us, the sky was a beautiful clear blue. Below, it was darker but we could see scattered white clouds reflecting the day's first sunlight. Below them, the blue-black sea was flecked with white caps. It was the first time that any of us—excepting the navigator—had been out of sight of land."

The sky and seascape was beautiful, but George was nervous nonetheless. "Of course, we all wondered what we would find when the clock showed our estimated time of arrival. Wolfe had pegged it at 1100. It was just a few minutes before that when the verdant green of the Hawaiian Islands came into view. It was like stumbling across paradise, and we praised Wolfe enthusiastically for his accuracy. And although we didn't need it, I was very happy to find that we still had two hours of fuel remaining." After a 13-hour flight, George and Parke put the aircraft down at Hickam without incident.

It had been less than two years since the Japanese sneak attack on Hawaii and the entry of the United States into the war. "They had long since cleaned up the debris," George said, "and most of the facilities had been repaired. But evidence of the attack was still everywhere in the form of bullet holes and damage from bomb blasts and shrapnel. And of course, the battleship *Arizona* was still resting on the bottom of Pearl Harbor."

George and the rest of the crew enjoyed Honolulu for several days while the large fuel tank was removed from *Jayhawk*'s bomb bay, and replaced with a smaller one. The remaining flights to Australia would be much shorter than that from California to Hawaii. "We did get a chance to go to Waikiki Beach," he remembered, "but mostly we just relaxed in town."

The news spread that a 499th crew had failed to reach Hawaii. Bernard Salmela's aircraft had simply disappeared. "Since there had been no bad weather along the route," George said, "we considered that perhaps the crew had—like us—fallen asleep." It was certainly a possibility, as no radio transmissions were ever received from the missing aircraft.

Another possibility was mechanical or engine failure. Regardless, in real terms—considering the destruction of Hyder's aircraft, and the loss of Salmela's aircraft and crew—it meant that George's squadron, the 499th, had already sustained real losses of more than 12 percent, as two of the squadron's roster of 16 aircraft were destroyed. And the 499th had yet to even leave Hawaii, much less enter combat.

"On the morning that we left Hawaii for Christmas Island," said George, "I ate breakfast at the officers' club with Clifford Bryant. He was a fun-loving boy from Kansas and one of my closest friends, as we had gone through pilot training together. He loved to play cards and was a good gambler. On our way out of the club he stuck a dime into one of the slot machines and won big. Dimes came clattering out of the machine and it seemed they wouldn't stop. He walked out with pockets that were bulging with coins. He was one of the luckiest guys I knew."

Only an hour or two later, on May 8, 1943, George checked *Jayhawk*'s engines one more time before taxiing onto the runway at Hickam. They gave no indication of trouble, and he released the brakes and let the aircraft roll onto the runway. When the B-25's nose was pointed squarely down the middle, he pushed the throttles forward and felt the aircraft accelerate.

BANG! BANG! BANG! There came a series of explosions from the left engine and George quickly pulled the throttles to idle. The racket ceased and George let the aircraft slow before calling the tower personnel to let them know he was aborting the takeoff. After making a perfect crossing from the mainland, it seemed that *Jayhawk* was behaving badly again.

After parking the aircraft, George steeled himself against the possibility that he might be left behind. He had no idea how long it might take to get an engine changed at Hickam—if one was even available. He climbed out with the rest of the crew as Jepson trotted off to get a maintenance stand. It was only about 20 minutes later that Jepson looked down from the engine and smiled. He waved a matted clump of brush and leaves and sticks down at the rest of the crew. Birds had built a nest in the intake which had choked the carburetor of the air it needed to operate at high power settings. Without that air, the engine had protested with the explosive backfires that had caused George to abort the takeoff.

George and his crew were airborne less than an hour later. Christmas Island, or Kiritimati, was only about six hours—1,200 miles—to the south. "I figured that if Wolfe got us to Hawaii with no trouble, then he could certainly find Christmas Island; it was only half the distance. I didn't bother setting the engines for maximum range. Instead, we just cruised at a normal airspeed, about 200 miles per hour."

Unnervingly, Christmas Island was nowhere in sight at the estimated time of arrival. The ADF, or automatic direction finder, was tuned to the proper frequency but was performing erratically. The needle swung 30 degrees to each side of *Jayhawk*'s nose. "Wolfe wanted to execute a square search pattern," George said. "We would fly a large square within which Christmas Island should be, and then fly a series of smaller squares until we spotted it."

George's heart beat faster. He was the aircraft commander. He was responsible not only for *Jayhawk*, but for the men flying with him. And for himself, and Betty and the baby she carried.

The ocean spread endlessly and unbroken in every direction. George squinted through the windscreen into the distance. He checked the fuel remaining. He looked at Parke and Wolfe. Again, he tallied the fuel. "We didn't have enough gas to do a proper square search," he said. "I decided to split the difference on the heading the ADF was showing."

His mind made up, George held *Jayhawk* on course. Anxious, but not panicked, he tried to act with as much confidence as his sensibilities would allow. With little else to do, he and the crew watched the horizon, the ADF and the fuel gauges. Although no more remarkable than any number of similar islands, Christmas Island was a very welcome sight when it appeared through the haze. Seldom had George been so happy to make a landing.

Happy or not, there wasn't much at Christmas Island other than palm trees and servicemen. Recreation was scarce and the men stationed there often entertained themselves by shooting at the sharks that lazed in the lagoon. George and his crew were happy to leave for Canton Island the next day.

The flight was unremarkable. Getting the aircraft parked after they landed was not. "I do not know how much of this I can stand," George wrote to

Betty on May 9, "but at present my crew and I are stranded on a treeless, barren island until we can get a new wingtip for the plane. I very carelessly ran the left wing into the side of a coral embankment as I was parking my ship."

"Of all the places I had to do it at," he continued. "It had to be here. It is hotter than Hades, and the white coral sand sends out an awful glare." The local maintenance officer wouldn't release *Jayhawk* until a replacement tip could be gotten and installed. George fumed at the delay. The tip had little effect on the flying characteristics of the aircraft, but the overcautious maintenance officer would not be persuaded. George was anxious at the thought that the rest of the squadron was going to pull away from him while he and his crew waited for a spare wingtip to be located, delivered and installed. Still, he was fully aware that it was his fault entirely.

"It was a miserable place," George said. "The officers' club was dug underground for protection from the sun. People did little during the middle of the day, unless they had to." Alcohol—to ease the boredom—was highly prized and sold at a premium; he and his crew were offered an incredible 90 dollars per quart for any liquor they had. Sadly, they had none to offer.

George and his crew were billeted in a little hut that some wag had dubbed, "The Hotel Astor." Showering was done with salt water which left the men feeling less than clean. "There is no point in using soap because you can't lather," George lamented. "I tried washing my hair the other day and only made a gluey mess of things."

Probably against censorship regulations he told Betty of Salmela's disappearance on the flight to Hawaii. He also noted a practical impact of the loss: "He had three mail bags on board, so all your letters are probably at the bottom of the Pacific."

"Still on our little island waiting on the wingtip," George wrote to Betty five days later, on May 14. "It is getting rather tiresome and annoying because we don't even know if they have one yet." He described how he attempted to break the mind-numbing routine of cards, paperbacks and sleeping into which he had fallen, by taking a ride around the island. "On one side the birds have a large gathering and you can walk right up to frigate birds, goonies and boobies. They don't seem to be afraid, and as far as I know, no one seems to harm them."

In fact, George seemed to have settled in at Canton Island to a small extent. "We have picture shows every night except Sunday. The theaters are in the open and the films are free—donated by the picture companies in the States." He also reported that Bill Parke had been going to the beach each morning to look for shells with which he might make his wife, Billie, a necklace.

*Jayhawk* was repaired a few days later and George and his crew flew next to Nandi, in the Fiji Islands. "After we landed," George said, "we learned that Cliff Bryant had gone missing after he'd left Nandi. A Navy PBY coming from the opposite direction at the same time reported a violent thunderstorm along Cliff's route. It's likely that he perished in that storm." No sign of Bryant—George's friend and the lucky gambler with pockets full of dimes—was ever found.

George and his crew showed up at *Jayhawk* the next morning and found that a finger exhaust on one of the engines was cracked. This was a trivial next-to-nothing as far as George and his flight engineer, Henry Jepson, were concerned but the local maintenance officer grounded the aircraft. George had seen this trap before, and would have none of it; there was no telling how long it would take to get the required part flown in. Under threat of disciplinary action, he loaded his crew, started the aircraft and took off.

Following an overnight stay at New Caledonia, with a cracked finger exhaust about which no one there seemed to care, George pointed *Jayhawk* toward Amberley Field, near Brisbane Australia. The flight was unremarkable until they neared their destination, over which a rainstorm was dumping prodigious quantities of water. Rain beat on the aircraft as George descended through the clouds. "The field was grass," he said, "and was covered with water. As I braked after landing, the plane hydroplaned."

*Jayhawk* might as well have been rolling across ice. "I could not stop," George remembered. "A line of trees at the end of the field loomed close," he said, "and I kicked in full rudder to ground loop the plane." *Jayhawk* obeyed and swung around, plowing up a huge plume of water and mud and grass. "We skidded to a stop, sideways," George said, "just short of the trees."

At last, George and his crew were in Australia.

\*\*\*

While George worked his way through flight training and the disorienting wonderment of marriage—and his subsequent journey to Australia—his father, mother and sister got on in the Philippines as well as they were able. Prisca, without Lawrence, had no regular income. As time went on, there were less and less manufactured goods and products to buy, and those that were available were very expensive. Prisca was compelled to make money however she could, even selling or bartering bunches of bananas from the trees that grew on the property. "We had no good way of making money," said Dorothy, "but our

Filipino friends and servants were very loyal and kind; they brought us food and other things we needed. We ate a lot of chicken and rice."

Early during the war, Prisca had been allowed to make short visits to Santo Tomas to visit with Lawrence. Dorothy remembered that they were also allowed to send food. "Mother often wrote messages on tiny, rolled-up ribbons that she would tuck inside the food."

Later, the Japanese stopped the spouses from visiting and from sending food. But for a time, they permitted children to visit their fathers. "My mother took me there and watched from a building across the street," Dorothy said. "I ran to the gate where all the fathers waited under Japanese guard and I hugged my father and told him that we were okay. And he held me and told me that he was fine and that he missed me, and those sorts of things. And he especially wanted me to tell Mother that he was well."

As the war began to turn against them, the Japanese stopped all physical contact between the prisoners in Santo Tomas and their families. "Early during the war when the Japs were winning," said Dorothy, "they wanted us to think they were kind and magnanimous victors. But later, when it was obvious that they were losing, they turned vicious."

## CHAPTER 7

# "She Was 'Knocked Up'"

"We stayed a few days in Amberley to acclimate ourselves while *Jayhawk* was checked out," said George. "They also issued us different types of tropical gear that we would need while flying combat operations. I didn't need them, but I was able to get two pairs of nice, fur-lined flying boots. I planned on taking them back to the States when my combat tour was over."

The group headquarters element and the 498th Bomb Squadron were sent more than 600 miles north to Woodstock, near Townsville, Australia, which was located on Australia's northeastern coast. The Fifth Air Force maintained a supply and repair depot at Townsville. It was raw, cattle country with a thin population. More raw, and more thinly populated was the nearby airfield at Reid River where the 499th and 500th Bomb Squadrons were sent. It was little more than a landing surface scraped into the dirt. The 501st made do at not-too-distant Charters Towers which was a legitimate town.

"We shared Reid River with the 22nd Bomb Group," said George. "Those boys were enjoying a period of rest and rehabilitation as they had been in combat since almost the beginning of the war and were just about spent. They flew B-26s which had suffered a bad reputation for being difficult and dangerous to fly. A couple of their pilots invited me along for a training flight and let me fly it for a while. I thought it was a delight. It was much lighter on the controls than the B-25 and quite easy to maneuver. I didn't find anything wrong with it at all."

George's experience with the B-26 was well after many of the kinks had been worked out of the type. The 22nd had arrived in Australia during April 1942 while still learning to fly and maintain it. During those dark days, the group had flown small raids of six or fewer aircraft with no fighter escorts against such distant and heavily defended targets as Rabaul and Lae. Each raid was an exhausting, multi-day affair as the crews first had to fly from Australia to Port Moresby, New Guinea. There, they were compelled to refuel their aircraft by hand. The following day they flew the actual combat mission and returned to Port Moresby. It wasn't until the next day that they flew back to their main bases in Australia.

The 345th's eager crews argued good naturedly with the 22nd's tired veterans about whose aircraft was better. Impressed as he was by the B-26, George still preferred the B-25. "It was strong, honest and rugged. And it could take a beating." Ultimately, this trading of barbs was for nothing as the 22nd later converted to the B-25, and ultimately to the B-24.

The 499th's crews kept their skills up during this period with occasional bombing practice and formation flying. And sometimes they simply flew alone. "I took my aircraft and crew out one day with the intention of seeing how high we could go," George said. "After takeoff we climbed into a solid deck of clouds at 2,000 feet and broke into the clear at 8,000 feet. I kept climbing, not really knowing exactly where we were. We put our oxygen masks on as we passed through 13,000 feet. Our rate of climb gradually tapered off until, at 25,000 feet, the aircraft was on the edge of stalling."

"At that point," George said, "I let the nose of the aircraft drop and started a gentle descent to the east. The clouds below us extended as far as we could see in every direction and I wanted to get past Townsville, across the coast and over the sea. I didn't want to inadvertently fly into a mountain while I was in the clouds."

Satisfied that he and his crew were beyond the shoreline and over the water, George nosed the B-25 down into the cloud layer. Minutes later, both he and Bill Parke gasped when *Jayhawk* popped into the clear between two peaks, one of which rose above their altitude. They had come down over the top of Magnetic Island, just northeast of Townsville. Shaken, but grateful that he and his crew weren't smashed to bits against the surrounding hills, George hauled the aircraft around in a turn to the south. A short time later he landed back at Reid River without incident.

During this time, keen to keep his men sharp, the 499th's commanding officer, Edison Walters, led the squadron's men on morning runs through an aromatic eucalyptus grove and up a hill, a mile or so distant. His interest in physical conditioning was not shared by his men, and there was much grousing. "He always prided himself on being the first to the top," George recalled. "One morning, Bill Parke, Ken McClure and I decided to surprise him. We found a shortcut up the side of the hill, slipped away from the group and scrabbled to the top. Walters was somewhat confounded—crestfallen even—when he found us waiting for him with smiles on our faces."

The crew of *Jayhawk*: George Cooper, Bill Parke, Henry Jepson, Harvey Green, Ralph Stevens and John Lipp. (USAAF)

Time was also made for social events with the locals. "They had a party for us one evening," said George. "I danced with a nice young woman who startled me when she admitted that she was 'knocked up.' I was a little bit embarrassed about questioning her further but was relieved and amused when I found out that 'knocked up' was an Australian expression for being tired."

\*\*\*

Most of the way around the world, on June 11, 1943, George's friend Hal Herrick fired his B-17's nose gun at the German fighters that dove through the formation. The noise and violence of it reverberated through his body. It had been just more than a year since he had washed out of pilot training. He had stood up at George and Betty's wedding during that same time. Since then, he had trained as a navigator and been assigned to the 379th Bomb Group which was now based at Kimbolton, England.

This was the 379th's second combat mission and Herrick's first. George and Betty, pilot training and almost everything else in his life were far from his mind. The target was the submarine complex at Wilhelmshaven, Germany, and the 379th—outside the range of American escort fighters—was being savaged by the Luftwaffe. His earphones crackled with interphone chatter as the crew called out the positions of attacking fighters. Other aircraft in the formation bobbed and skidded as much as they dared in order to throw off the aim of the enemy pilots.

The fight came to no good end for Herrick and his comrades. Their aircraft, afire now, fell back from the formation before going out of control and spiraling earthward. A single crewman tumbled away and fell for several seconds before his parachute blossomed. It was not Hal Herrick.[1]

\*\*\*

George flew low, lazy and slow along the line of the beach. He and his crew were on a familiarization sortie—little more than a joy ride—along New Guinea's southern coast where there was virtually no chance of encountering Japanese aircraft. Ahead, he spotted a lone, nearly naked figure holding a spear. The dark man had already spotted *Jayhawk* and watched it approach. George dipped his wings slightly and pointed the aircraft directly toward him. Just as the B-25 was about to pass over his head, the native stepped out of his relaxed stance and hurled his spear at the big flying machine. The weapon fell harmlessly behind. The juxtaposition between the primitive nature of New Guinea, and the nation that had manufactured the B-25 and sent it to war under George's command, could not have been more stark.

\*\*\*

The 345th's crews started moving from their bases in Australia to Port Moresby, New Guinea, during the middle of June. "We flew individually to New Guinea," George said. "It was more than a 600-mile flight, almost entirely over water. I purposely flew so as to hit the New Guinea coast well to the west of Port Moresby. By doing that, I knew that all I had to do upon making landfall was to make a right turn and follow the coast until I arrived at Port Moresby."

George and his crew made the trip without incident, however George's friend and squadron mate Jack George lost his way and was forced to land on a stretch of beach. "They sent me out to find him, which I did," George

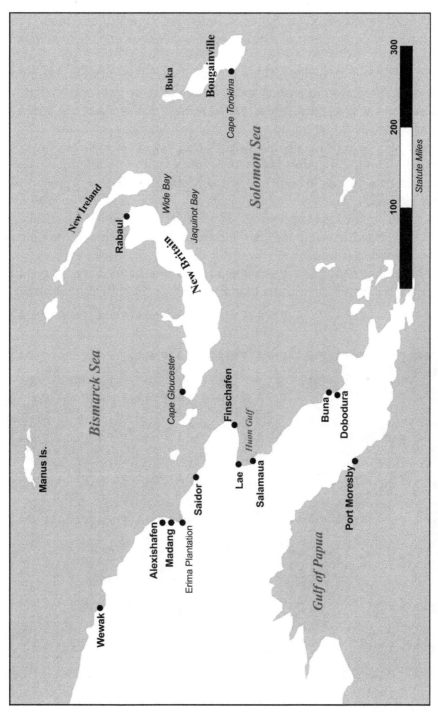

George Cooper's first combat tour was concentrated in and around New Guinea, July 1943 to March 1944.

said. "I dropped him some supplies and they got some fuel out to him via a landing craft of some sort so that he was able to take off and rejoin us within a week."

Port Moresby, aside from being a harbor, was also a complex of several airfields. There was not enough room on any of these to host the 345th in its entirety so the group's squadrons were sent to three different airfields. George's 499th Bomb Squadron was sent to Durand, named after a P-39 fighter pilot who had gone missing the previous year. It was also known as "17-Mile Drome." This dispersal of the 345th's squadrons to different locations made it more difficult to build face-to-face camaraderie across the group. "We didn't know everyone in the other squadrons," George said, "but we grew very close with our own squadron mates." Nevertheless, the training the squadrons had done together before leaving the States helped to ensure the group still operated well as a whole.

"I like the country," George wrote of New Guinea to Betty. "It is quite pleasant here and I like it better than the old place [Reid River, in Australia].

Straight lines and military spit and polish did not characterize the 499th's squadron area at Durand, in the Port Moresby area. (USAAF)

It is all jungles and rather interesting. The growth is much like you'd find in the Philippines."

A nearby range of hills nestled a cradle into which the 499th settled. "The operations and administrative buildings were built on the flat sections," said George, "and the living sections were set up on the slopes to either side. Next to our camp were large trees that were often filled with white cockatoos. And there were many colorful varieties of parrots. Aside from birds, wallabies—which looked like small kangaroos—were very common. Initially, we were concerned that they would get out on the runway and cause problems for us, but that wasn't the case and we soon ignored them."

"Large fruit bats swarmed in the evening," George said. "Their wingspan was two feet or more and they looked like small red foxes with wings. The natives hunted them for food."

It was the insects more than anything else that made rough living in New Guinea less than what it could have been. During certain parts of the year the mosquitos were almost inescapable—fierce. "The rainy season seems to

This photograph was originally captioned: "Lt. Cooper, Doc Archy Brown, No. 1 Boy." It was taken in the Port Moresby area during the latter half of 1943. (USAAF)

have started," George wrote to Betty, "and with it, an increase in mosquitos. It is unbearable in the tent, and I have to do most of my writing elsewhere." At night, the men slept under mosquito netting they hung from frames that were set over their cots. The men took daily and compulsory doses of Atabrine to stave off malaria. The medicine gave them a yellow pallor that did not fade until long after they returned to the States.

The men paid the indigenous people, nicknamed "Fuzzy Wuzzies," to do their laundry, or they did it themselves. "Parke fixed a 50-gallon steel drum as a tub for our washing," George wrote to Betty. "We have it heating now, over a fire." But if he was washing his clothes in much the same way he would have washed them hundreds of years earlier, that wasn't the case with his shaving. "I am able to use my electric razor now that we have lights in our tent. Am sure glad too, because it's so much easier on the face."

Clothes were never laundered enough. The men didn't bring many uniform pieces and what they did have with them was quickly soiled. It was hot in New Guinea and the men sweated. It was dirty in New Guinea and the men got dirty. And there were no special flying suits. "We just flew in our regular khaki uniforms and shoes," George said. Consequently, their clothes became stained with fuel and oil, not to mention ripped and torn. Too often, as replacement clothing came available, it was the wrong size. Some men cut their trousers into shorts, and they often lounged shirtless when they were off duty. As time wore on and different parts of their uniforms disintegrated or became otherwise unserviceable, the men looked more and more disheveled, although most kept at least one set in good condition for special occasions.

"Our first missions were supply drops to Australian troops," George said. Roads into the interior of New Guinea were virtually nonexistent and the best way to get needed material to the men in the jungle was to drop it on top of them. It wasn't the most efficient way to keep an army provisioned, but I know that the Aussies were appreciative of whatever we were able to deliver to them."

"The supplies," George remembered, "were bundled into large canvas sacks onto which parachutes were attached. Then the entire package was attached to shackles in the bomb bay, and there was a lanyard—much like a ripcord—that ran from the parachute to where it was tied off in the bomb bay. When the package fell away, the lanyard extended to a certain point until it deployed the parachute. Then, the whole thing fell away and floated to the ground."

"We were given coordinates of where we were supposed to drop," said George, "as well as other information such as the expected weather and the likelihood of encountering the enemy. We flew these missions as single aircraft rather than in formation. Many times, we couldn't see anything on the ground because the jungle was so thick, so we simply dropped the supplies at the location we had been provided. We released the packages just like a bomb, using the bomb release button on the control yoke. The missions weren't very exciting, but they gave us some familiarity with flying through the weather and around the mountains."

In fact, the 345th lost a crew when Lee Ow of the 500th Bomb Squadron flew into a mountain during one of these missions. Another aircraft was almost lost when its life raft broke loose and became tangled with the controls in the empennage. The 345th's crews were learning that there were many ways to die in the Pacific theater of war.

*** 

The 499th's commanding officer, Edison Walters, continued to torment the squadron with his particular brand of West Point jackassery. "No one argued against the need for discipline and good order," said George. "But we were entering combat and he was treating us like we were brand new cadets."

"He held weekly inspections," said George, "during which he and the adjutant marched around to all the tents to ensure that we were maintaining everything in a clean and tidy fashion. As he approached, we were supposed to snap to attention, and the poor adjutant had to record all our infractions on a clipboard. On one particular inspection, someone had thrown an orange peel into a grill pit that we had made outside. Walters saw that orange peel as an affront and had it recorded as a violation. As punishment, he ordered me and Stevens and Parke to live in a pup tent for a week. It was ridiculous."

Aside from being disliked as a leader, Walters was not respected as a pilot. "He had no regular crew," George said, "and no one wanted to fly with him." Indeed, on his first combat mission, a medium-altitude strike to the Salamaua area on July 8, 1943, Walters had himself assigned as copilot to Claude Burger. Burger, in turn, was flying as wingman to the formation leader, Orlen Loverin.

On takeoff there was confusion in Burger's cockpit between him and Walters about who was supposed to raise the landing gear, and when. As a result, Burger crashed beyond the end of the runway. The aircraft was torn to pieces and both Burger and Walters were hospitalized, as was the navigator who suffered two fingers sliced away. Neither Walters, who suffered a fractured skull, nor Burger, returned to flying duty with the 345th.

Julian Baird, the squadron's operations officer, took over as the acting squadron commander. "Baird was a Texan, a graduate of Texas A&M," said George. "Before the war, he had been a teacher. He was pretty easygoing, and we treated him like any other pilot. For extra protection he had armor plate installed on his aircraft on the left side of the cockpit. There was only a small opening for him to peer through and we kidded him that he was a formation flight risk because of the limited visibility he had through the armor."

*** 

The 345th's arrival in New Guinea coincided with the shift of strength from the Japanese to the Allies. The Allies were growing stronger and were increasingly on the offensive, while the Japanese struggled to hang on to bases and territory they had seized during the early days of the war. The dark time, during which it seemed the Japanese would take all of New Guinea, had passed.

And much of the credit belonged to George Kenney and his Fifth Air Force which was responsible for the USAAF's air operations in that theater. A forceful, get-it-done personality, Kenney was a World War I veteran and had scored a brace of aerial victories during 1918. When he arrived in the southwest Pacific during the latter half of 1942, he cleared his staff of non-performers and revamped the entire organization, to include changing its designation from the Far East Air Force to the Fifth Air Force. Despite the thin resources available to him in terms of men, material and aircraft, the results were telling. His newly motivated and streamlined team began to achieve results that increased in pace and import as new units arrived in theater.

The 345th was among those new units. To that point, the Fifth Air Force and its predecessors had fought with tired, partial-strength units, many of which were survivors from the start of the war or were ad hoc organizations that had been slapped together from pieces of other units. On the other hand, the 345th was the first bombardment group to join the Fifth Air Force that had been wholly organized, trained and equipped in the United States—with full complements of men, material and aircraft. It had shown up ready to fight, and Kenney was anxious to have it do just that.

CHAPTER 8

# "I Hated Flying Straight into that Flak"

George's hands and feet worked almost automatically to keep *Jayhawk* in position only a dozen or so feet from the right wing of Alden Thompson's B-25. On the other side of Thompson's aircraft, he saw Jack George working to hold his own place in the three-plane formation. They were not just one of the 499th's designated three-aircraft flights, they were good friends, having trained together and played together since the 345th was formed.

The sun streaked through the scattered clouds above them and bounced back up, bright and blinding, from the layers below. The light it created was filtered by a tropical haze that rendered the brilliant green of the approaching New Guinea shore a dull gray. Likewise, the rich dark blue of the sea over which they flew appeared leaden.

However, the explosions of the antiaircraft fire that reached toward them were a vivid, terrifying orange and black.

***

"I never liked to bomb from medium altitude," George said. "For the actual bomb run, you had to turn control over to the bombardier and follow his directions while he used the bomb sight to fine-tune the drop onto the target. I always felt like a sitting duck, with nothing to do but get shot at. We couldn't maneuver to get out of the way of fighters or flak because it would destroy the bombing solution." Of course, getting bombs on target was the entire reason for the 345th's existence at that point, so he and his crew really had no choice but to buckle down and endure it.

This grim reality was driven home on July 13, 1943. On that day, the 499th sent nine B-25s aloft, together with nine aircraft each from the rest of the group's squadrons, and another squadron from the 38th Bomb Group. The target was a set of antiaircraft gun emplacements at MacDonald's Junction, near Salamaua on New Guinea's northeast coastline. Considering the obvious fact that the guns were purpose-made to knock down aircraft such as the B-25, the mission was akin to a herd of elephants attacking a group of hunters armed with elephant guns. Someone was going to get hurt.

George was flying *Jayhawk* on the right wing of Alden Thompson who was leading the squadron that day at the controls of his ship, *Jelly Belly*. On Thompson's left wing was Jack George and his crew. The morning takeoff was normal and Thompson made a wide circle around Durand while the rest of the squadron's aircraft took off and joined the formation. That done, Thompson rendezvoused the squadron with the rest of the group as it took up a heading for Dobodura.

The group droned in circles over Dobodura waiting for an escort of fighters that was 30 minutes late. The leg to Salamaua was unremarkable other than that it was the first combat sortie for a few of the crews which created at least some degree of anxiety. The weather was spotty with layers of broken clouds here and there, and some of the squadrons lost sight of others as they readied for their separate runs on the target at an altitude of 10,000 feet.

Thompson, with George Cooper and Jack George on his wings, and two other three-ship formations in trail, made a couple of spacing turns in order to deconflict with the other squadrons and to hit the target at the prescribed time. Overhead, the escort of P-47s went without trade; there were no enemy fighters in sight.

Finally, Thompson rolled out on course for the target. George ordered the bomb bay doors open and felt *Jayhawk* shudder as they came apart and exposed the payload of bombs to the environment. Ahead of him there appeared a heavy barrage of antiaircraft fire, or flak. Bright orange bursts gave way to oily black smudges that dissipated slowly even as new bursts appeared. "On the earlier missions," said George, "the Japs had missed low or high, but this time, they got our altitude right."

"I didn't like that," he said. "I hated flying straight into that flak." The antiaircraft fire increased in intensity as Thompson's aircraft—at the head of the 499th—approached the release point. And then, just as bombs from the previous squadron exploded on the target, *Jelly Belly* reached that perfect three-dimensional point in the sky at which its bombs—if released—would strike the target. And indeed, at that very instant, *Jelly Belly's* bombs fell clear. The bombs from *Jayhawk* and Jack George's aircraft likewise dropped earthward.

"Just at that moment," said George, "there was a sharp crack and a chunk of shrapnel came up through Stevens' seat and smashed into his handheld computer." Ralph Stevens, the bombardier, had earlier set his E6B "whiz wheel" on his seat before kneeling at the bomb sight. "He seemed pretty upset and shouted that, 'the bastards shot my computer,'" said George. "I told him that he ought to be glad he hadn't been sitting down—he might not have been able to complain. In truth, he would have been dead."

While Stevens was reconsidering his luck, George saw that Alden Thompson and Jack George had not been nearly so fortunate. *Jelly Belly* was hit in the right wing between the engine and the fuselage; the engine nacelle caught fire. George had a front row seat from where he was flying, only about 50 feet from the stricken aircraft's right wing. "Thompson was feathering his right engine," he said, "and there was a fire going behind him in the navigator's compartment where Lawrence Davis was. George Cagle, his copilot, was out of his seat and fighting the fire. And John Yarborough, the bombardier, had crawled through the tunnel under the cockpit from his position in the nose, and up to the navigator's compartment. I could see that there was something wrong with him—he was wounded."

In fact, Yarborough had been hit in the face and one of his eyes was knocked out of its socket. "Cagle went back to his seat," said George, "while Yarborough, horribly injured, fought the fire. At about that time, the left engine also went dead." From that point, *Jelly Belly* was little more than a poorly flying glider. And it was afire.

"While all this was going on," said George, "Jack George had also been hit." In fact, Jack George's ship had been hit in both engines, the Plexiglas in the top turret was blown away, and the bombardier had nearly been hit by a piece of shrapnel that ripped through the compartment. With two sick engines, Jack George slid his aircraft out of the flight and back toward Port Moresby.

"I throttled back to stay with Thompson," George said. He and his copilot, Bill Parke, and the rest of the crew, watched as the other aircraft's nose dropped steeply toward the water in order to maintain flying speed. Closer to the water, George brought *Jayhawk* into level flight as Thompson lifted *Jelly Belly*'s nose and eased its descent toward the waves. "The water was rough and they hit pretty hard and threw up a lot of water," George remembered. "The aircraft broke into two pieces behind the wings."

George added power and circled the downed crew. He counted five men in the water. Although he didn't know it, Yarborough, who had so bravely battled the fire in the navigator's compartment—despite the injuries to his face and eye—failed to escape the sinking aircraft. "I stayed pretty low over them, and told the crew to watch out for sharks. I instructed them to shoot any sharks they saw." Although sharks were a real danger, none were spotted.

Thompson had put his aircraft down several miles from shore at a point that was a couple of miles behind the Japanese lines. George marked the position and struck out for the coast on the Australian side of the lines. There he found an Australian Army encampment over which he flew at very low altitude and wagged his wings. "I made several passes and dropped a message telling them that there was an American crew out there. In truth, Thompson had gone down close enough to shore that there was a good chance that they had seen him."

George wheeled *Jayhawk* back out to sea to check on his squadron mates. He spotted them again and rocked his wings. No doubt they drew some comfort at the sight of the B-25, knowing that someone was aware of their location and plight. On the other hand, George worried that the Japanese might take a cue from where he was flying and send a boat to investigate.

He pointed his aircraft back to the Australian position again. There, he could see a handful of soldiers helping some natives to push a pair of dugout canoes through the breakers that crashed onto the beach. They had no success—the waves were too big. Frustrated and worried about his friends, but low on fuel, George turned for home and started a gentle climb.

Still far from shore, Thompson and his crew, buoyed by their Mae West lifejackets, clung to each other and paddled slowly toward shore. Their progress was hampered as they nursed the navigator, Lawrence Davis. Both of his legs were nearly cut off below the knee and after several hours he died, likely from shock and loss of blood. His comrades had little choice but to let him slip beneath the surface and leave him behind.

Jack George made it safely back to base, as did George and the crew of *Jayhawk*. When the 345th's deputy commander, Clinton True, learned that Thompson's crew had gone down, he ordered an extra life raft loaded aboard a B-25 and took off for Salamaua without any sort of escort. There, he searched the waves but his efforts went unrewarded; he failed to spot them. They were in fact still swimming to shore and saw him, but had nothing with which to signal, and could do little more than wave when his aircraft came near.

The beleaguered men finally stumbled ashore at dusk. It was perhaps fortunate that it had taken them so long. They were behind Japanese lines and the deepening gloom helped to hide them. Barefoot, exhausted and essentially unarmed, they crept through the jungle until reaching an Australian outpost. Finally in safe hands, they were returned to the 345th a few days later.

"I was very excited and heartened to see Thompson and his crew back safe," George said. "Alden was a great pilot and friend. He was steady and a bit more mature than most of the boys, and we enjoyed talking about different

Alden Thompson's crew was shot down on July 13, 1943, during an attack on Salamaua. Thompson, with head bandage, was one of the four survivors who made it to Australian lines the following day. George's best friend, he was killed a few months later. (Via Australian War Memorial)

sorts of things. We'd known each other since we had started flying the B-25, and Betty got to know his new wife, Marian, during our time together in Columbia. Anyway, along with my copilot Bill Parke, Alden was my closest friend in the squadron."

Along with food and shelter, letters from home were of primary importance to the men. "Mail tied us to our loved ones and to our past," George said, "and brought us promises of the future. Betty's letters were always sealed with a kiss, imprinted in lipstick. They always made me long for her embrace. I also enjoyed corresponding with other family and friends, but Betty's letters were what I watched for when mail was passed out."

Those letters took too long to arrive and came in fits and spurts and often out of order. "Received three letters from you," George wrote in early July. "May 24, May 26 and June 18." Because of these erratic patterns, George and Betty started numbering their letters so that they might be read in order.

George always addressed his letters to "Pretty," rather than Betty. It was his pet name for her. "When we were dating," he said, "the topic of beauty came up and Betty surprised me by saying that she did not believe she was beautiful. I told her that when I was growing up, we used the expression, 'pretty as a picture,' meaning a natural beauty not only in regard to features, but also a natural beauty without makeup and jewelry and stylish clothes. It also applied to character. She loved it, and it was true—she had all the elements of natural beauty."

The 499th's censor frustrated George. The officers in most units were trusted to censor their own mail, and most squadrons rotated the chore of censoring the letters that the enlisted men wrote between all the officers. But the 499th had a designated censor who was over-zealous and checked everyone's mail, officer or not. "I once sent a photograph of my aircraft and crew," George said, "and was told I would have to cut out the portions that showed the guns. This was absurd. The Japanese saw our guns every time we flew a mission. To think that cutting out the guns in that photograph was somehow protecting secrets was ridiculous."

As might be expected, Betty and the unborn baby were never long out of George's mind, especially as July wore on. "I have been expecting some word of the baby for some while now," he wrote. "[Orlen] Loverin has been kidding me, asking how my little baby girl is. Really, I would be just as tickled with a girl as with a boy." Indeed, his longing for letters from Betty was heightened even more as he waited—impatiently—for the big news.

That news finally reached him on July 21, 1943. "I finally received the letter that I have been looking so anxiously for," George wrote to Betty. "I really laughed to myself when I read the name, 'Pris.' I had been telling the boys that I would have a son, when all along I really knew it would make no difference. I am so glad that there were no complications, and that you are up and around."

Priscilla Jean Cooper had been born on June 20, 1943. The labor came suddenly but Betty was rushed to a midwife and the delivery went well. Small at birth, but healthy, Priscilla, or "Pris," was named in part to honor George's mother, Prisca.

Not long after arriving at Durand, the officers and enlisted men of George's 499th Bomb Squadron started construction on their respective clubs. "The officers," George remembered, "pitched in to help the squadron carpenter build a structure that included a bar and enough room for tables and chairs. One of the officers was a skilled artist and he painted a nude woman behind the bar; the painting was large and quite good."

The club was put up right next to George's tent which was handy, but it could also be annoying when the merrymaking grew too loud. Still, he enjoyed using it. "It was a central point for us to gather and socialize. It wasn't just for drinking," he recalled. "Sometimes there simply wasn't any liquor to serve. I often went there to write letters or to play cards—poker or bridge—or sometimes just to talk with some of the other men."

Still, when it was available, George did appreciate a drink or two. If he drank more, he often suffered from the Asian flush. But many of the men, his close friends included, often enjoyed a drink or nine. "Most of them moderated their drinking," George said, "and it was only very rarely that there were problems with offensive behavior. The ability of one of our officers, Carl Conant, to maintain his demeanor while drinking was remarkable. He consumed enormous quantities of alcohol with seemingly no ill effects whatsoever—no slurring or stumbling or garrulous conduct. And then, when he reached a certain point, he simply passed out and fell forward or backward, or crumpled in place, depending on where his center of gravity was at that particular instant.

"On the other hand, my bombardier, good friend and tent mate, Ralph Stevens, often drank too much and could be a handful. For a time, he would get drunk and then come back to the tent and try to tip me or Bill Parke over in our cots. This continued until we ganged up on him one night and gave him a good going over."

George was typically mindful of the censor when he wrote to Betty of losses that the group or squadron sustained. "It seems that every now and then someone leaves us," he wrote on July 27. "[James] Banks went today, and with him [Allan] Bardwell." In fact, Banks took off with Bardwell, the group's weather officer, in a Piper L4 Grasshopper—a light utility aircraft. Banks tried to put on a show by flying down the airstrip as low and fast as the little aircraft would go. He ran into a tree at the end of the runway, killing both himself and Bardwell.

\*\*\*

The B-25 was designed to bomb from medium altitude, just as the 345th had used it on the day that Alden Thompson was shot down. And it was effective as a medium-altitude bomber so long as the targets could be readily seen. It was easy to see and bomb an airfield or harbor or supply depot or other similarly large installation. But many of the targets that George Kenney and his Fifth Air Force staff wanted hit were not suitable for medium-altitude bombing.

For instance, it was paramount to interdict the maritime traffic—especially barges—with which the Japanese kept their forces in New Guinea supplied. It was nearly impossible to hit those sorts of vessels from medium altitude. Likewise, Japanese units in the thick scrub and jungle were difficult to find and hit. And although harbors and airports were large targets, they included much dead space—area that included nothing important. Bombs that fell there were wasted.

This problem was recognized long before the 345th arrived in theater. And it was addressed by an unlikely character. Paul "Pappy" Gunn was a colorful and near-mythic personality who started his military career just after World War I as an aircraft mechanic in the Navy.[1] A hard drinking, hard playing, teller of tall tales—and an inveterate tinkerer—Gunn's passion to fly was eventually rewarded when the Navy accepted enlisted personnel as pilots. He grew a reputation as an expert and innovative fighter pilot and was very well regarded by the time he retired in 1937.

At the time of the Japanese sneak attacks on Hawaii and the Philippines, Gunn was running a small airline near Manila. He was almost immediately pressed into service in the Army Air Forces as a captain and was especially close to George Kenney. He fixed airplanes, transported people and material, and flew combat missions for which he was awarded the Silver Star, several instances of the Distinguished Flying Cross, and the Purple Heart—among others. When he was away from the Philippines, the Japanese marched into Manila and interned his family in Santo Tomas, where George's father Lawrence was being held.

It was Gunn's combat experience that motivated him to create what George Kenney called "commerce destroyers." These were aircraft specifically designed to destroy shipping. Tinkering first with the A-20, and then the B-25, Gunn stuffed their noses with machine guns and helped develop bombs and tactics for making wave top-level attacks.

On the B-25 specifically, his design put four .50-caliber machine guns in the nose, and two on each side of the nose, just below and behind the cockpit. This concentration of heavy machine guns was capable of shredding most targets, and of forcing enemy antiaircraft gunners to go to ground during an attack. At low level—rather than at medium altitude—the pilots could see and strafe specific targets in a way that had never been done with the B-25.

Of course, the B-25 was a bomber and that aspect was not neglected. Different sorts of bombs were fielded that could be safely and effectively dropped from low altitude. For instance, a conventional bomb with a contact fuze dropped at low altitude—100 feet or below—would blow the aircraft out of the sky when it hit the ground. But fitted with a parachute, the bomb would decelerate immediately and descend more slowly to the ground. By the time it made contact, the aircraft would be safely out of the fragmentation pattern. Delayed fuzes added a margin of safety.

Several types of bombs were fielded. Small, 23-pound, parachute fragmentation bombs—or parafrags—could be dropped in great numbers and were effective against "soft-skinned" targets such as aircraft and trucks and personnel. Larger parachute demolition—or parademo—bombs came in sizes of 100, 200, 300 pounds and larger. These were effective against bigger, harder targets such as buildings. They were sometimes wrapped in heavy wire which broke up on detonation and created lengths of whistling scythes.

For anti-shipping missions, conventional bombs with delayed fuzes were used. Tactics were developed whereby the pilot—flying just above the water—pressed in close to a ship and released his bomb such that it slammed directly into the vessel or skipped across the water and then smashed into it. A fuze delay of several seconds gave the pilot time to put distance between his aircraft and the ship before the bomb exploded.

Parafragmentation bombs drift down toward a Ki-43 "Oscar" fighter. (USAAF)

Gunn, with technical help, manpower, and resources from a gamut of organizations, converted a small number of B-25s with great success. They were essentially custom-crafted aircraft with none of the reliability and safety features that a factory design would have integrated. But they worked—and spectacularly. Eyewitness accounts from the battle of the Bismarck Sea during March 1943 described masses of enemy soldiers being ripped to pieces as they huddled helplessly on the decks of their transport ships.[2]

By August of 1943 when the 345th was directed to stand down while its aircraft were similarly reworked, a true modification line with skilled workers and proper parts and materials had been set up at Garbutt Field, in Townsville, Australia. There, the group's aircraft—which numbered more than 60—were modified in less than a month. Of course, during that period, no combat operations of any note could be flown.

So, the men were sent to Australia to relax. "I will try to be on my best behavior, Pretty," George teased Betty in early August, "and not flirt with the women. But it will be a sight to see one—and in civilian clothes!" George had no intention of chasing after Australian women, although he certainly was looking forward to getting back to civilization after so much time living rough.

He was sent to Sydney, Australia, as were most of the men, and he wasn't disappointed. "Uncle Sam takes care of his men on the front," he declared, "and the Red Cross does a good bit to aid him." He stayed with Bill Parke and other squadron mates in Red Cross lodgings with clean rooms, good dining and lounges for reading and listening to music. "And," he said, "the expense is only about half of what it would be for a cheap hotel in the States."

If George wasn't too interested in hard drinking, and carousing and chasing skirts, many of his comrades were. And except for isolated exceptions, the Australians were gracious hosts—especially the young women. Many of their Australian male counterparts were in uniform and out of the country. Accordingly, American servicemen were ready and willing to fill the gap. They were interesting to the Australian women in large part because they were different. But they were also relatively well paid, attentive and had demonstrative manners. Many Australians were surprised at the American habit of showing physical affection in public.

At times there was resentment which boiled over into fistfights or worse. In fact, the "Battle of Brisbane" was a clash between American servicemen and Australian servicemen and civilians that took place during November 1942. It ended with one dead Australian and scores of injured on both sides.[3] For its part, the Australian government tried to forestall such altercations through goodwill campaigns, and by limiting when and where alcohol could be sold, and to whom. For instance, women could not be served in public bars, and the drinking age for women was 21, whereas it was 18 for men.[4] The government felt that women under the influence of alcohol were more inclined toward immoral behavior, which led nowhere good.

But in fact, such curbs had little effect. Booze was readily available, promiscuity was the order of the day, and few American servicemen lacked for company when and where they wanted. Some units, including the 345th, bought or rented houses through which they rotated their men for "rest." A few of the more enthusiastic women likewise rotated their men. That enthusiasm was much appreciated.

For his part, George went shopping and bought a sheepskin rug for Betty and Pris. And he went to see the operetta, *The Merry Widow*. He was additionally quite taken with an Irishman that he and Bill Parke hired to take them fishing. "He was well versed in all subjects," George declared, "being able to carry on a conversation by himself—not at all dull to us. He was in the last war [World War I] and now seems to be living an easy existence with his motorboat and fishing."

All in all, George found Australia and the Australians very much to his liking and thought that Sydney was a beautiful and cosmopolitan city. But when it was time to return to combat, he was ready. "It was rather pleasant," he wrote, "but I am glad that it is over. It seemed like I was prolonging the war by taking time out. It seems that way every time I am inactive."

## CHAPTER 9

# "I Will Tell You About It Some Day"

"My copilot and friend, Bill Parke, was assigned his own aircraft and crew when we got back from Australia," said George. "I was both happy for him, and proud of him. He had been an excellent copilot, and I knew that he'd do a great job commanding his own aircraft. And I also liked to think that, as his pilot, I had played a part in his development and success."

It was at about this time that a pilot who had played a part in George's own development and success left the 345th. The group commander, Jarred Crabb, had been fingered by General Kenney as exactly the sort of talent he wanted on his staff. He was sent to Fifth Bomber Command, and was succeeded by Clinton True, an aggressive leader and talented pilot. "I thought the world of Colonel Crabb," George said. "Although he didn't spend much time with us once we started flying combat, he was the one responsible for shaping and training us for our future successes."

***

The 499th circled over Marlinan on the morning of September 9, 1943. The 12 aircraft, with George's friend Alden Thompson at the head, had been motoring above the newly constructed airfield for nearly half an hour when a squadron of P-39s appeared. The 499th's escort to the target, which was the airfield complex at Alexishafen, about ten miles north of Madang, was supposed to be a P-38 unit. However, Thompson guessed that the assignment had changed and turned north on course, expecting the little fighters to attach themselves to his formation.

After several minutes it became apparent that the P-39s had business other than the 499th, as they failed to join the B-25s. The collective, tired sigh of the bomber crewmen was almost audible as Thompson reversed course and returned to Marlinan. It was only after they made several more orbits that they were finally joined by their escort of P-38s.

The flight to Alexishafen, on New Guinea's northern coast, was uneventful. Thompson started a descent south of the enemy base and circled inland to set up for an attack from west to east. Behind him, the two other flights of four aircraft each, took separation and fell into trail, one behind another. And then, as he closed on the target, Thompson signaled the three members of his own flight to fall back into a single-file formation. Following immediately behind Thompson was his wingman, Jack Snyder. George followed Snyder, and Bill Parke—commanding his own aircraft now—brought up the rear.

The Japanese at Alexishafen had been beaten down for some time, and the Fifth Air Force staff wanted to keep it that way. Although there were few aircraft on the airfield, there was still material and infrastructure capable of supporting many more if they should stage there for a raid or make themselves a more permanent presence.

Specifically, Thompson and his flight were tasked with bombing and strafing the motor pools, and ammunition and fuel dumps at each end of

George's 499th Bomb Squadron is at the head of this 345th formation. (The San Diego Air & Space Museum)

the installation. That done, they were supposed to continue east to hit the antiaircraft guns that were dug into the peninsula that jutted into Bostrem Bay. Racing at nearly 300 miles per hour now, only 50 feet or so above the ground, the crews checked the switches for their guns and bombs.

Machine-gun fire reached up at them in thin streams as they approached the perimeter of the airfield. "Lieutenant Cooper," recounted the squadron's mission summary report, "made a run on Target #1 [the near end of the airstrip], saw his bullets strike vehicles, pulled up sharply and down again on Target #2 [the far end of the airstrip]."

"I sprayed the revetment areas with machine-gun fire," said George, "and as I was about to pull up, a gasoline tanker appeared at the end of the runway." Anxious to shred the enemy truck, he shoved the nose of *Jayhawk* down to bring his guns to bear. The negative g-force from George's abrupt control inputs was too much. Not only were he and his crew lifted out of their seats, but the ammunition belts that fed the guns came out of their cans.

"All the guns jammed," George said. He pulled back on the control yoke and climbed the aircraft away from the ground before turning to follow Thompson and the rest of the flight. Unfortunately, it wasn't just the guns that had failed during the maneuver. The mission summary report noted, "Two bombs broke loose, taking shackles and damaging the bomb bay doors." Still, *Jayhawk* held together and George caught the other crews.

Speeding across Bostrem Bay, the 499th's crews hosed more than a dozen barges with fusillades of machine-gun fire. Medium-caliber antiaircraft guns lashed back, pocking the sky around them with orange and black explosions. George, frustrated at his inability to bring *Jayhawk*'s weapons to bear, dodged the enemy shells. At that point he was essentially little more than a gunnery target for the Japanese, and moral support for his squadron mates.

The squadron rejoined over Sek Island, east of Alexishafen. After counting heads to make sure no one had been downed over the target, Thompson pointed south along the coast toward Madang and let the squadron separate into loosely formed flights. The second half of the mission was to be a barge sweep, and the crews would have more success at finding worthwhile targets if they weren't bunched together into a tight formation.

The B-25s flew low along the coast bombing and strafing targets—especially barges—as they were found. The barges were usually tied up along the coast during the day, camouflaged with branches and such material as was handy. They were not typically well defended and certainly posed no real threat to a squadron of B-25s. The same was true of whatever casual targets were found ashore—usually scattered outposts or supply dumps rather than heavy troop concentrations.

The Japanese relied heavily on barges to keep their units in New Guinea supplied. The 345th was frequently tasked to find and destroy them. (USAAF)

But given an opportunity, death could be resourceful. Alden Thompson dove against a target in a native village near Yula plantation. The squadron mission summary report described how he failed to pull up in time. "He mushed into the trees, pulled off the tail assembly and crashed, burning. It is believed that his bombs exploded as well as his fuel tanks."

The explosion and fire that had once been Thompson, his aircraft and his crew was spectacular. George, like most of the squadron, never saw Thompson hit the ground. In fact, trailing crews believed that the towering column of fire and smoke was a Japanese supply depot that another crew had hit. Many of them dumped their own bombs atop the site.[1]

"I didn't know that it was Thompson that had gone down until we all landed and he wasn't among us," George said. "It was a great shock to me because he was such a talented pilot. And his copilot was very sharp as well—I just didn't see how both of them could have made that sort of mistake. Alden was someone I looked up to; he was a leader in the air and on the ground. And he was a very good friend. It took me some time to reconcile myself to the fact that he had actually flown into the trees."

George took on the unhappy task of telling Thompson's crew chief, George Mottern, what had happened. "When I told him, he cried," George said. "Crews were very close." George also volunteered for the miserable job of packing Thompson's personal effects and readying them for shipment back to the States. "I wanted to make certain that everything that was his made it back to his folks. Sometimes things disappeared."

His mood was melancholy when he wrote to Betty later that day. "I wish your letters were spaced so that I could count on getting one every other day," he wrote. "They are an awful comfort to me." His next line, no doubt told Betty of Thompson's death. It was cut away by the censor. "I will tell you about it someday," he wrote in the line that followed the gaping hole.

Later in the letter he returned to Thompson, explaining to Betty that Thompson was supposed to have been assigned as the deputy squadron commander. Again, the censor slashed away the meaning. That the death of his friend had a real impact on George was belied by his next sentence. "I have not been as careful as I should have been, but today taught me a lesson. Don't worry—I'll be alright."

Although he tried to distract himself by helping with the never-ending improvements to the squadron's officers' club, and by reading, letter writing and other activities, September 1943 continued to be a hard month for George. He groused about the organized morning calisthenics that continued despite the fact that the disliked squadron commander, Edison Walters, had been sent away following his takeoff accident.

George continued to grieve Alden Thompson's death. "Ever since Thompson went," he wrote to Betty, "nothing has run smoothly for me. I miss him more than I would anyone else in this squadron. It is when things go wrong that I wish to God that I could go to you and just sob out my troubles."

George's friend, his bombardier and his tent mate, Ralph Stevens, was sent away during this time. As the intention was to operate the 345th's aircraft as low-level strafers and bombers, there was no need for a full complement of bombardiers; the bombsights weren't even carried. A few bombardiers were kept in the event that there was a need for the group to fly medium-altitude missions—and to fill staff positions—but the majority were sent to B-24 units which had more legitimate needs for trained bombardiers. "I was sorry to see Ralph go," George said. "He was a good friend and a reliable crew member."

George had an ugly quarrel with Julian Baird, the squadron's operations officer who had been acting as the commanding officer since Walters was injured, and who was scheduled to officially assume the position in the near term. "He has always been so damn sweet and ready with compliments for me," George wrote to Betty. "I was really taken in until the other day when I found out that he has talked against me for some while."

"He didn't like what I told him," George continued, "but when I got through, I told him that I would speak when and what I damn well thought, of anything that he or anyone else did that concerned me. I know that won't get me advanced far, honey, but that is my temperament, and that is the way I will stay."

George was aggressive by nature, but also a team player who believed that ideas and criticisms ought to be shared up and down the ranks. They were there to win a war, and if someone had ideas about how something ought to be done, or not, it was worth discussing. It is quite likely that some of what George vocalized rubbed Baird the wrong way. But George did not believe it justified Baird's disingenuous behavior.

The run-in with Baird had no immediate negative affect on George. He was assigned to take over Thompson's flight—a decision that had to be made by Baird. It was additionally an endorsement of George's skill as a pilot and a leader as it meant that he would be entrusted, on a rotating basis, to lead the entire squadron on combat missions. Whatever animosity there was between Baird and George was put aside.

George embraced his new responsibilities as a flight leader with enthusiasm and purpose. "On days that we weren't scheduled for missions, I took Bill Parke and Jack George and some of the other wingmen on training flights. We worked especially hard on formation flying. I liked to fly as close as possible to my flight or squadron leads, and I wanted my wingmen to be skilled and comfortable with flying as close as possible to me, while still staying safe."

This ability to fly close formation served several purposes. In the event that the squadron or flight had to penetrate through clouds or heavy rain, it kept the aircraft together. If they became separated in bad weather, there was a danger they might inadvertently collide. Also, it took time and fuel to get rejoined once they cleared the clouds.

Close formation was also important when maneuvering to set up for a run against the target. If the flight leader had to make an aggressive turn and the wingmen were widely separated, the wingman on the outside of the turn would get left behind, while the wingman on the inside of the turn could not fly slowly enough to maintain his position. On the other hand, if they were closely tucked in to their flight leader, they could stay with him, and then spread into an attack position once he settled on a final attack heading.

Finally, in the event that the formation was attacked by enemy fighters, the concentrated fire put up by the guns of close-flying B-25s was more effective

Maintenance of the B-25 in the primitive conditions of New Guinea was grueling work—a fact appreciated by George and his crew. (The San Diego Air & Space Museum)

than that of loosely formed aircraft. Indeed, aircraft flying too far from the rest of the formation could be "cut from the herd" and more easily shot down. George was not about to lose a wingman—a friend—because of indifferent formation flying skills. "Some thought that I was overdoing it," he said. "They felt that I was making my wingmen fly too close—that it was dangerous. But we never had any trouble and it worked out well for us."

Toward the end of the month, George, and Bill Parke cleared their original tent and moved into the one that their dead friend Alden Thompson and his crew had occupied. It was farther from the officers' club—and its noise—and was situated so that it more readily caught the cooling breezes. It was during this time that the 499th moved its aircraft to Schwimmer Field, also known as "14-Mile Drome," from where a sister squadron, the 501st, also flew.

\*\*\*

"Chandler Whipple was a nice, quiet fellow," said George. "Originally he was assigned as Jack Broadhurst's copilot. But Broadhurst kept complaining of discomfort from a bad case of piles [hemorrhoids]. He was transferred out of the unit in September after only a couple of months of combat. So, then they made Whipple the aircraft commander in Broadhurst's place. He was young, and still a second lieutenant. Most of us were first lieutenants and well on the way to being captains."

The 345th continued to play an active role in the Fifth Air Force's concerted efforts to destroy the supply lines through which Japan kept its forces in New Guinea fed, clothed and armed. Without them the Japanese army would literally starve to death. And that, in practical terms, is exactly what the Allies were trying to make happen.

On October 5, 1943, the 499th was sent to troll the northern coast of New Guinea from Fortification Point to the mouth of the Gogol River. They were to kill whatever Japanese they might find, or destroy whatever they discovered that could be useful to the Japanese. The squadron put up 12 aircraft on the mission which—except for one aircraft which turned back due to engine trouble—threaded their way through heavy weather to the airfield at Marilinan. There, they were supposed to meet their fighter escort.

The squadron, with Jack Snyder at the head, spotted a flight of eight P-47s, but thick rain clouds turned their attempts at getting together into a dangerous game of hide and seek. One of the B-25 crews—unable to keep tight formation—became hopelessly lost in the weather and turned for home. Despite Snyder leading the formation through five orbits over the rendezvous point, the P-47s failed to join the 499th and he finally gave up and proceeded on the target route without them.

Upon reaching the coast, the remaining ten aircraft separated into three flights and accelerated as they descended to low level. Like dogs on the hunt, they moved fluidly in no particular formation as they motored into, over and along likely hiding places. The crews peered into the dark shadows created by the thick foliage that hung over the beach, and they looked higher into steaming, rain-wet clearings where the enemy might have encamped, or staged equipment or material. The hunting was good, and they bombed and strafed a number of barges. But aside from the barges, essentially anything that was manmade was machine gunned and bombed, including native villages, random buildings and bridges.

When they arrived at the terminus of their route, the 499th's crews tore into Erima Plantation where the Japanese had stockpiled supplies that were protected by several antiaircraft gun pits. The crews in those pits were alert as they had endured an attack by high-flying B-24s only an hour or so earlier. Accordingly, the 499th B-25s racing low and fast from over the water had no element of surprise.

Chandler Whipple—flying his first mission as an aircraft commander—was caught by a curtain of antiaircraft fire that was set to detonate at minimum altitude. His aircraft was hit in the nose and the hydraulic fluid that operated the landing gear caught fire. A great clot of flames streamed back over the cockpit and all the way past the wings. Seconds later, the flying torch that was Whipple's aircraft nosed over and exploded as it smashed into the ground.[2] There could have been no survivors. Orlen Loverin, Whipple's flight leader, called over the radio for his squadron mates to stay away from the plantation. But his calls went unheard or unheeded.

George not only saw Whipple's crash, but he saw the guns that shot him down. "Whipple was young—he had just turned 20 only a day or so earlier," George said. "I turned and flew straight at the gun pit. It was a very odd feeling to fly directly at the guns—almost like a duel. I saw my bullets and tracers hitting all over the gun pit, and saw the Japanese firing back at me. I could see their faces. I don't know how they missed—I kept expecting my windscreen to explode in a shower of glass." George pulled out of his firing run only just in time to keep from flying into the enemy gunners.

George and the rest of the 499th strafed and bombed the Japanese at Erima Plantation until no worthwhile targets remained.

"I don't think I ever hated the Japanese," George said. "Hate wasn't the right word. But I certainly didn't hesitate to shoot them—they could be very cruel. I'd shoot at whatever came up in front of me. I guess my motivation was revenge, rather than hatred. Revenge for the war they started and for the friends I lost."

*** 

Just at the limits of his vision, George spotted the vessel—a barge or landing craft of some sort. It pushed up through the swells and then slid down the other side, making for the shore. George banked slightly to put *Jayhawk* on a course to intercept the boat before it reached the beach.

Glancing out both sides of his aircraft, George saw his two wingmen slip into trail so that they could follow his attack with minimal maneuvering. The boat grew in size as the three, olive-drab bombers closed the distance. George checked that his guns were armed and squinted through his windscreen.

Something wasn't right. Just as he came within range, he took his thumb off the firing button, hauled *Jayhawk* left away from the target, and simultaneously called his wingmen off their attacks. Rolling back toward the boat he flashed past and looked down at the upturned white faces that belonged to the men who waved at him.

"It was their uniforms, George said. "At the last instant I could tell that they were Americans. I don't know what I would have done had we shot up some of our own boys."

\*\*\*

If neutralizing the Japanese in New Guinea was essential to Macarthur's strategy in the Pacific, then it was imperative that the great Japanese bastion at Rabaul also be emasculated. Situated about 500 miles northeast of Port Moresby on the northern tip of the island of New Britain, it was characterized by a fantastic natural harbor, protected by low mountains. Since seizing it from Australia in early 1942, the Japanese had garrisoned it with more than 100,000 soldiers, sailors and airmen—as well as additional laborers. They created a complex of five airfields from which fighters could be launched to protect the area. The airfields were also used to stage bombing raids on Allied positions to the south.

Rabaul's location was ideal for the Imperial Japanese Navy to stage its warships prior to making sorties against Allied forces in the Solomons, and in the waters around New Guinea. Likewise, men, material and equipment sent from Japan were transshipped to smaller vessels before being sent to New Guinea or other outposts in the region. In short, so long as Rabaul remained in business, so would the Japanese forces in New Guinea.

Macarthur needed to stop that business in order to continue his drive across the top of New Guinea and on toward the Philippines, and ultimately Japan. Initial plans for an amphibious assault and seizure were dropped as too costly in men, material and time. Instead the decision was taken to wreck the Japanese infrastructure there, isolate the garrison and keep it beaten down.

Many raids had been made against Rabaul since early in the war, but they were mostly small, harrying efforts that did no lasting damage. Indeed, most of them did little more than provide experience to the crews involved and to the defending Japanese. Macarthur wanted more substantial damage done, and he put the Fifth Air Force's commander, George Kenney, in charge of making it happen.

\*\*\*

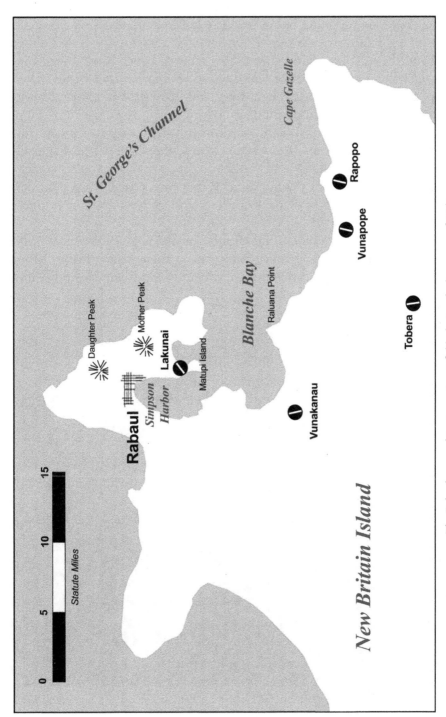

The Rabaul area and its protective airfields during the latter part of 1943.

George pressed the firing button and felt *Jayhawk* rumble as its .50-caliber machine guns sent rounds into the enemy encampment. The bullets turned parts of the buildings into flying debris, some of which was still tumbling through the air as George flashed overhead and dropped two six-bomb clusters of parafrags. Bill Parke on his right wing, and Bill Cabell on his left, likewise fired their guns and released parafrags.

The rest of the 499th Bomb Squadron stretched away to his right in a broad, line-abreast front. The formation of 11, olive-drab B-25s, flying only 50 feet or so above the ground, made up a great, flying scythe. The target was Vunakanau, one of the five airfields that protected the great Japanese air and naval bastion at Rabaul on the island of New Britain's northern tip.

The line-abreast formation was effective in that it gave the squadron the ability to cover an expansive target. But it was not maneuverable in the slightest and limited the ability of an individual aircraft to attack anything other than

The view from *Jayhawk* at Vunakanau on October 12, 1943, was very similar to this. (USAAF)

what was in its flight path. If a pilot turned to engage a target not directly to his front, he risked plowing into another aircraft.

Such was George's bad luck; he and his flight were overflying the extreme western edge of the airfield. Although he could see enemy aircraft parked across Vunakanau's different dispersal areas, he could not bank toward them. Instead, he had to trust that his squadron mates would destroy them. Bright flashes of fire and clots of smoke indicated they were doing just that.

A set of neatly groomed garden plots were all that sat in *Jayhawk*'s path. He ripped them with his machine guns and additionally sowed them with clusters of parafrags. It was better than bringing them home.

And then, incredibly, a Japanese fighter lifted from the runway in front of the 499th's B-25s. The pilots went for it like hounds for a hare. All sense of discipline broke down and several aircraft, machine guns blazing, chased after it, directly into George and his flight.

Japanese aircraft at Vunakanau, near Rabaul, about to be destroyed by parafragmentation bombs dropped by the 499th on October 12, 1943. (USAAF)

George, Parke and Cabell were forced into a hard, left turn to avoid their squadron mates. Disaster was narrowly averted, but the attack on Vunakanau was over. The Japanese pilot, unmolested, escaped over the horizon. Likewise, the 499th regrouped without incident and returned to the airfield complex at Dobodura, from where they had staged for the long-range raid. Although they had been told that Rabaul would offer a stiff defense, the 345th's crews were unimpressed.

That multi-group attack on October 12, 1943, marked the beginning the 345th's participation in the focused effort that George Kenney and his Fifth Air Force were mounting to neutralize Rabaul.

***

The 345th had flown from Port Moresby to the airfield complex at Dobodura, near New Guinea's northern coast on October 11, the day before the mission to Rabaul. Dobodura was closer to the enemy bastion, and its proximity ensured that the group's B-25s would have adequate fuel to make the attack. This sort of staging was something that the Fifth Air Force and its predecessors had practiced in the past, but it taxed not only the aircraft and crews, and the men who maintained them, but also those who maintained the logistics lines that provided the necessary fuel, bombs, aircraft parts and other material.

***

Rabaul was Japan's center of gravity in the southwest Pacific, and Wewak—regularly provisioned and reinforced via Rabaul—was its main airbase in the eastern part of New Guinea. Located on the northern coast, it was actually a complex of four airfields: Wewak, Dagua, Boram and But. The Japanese regularly mounted both offensive and defensive air operations from the well-protected airfields, and it was a thorn in the side of Allied operations that MacArthur wanted removed.

To that end, George Kenney's Fifth Air Force had been mounting attacks against Wewak for more than a year. However, it was only during the previous few months that the attacks had enjoyed any lasting success. Most effective were raids executed from August 17 to August 21, 1943, during which time the 345th's aircraft were being converted to strafers. Those raids destroyed more than 100 enemy aircraft and much difficult-to-replace material.

A 499th B-25 flies through smoke at a target in New Guinea. (USAAF)

Notwithstanding those successes, the Japanese replaced their losses and continued to maintain the Wewak complex as a viable, if less effective, forward base. Consequently, it remained a primary target for Fifth Air Force units. George and the rest of the 345th had participated in a big raid on September 27, and headed back on October 16. Loaded with wire-wrapped, parachute, demolition bombs, they were tasked with hitting aircraft and material at both Boram and Wewak airfields.

On that day, George led the 499th Bomb Squadron's second flight. The antiaircraft fire was only moderately intense but it was accurate. He brought his flight, including Bill Parke, low and fast on a westerly heading, down the north side of Boram. Above the group he saw Japanese fighters tangling with the escort of P-38s and P-40s. A Zero, afire, fell into the sea. A short time later, a P-40 was also observed falling to earth.

George let go with bursts of gunfire and released his bombs singly whenever a worthwhile target presented itself. Those bombs turned three Japanese aircraft into fiercely burning pyres.

A 345th B-25 flies low over one of Wewak's airfields. (USAAF)

Past Boram and over Wewak, George hit a supply depot and dumped more bombs into an aircraft dispersal area. He led his flight over the water and turned toward Muschu Island. A couple of miles southwest of the island he spotted a patrol boat. He dipped a wing to change his course slightly and barreled after the enemy vessel. At the last instant he released his final bomb which scored a direct hit.

A flight of enemy fighters plummeted through the protective screen of P-38s and P-40s to attack George's flight. Behind him, George heard Jepson's guns boom in the top turret. One of the enemy aircraft fell flaming into the water. Jepson's victory was confirmed by Parke's crew.

One of the 500th Bomb Squadron's aircraft, piloted by Donald Stookey, was holed by antiaircraft fire and forced down into the water. The crew was observed on the wing of the downed aircraft and several squadron mates dropped life rafts and other gear. Following the 345th's return to base, several attempts were made during the next few days to locate and rescue Stookey and his men.

It was no good. The crew had been captured by the Japanese. They were all dead within the next several months.

***

There wasn't an American in uniform who wasn't aware of Japanese cruelties. "Aside from the monstrous things they had done to innocent civilians in China," George said, "we heard about atrocities they committed during the fighting in New Guinea—they were terrible stories and I found myself regularly wondering if I could withstand being tortured. One day I took my pen knife and poked and cut myself to see what sort of pain I could bear. But it wasn't long before it occurred to me that it was a pretty stupid idea. It wasn't something a person could practice, and I could save myself some trouble and pain by simply waiting until I was shot down and captured. If that ever happened there was no doubt that I would discover what sort of agony I could, or couldn't, endure."

***

After a midmorning takeoff from Dobodura on October 18, 1943, George worked *Jayhawk*'s controls to keep his flight in position as the 499th, headed by Orlen Loverin, joined with the rest of the group. William Cabell flew on George's left wing, and Bill Parke flew on his right. Cabell had been Thompson's wingman before Thompson and his crew were killed. Now, along with Jack George, he regularly flew as one of George's wingmen.

This raid to Rabaul was to be a massive and complex effort that included not only 36 B-25s from the 345th, but two more squadrons of B-25s from the 38th Bomb Group, as well as three squadrons of P-38 escort fighters. Also participating were eight squadrons of B-24s protected by P-40s. It was to be the biggest strike against Rabaul yet mounted.

The plan was clever and focused primarily on gutting the Japanese fighter forces based at the airfields protecting Rabaul. Without Rabaul-based fighters to intercept their bombers, the Allies could isolate the enemy stronghold at their leisure. The four-engine B-24s were to attack first, from high altitude. Their targets were the airfields at Lakunai and Vunakanau. The fighters from all of Rabaul's airfields would be compelled to climb after the B-24s—fighting through the escorting P-40s as they did so.

Then, low on fuel and ammunition, and with Lakunai and Vunakanau cratered by the B-24s, the Japanese fighters would be forced to land at Rapopo and Tobera just as the B-25s from the 345th and the 38th swept in at low altitude. Caught in the middle of refueling and rearming, the enemy aircraft would be shredded by machine-gun fire and bombs. The 345th's 500th Bomb Squadron was the only exception; it was to hit material and shipping at Vunapope.

The 345th's commanding officer, Clinton True, led the B-25s at the head of the 498th Bomb Squadron which was followed by the 501st, 499th and 500th. The 38th Bomb Group's two squadrons followed the 345th's. The initial part of the mission went well, but past the halfway mark a dark line of storms appeared on the horizon. As the crews continued on course it became apparent that they would have to penetrate the roiling weather or turn around and return to Dobodura. A radio message was transmitted which cancelled the mission. High above him, George spotted the B-24s and their fighter escorts headed in the opposite direction. The P-38s that escorted the 345th and the B-25s of the 38th Bomb Group also reversed course.

"People later debated as to whether or not True heard the message," said George. "There is no question. He heard it, I heard it—we all heard it." That True continued toward Rabaul was in contradiction to a Fifth Air Force standing order that bombers would not fly without fighter escorts unless directed otherwise. True had not been directed otherwise.

"I saw True and the rest of the 498th disappear into a solid cloud bank," George said. "The 501st followed the 498th and our squadron went after them. Although there wasn't much turbulence, the rain was torrential and it was difficult to keep sight of the other flights."

Fearful of running into the other aircraft, and wary of getting caught in their prop wash, George slid his flight out of the squadron formation and dropped down to 50 feet, just above the wave tops. "I could see almost nothing looking ahead through the heavy rain," George said. "Knowing that I was going to get wet, I opened my side window so that I could better judge how high we were above the water. Parke and Cabell did a nice job flying formation and staying tucked in to my aircraft—just as we had practiced so many times."

George and his flight punched clear of the weather less than 100 miles from Rabaul. "At first, I didn't see anyone else," George said. "But we continued on course and gradually spotted other parts of the squadron. It was remarkable, but the 499th managed to get back together before we reached the target area, although the group formation was never reconstituted."

Orlen Loverin led the squadron through a complete 360-degree turn in order to give the 498th and the 501st time to complete their attacks on Rapopo. As he rolled out of the turn, antiaircraft fire of all calibers streaked after the squadron from several directions. To stay clear, Loverin wrapped his aircraft into a tight left turn.

George was on Loverin's right side, but because he had tucked his flight so close to Loverin, they were able to stay with him despite the sharpness of the turn. But Loverin, from where he sat on the left side of his aircraft, could not see that George's flight was still in position. When he rolled out of the turn and pointed north toward Rapopo, he thought that George's flight would need time to catch up and consequently didn't advance his throttles for the attack. However, George shoved his throttles forward to accelerate. He and his flight flashed past Loverin and into the lead. Julian Baird's flight also sped by Loverin. Loverin and his two wingmen—the lead flight—brought up the rear. So then, rather than attacking the airfield in a roughly line-abreast formation of nine aircraft, the 499th attacked Rapopo in three separate flights.

And they tore it up. George let *Jayhawk*'s nose drop toward an antiaircraft position that included a heavy-caliber gun, and three medium-caliber guns. Muzzle flashes belied the fact that the enemy gunners were targeting his squadron mates. In range, George fired his .50-caliber machine guns and watched tracer rounds arc into the position. The enemy guns went silent.

He likewise strafed several aircraft parked at various dispersal areas across the airfield. "We were carrying 12, wire-wrapped, 100-pound, parachute, demolition bombs," he said. "When the bombs exploded the heavy-gauge wire was fractured into short lengths which slashed up whatever they hit. The wire-wrapped bombs were particularly effective against aircraft and vehicles and personnel."

Once clear of the airfield, George held his course for a few seconds until *Jayhawk* was over Blanche Bay. Then he turned right toward home and watched Parke and Cabell maneuver to get into position on either side of him. Parke failed to close the distance and George slowed to facilitate the rendezvous. "As he got closer," George said, "I saw that he had a big hole in his right wing, near the engine. I wasn't sure the wing would hold up if he applied too much power to it, so I stayed at 200 miles per hour. At the same time, I saw Baird and his flight coming up fast from behind me and to the left, and Loverin's flight trailing them."

George also spotted a formation of about 15 enemy fighters a few thousand feet above him, and a B-25 down in the water. The downed aircraft had been flown by the 500th Bomb Squadron's Lyle Anaker who had been part of the attack against Vunapope. Both he and his squadron mate Harlan Peterson were chopped out of the sky by the enemy fighters. Between the two crews, only two men—both from Anaker's aircraft—survived.

The Japanese fighters were proving deadly and it was imperative that the 499th's crews got back together for mutual protection. "I fully expected Baird and Loverin to slow down and join my flight—that was standard procedure and the smart thing to do," said George. "Flying tightly together our concentrated defensive fire would help keep the Japanese fighters away."

Baird raced past, to *Jayhawk*'s left, and kept going. "And Loverin followed him," George said. "They left me and Cabell to shepherd Parke back on our own. I was almost in disbelief. I'm not sure if they expected me to accelerate and catch them, or what. But I wasn't going to leave Parke behind."

And then the Japanese fighters dove on George and his flight. "I had brought us down to just a few dozen feet above the water," George said, "so that they couldn't attack us from below. And neither could they dive on us too steeply, or they'd fly into the water. So, they attacked us from the rear, the sides and the front."

The crew called out the attackers to Henry Jepson who manned the top turret. Jepson's two guns rumbled as the Japanese fighters—identified as Zeroes—made their attacks. Two of them crashed into the ocean, sending up great geysers of water. "Jepson shot down one of them," said George, "and the top gunner in one of the other aircraft shot down another."

George and his two wingmen soon dissuaded the enemy pilots from frontal attacks. "Each time they tried a head-on pass, I turned our formation into them. When they got into range, we opened up with our .50-caliber machine guns. Those concentrated streams of bullets were too much for the Japanese pilots, and they soon returned to harassing us from the flanks and the rear."

As George and his flight stretched the distance from Rabaul, the Zero pilots grew fewer and less aggressive until the last of them turned away. It was more than two hours later that George got his flight safely on the ground. "We were the last aircraft in the squadron to return to Dobodura," he said. "The mission was over. I was tired and I didn't see any value in confronting Loverin or Baird about their failure to join with my flight. And Baird was our commanding officer by that time, and he and I had already bumped heads about a month earlier. Then, for whatever reason, he came up to me and said, 'Coop, I like you.' I'm not sure why he said that, but we didn't have any more arguments after that."

The 345th's commanding officer, Clinton True, was called to task for continuing the mission without a fighter escort. But at the same time that the Fifth Air Force's leadership was contemplating disciplinary action against him, newspapers trumpeted the audacity and success of the attack. Although the number of Japanese aircraft that were destroyed might be debated, a conservative estimate was in the dozens—at a cost of the two 500th Bomb Squadron B-25s. In light of the raid's accomplishments and the spectacular attention it received from the press, True was let go with a stern warning and the nation's second highest award for valor, the Distinguished Service Cross, or DSC.[3]

"I don't know whether or not he deserved the DSC for that mission," said George. "But I certainly admired his courage and aggressiveness. We were there to kill the Japanese, and that is what Colonel True's attitude was when he led us into combat. In that regard we were like-minded."

***

Combat flying was obviously the dominant activity in George's life and in the lives of his comrades. But the truth was that it occupied only a very small fraction of their time. Because of the vagaries of weather, crew rotations, operational tempo, illness and other such factors, it was not unusual for a man to go a week—or much longer—without flying a mission.

As did almost all the men, George and his comrades went into the bush to meet with the native New Guinea people. Referred to as Fuzzie Wuzzies by the Australians because of their shockingly thick and kinky mats of hair, they had been invaluable earlier in the war during the campaigning along the Kokoda track. They served as skilled scouts and indefatigable and gentle stretcher bearers. They were especially noted for their ability to carry large, much-needed loads of material and ammunition through the punishing jungle.

After a series of heavy rains, George and a friend bumped their jeep along a slippery mud path until a river blocked their way. They forded it on foot, carrying canned goods and coffee which were especially desired by the natives. "They met us at the river and set up an excited chatter as they eyed the canned goods," reported George. "Most of them seemed to speak pidgin English but it was still difficult to haggle with them."

George and his friend followed the natives to their village which George found markedly unappealing. "The grounds were spotted with human filth," he said, "and [this stink] was strengthened by the smell of pigs and dogs. The children were bare and usually coated with mud on their fannies, and generally covered with dirt although some were cleaner than others. As a whole they seemed healthy except for a few who had the yaws, or beriberi."

As it developed, the natives had nothing with which to trade. George and his friend found their way to another village which, although its inhabitants

The New Guinea natives were a curiosity to George and many of his comrades. (George Cooper)

likewise had nothing to offer, seemed tidier. Still, despite his lack of success at trading for something interesting, he seemed to find goodness in New Guinea and its people. "Things seem to have a touch of beauty here. Perhaps it was the nature of the people, but I am inclined to say it was the fresh verdure which fresh rains bring."

\*\*\*

On October 22, 1943, young Dorothy Cooper wrote to her father, Lawrence, who was missing both her and Prisca from the confines of the Santo Tomas Internment Camp. "Three of my little tame chickens were stolen," she said, "and I was very unhappy. They are so tame that anybody can pick them up." Food was growing scarcer in Manila and there is little doubt that Dorothy's pets had already been eaten by the time the letter reached Lawrence.

Notwithstanding the fact that the Philippines had been seized by the Japanese, Dorothy escaped the cruelties they often visited upon the people whose countries they conquered. "We were lucky," she remembered. "The Japs left us alone for the most part. My mother's lineage was partly Spanish and Japan was not at war with Spain. As I was still a child, I could go outside and play with other children my own age. The Japs didn't bother us kids, so that aspect of my life was relatively normal."

What was decidedly not normal, however, was the maggot-infested body that Dorothy and her friends found in the stream that ran by the neighborhood. "I have no idea who it was," she said. "And we ran away."

"My mother had been a teacher and then a school principal," said Dorothy. "And she ran a school out of our house for a while. She had about 20 pupils and held classes on the wide porch that ran around the house. She taught all the typical classes, and we often sang songs—sometimes they were patriotic American songs! Anyway, because of this, my schooling didn't really suffer during the war."

## CHAPTER 10

# "I Might Not Get to Write You Again"

"Even before we went there the first time, our stomachs sort of tightened up every time Rabaul was mentioned," George said.

Indeed, Rabaul was mentioned with more emphasis and frequency as October gave way to November 1943, and accordingly the 345th was staged forward to Dobodura. "I might not get to write you again for a few days," wrote George to Betty on October 29, "as I will be on the move again." In fact, the Marines were scheduled to make an amphibious assault on Bougainville at the northwest end of the Solomon Islands, and it was certain that the Japanese would send Rabaul-based air and sea forces to interdict them. As it happened, on November 1 when the Marines went ashore at Cape Torokina in Empress Augusta Bay on Bougainville, they encountered little resistance. And early the next morning, the Navy's protective screen of cruisers and destroyers turned back the more powerful Japanese task force sent to rout it. However, it was certain that the Japanese weren't going to give up.

As expected, reconnaissance reports confirmed that Rabaul's Simpson Harbor was bursting with shipping—both warships and freighters—during the days leading up to the amphibious assault. However, poor weather precluded air attacks. George remembered that the rain was almost continuous and, "on one occasion there was so much water that it flooded the floor of the tent." Finally, with promising conditions on the horizon, George Kenney, the Fifth Air Force's aggressive commander, ordered his men to attack.

At the 345th there were many tight stomachs.

That tightness wasn't unwarranted. Determined to scrape the Marines back into the sea, Japanese commanders put their forces at Rabaul on a heightened state of readiness. Moreover, Rabaul's air defenses had just been augmented by more than 150 naval fighters from the Japanese air and naval bastion at Truk, in the Caroline Islands.[1] The aircraft had been "loaned" from Imperial Japanese Navy aircraft carriers, and their pilots were skilled and aggressive.

The strike on November 2 was to be an all-B-25 show with the exception of an escort of 80 P-38s. The B-25s from the 3rd Attack Group, together with those from the 38th Bomb Groups, were charged with making low-level strafing and bombing attacks at Simpson Harbor. George's group, the 345th, was to play a supporting role. They were to bomb and strafe the Japanese gun positions that protected the harbor, and two of the squadrons—including George's 499th—were tasked with dropping 100-pound white phosphorous bombs. These bombs burned slow and hot, and generated enormous plumes of choking white smoke. This smoke would make it difficult for the enemy gunners to see the 3rd Attack Group and the 38th Bomb Group as they hit the mission's primary target—the ships that sat at anchor in Simpson Bay. Specifically, the 499th was to neutralize or destroy a group of 83 antiaircraft guns that occupied the Sulphur Creek area, just south of Rabaul.

"I was a little disappointed that we weren't given the primary role of attacking the ships," said George. "A lot of us were. But it was a team effort, and the job that we were given was essential to the success of the overall mission. We understood that, and were committed to doing what we were ordered to the best of our ability."

Regardless of who was assigned to do what, the weather still got a vote. The 499th, along with much of the rest of the 345th, got airborne before 0800 only to be recalled because of storms over the target area. Back on the ground, the group's B-25s were checked and refueled while the aircrews stood by and waited for the skies to clear. No doubt, at least a few of the men hoped that the mission would be scrubbed, but they also knew if it was, the respite would be only temporary. If they didn't go to Rabaul on that day, they would have to go sometime soon.

As it developed, they went that day—the signal to launch came less than two hours after they had landed. George, the 499th and the rest of the 345th were on their way to Rabaul by 1100. The group's four squadrons, with the 499th bringing up the rear, were at the head of the strike force. George led the second of the 499th's three flights of three aircraft each. Flying just off his left wing was his good friend Jack George. Flying to his right was his good friend, tent mate and former copilot, Bill Parke. The three of them held their place on the right side of the squadron's formation. Each of them—and the men that made up their crews—were anxious as they considered what waited for them at Rabaul. All of them had been there before, and all of them knew that the Japanese were capable of putting up a stiff, bloody defense.

The plan called for a different route than the ones they had previously flown. Rather than approaching their targets from the south and east, the B-25s and their P-38 escorts were to fly northwestward up St. George channel between New Ireland and New Britain, and then past Duke of York Island and the adjacent islets as they descended to low level. At that point the formation was to turn west to make landfall, and then climb through the gap between Mother and North Daughter peaks. On the other side, with both the town of Rabaul and Simpson Harbor in front of them, they were to drop down to treetop level to make their attacks.

The flight proceeded more or less as planned, but there was no element of surprise as Japanese observers and radar stations detected the approaching Americans. Scrambling fighters whipped clouds of dust into the air at the bases surrounding Rabaul, and antiaircraft gun crews hurried to pull the covers from their weapons and to stage cases of ammunition nearby. Enemy warships in both Simpson Harbor and Blanche Bay—into which the harbor opened—likewise readied for the coming attacks.

And they were ready in time. "As we came up through St. George Channel, a frigate opened fire, but did no damage," said George. A pair of destroyers likewise lobbed shells at the B-25s but scored no hits. The escorting P-38 pilots released their external fuel tanks and climbed ahead of the bombers as they prepared to engage the Japanese fighters that were just starting to marshal over the target.

It was only minutes later that the battle began in earnest. A seemingly impenetrable screen of exploding antiaircraft shells filled the gap between Mother and North Daughter peaks. Red and yellow tracers arced back and forth across this screen to create a barrier through which no aircraft could pass without, at a minimum, sustaining heavy damage. George saw the B-25s in front of him spray the enemy gun positions with their .50-caliber machine guns before pulling sharply up and over the Japanese fire. Subsequent flights—George's included—similarly ripped the enemy positions with their own machine guns before also hopping over the deadly screen. Once clear, the 499th took a southerly heading and flew directly at Rabaul.

"It was like something out of a movie," George said of the scene that stretched before him as the 499th descended to just above the treetops. "There were dogfights high above us, and explosions, and trails of black smoke as burning aircraft fell out of the sky. In the harbor I saw bright orange flashes as the warships fired their guns. And I could see a couple of our own B-25s on fire." One of those B-25s was piloted by Albert Krasnickas. An enemy shell hit his aircraft and set his load of phosphorous bombs afire.

The aircraft hit the ground and crumpled into a great sheet of flames. There were no survivors.

Orbry Moore's aircraft was also hit and his right engine immediately caught fire. Trailing flames, he turned to make a water landing and was subsequently left behind as his squadron mates—unable to aid him while under fire—continued their attacks. He and his crew were never heard from.

George had no time to consider the chaos that boiled in the distance. Enemy fighters attacked the squadron and Charles Banz, in the flight to George's left, flew in front of and above *Jayhawk* as he tried to get a shot at one of the Japanese aircraft. "Instead of returning to his position," George said, "Banz opened his bomb bay doors. I cursed him over the radio and quickly moved my flight out from under him just as he released his bombs. They only barely missed us."

George wrenched *Jayhawk* into a series of abrupt, jinking turns to make himself and his flight difficult for the enemy gunners to hit. Roaring down the east side of Rabaul and over Sulphur Creek, he continued to fire his

The phosphorous bombs dropped on Rabaul on November 2, 1943, by the 345th Bomb Group shrouded the Japanese antiaircraft crews with great, choking clouds of smoke. (USAAF)

guns and release his bombs. Behind him, Jepson added to the cacophony with gunfire from the top turret. The white phosphorous bombs burst into cotton-white clouds and sent grasping tendrils of burning material in every direction. The entire town of Rabaul, as well as the surrounding area, was smothered by ghostly, tentacled mist-monsters that gradually dissipated into a continuous choking fog.

Jack George and Bill Parke clung tightly to George, but it did little to save them from the enemy gunfire. To the right of *Jayhawk*, Bill Parke's aircraft took a hit in the bomb bay. One of the bombs caught fire and filled the aircraft with white phosphorous smoke. George saw Parke's aircraft drift to the right as he and his copilot tried to wave the eye-stinging vapors away. Seconds later, Parke salvoed his bombs. The smoke in his aircraft cleared quickly and he snugged back into position with *Jayhawk*.

Flying low and fast down the harbor's edge and approaching Matupi Island, George and his copilot, Richard Reinbold, caught sight of a line of enemy floatplanes. They were Nakajima A6M2-N fighters, which were derivatives of the famous Mitsubishi Zero. Code-named "Rufe," they were dangerous aircraft that rendered the Japanese good service. Catching them moored and helpless in shallow water was a stroke of good fortune.

"Reinbold was new and had been assigned to me so that I could help train and bring him up to speed," said George. "He was a good copilot, and a West Point graduate, but he got really excited on this mission. He kept pointing and shouting, 'Get that one,' or, 'Look over there!' I could see everything he could see, so it was a little bit annoying, but also—even at the time—kind of funny. He was very enthusiastic."

George lowered *Jayhawk*'s nose slightly and let go a burst of machine-gun fire at one of the enemy float planes. The B-25 shuddered and flames spat from the gun barrels. His aim was good and the .50-caliber rounds shredded the aircraft and kicked up small geysers from the water around it. Reinbold grew quite animated as George raked the line of Rufes with several hundred more rounds before pulling up to keep from slamming into the water. He and his flight continued south. Behind him, other members of the squadron confirmed that at least four of the enemy fighters were afire and several more were smoking or otherwise damaged.

"Past Matupi Island," said George, "we spotted a P-38 with a smoking engine passing in front of us from left to right. Hot on his tail were three Zeroes. As he came close, I brought the nose of my aircraft up and mashed down on the firing button in an attempt to shoot the Zeroes off his tail." The 90-degree deflection shot was almost impossible and none of the enemy

The aircraft that George destroyed on the November 2, 1943, raid to Rabaul were A6M-2N floatplane fighters, which the Allies codenamed "Rufe." (Wikimedia Commons)

aircraft were hit. "We were very sad when the P-38 crashed into the water. The pilot could not have lived."

George led his flight across Raluana Point where it was caught by a barrage of antiaircraft fire. At the same time, Zero fighters dove down on them. To his left, Jack George's aircraft was struck by antiaircraft fire and then jumped by a Zero and hit again. His guns were rendered inoperable and hydraulic fluid sprayed across the windscreen. He struggled not just to keep his wavering B-25 in formation, but to keep it from smashing into the water. Jack George's copilot, Mack Simms, was injured—shot in the leg—but still left his position to climb to the rear of the aircraft on two different occasions to render first aid to the flight engineer, William Parkhurst, and the radio operator, Ken Andrews, who had both been more seriously wounded.

The Zeroes also hit Bill Parke's aircraft, to George's right. One of his main landing gear tires was shot up, as was part of his hydraulic system. Happily, none of the crew was injured and the aircraft remained controllable.

The Japanese fighter attacks did no further harm and as the enemy pilots winged away George put *Jayhawk* in a gentle climb back toward Dobodura. By that time the 3rd Attack Group and the 38th Bomb Group were starting their attacks against the ships clustered in Simpson Harbor. It was the purpose of the entire mission; it was the reason that George and his two wingmen, and their squadron, and the rest of the 345th risked—and in some instances, gave—their lives.

It turned into an air-versus-sea slugfest. The crews from the two other groups, only dozens of feet above the water and traveling at nearly 300 miles per hour, hurled themselves at the Japanese ships. The attack was confused and frantic. The phosphorous smoke that George and his comrades laid down had drifted over the water in patches. It not only masked aircraft from ships, and ships from aircraft, but also ships from ships and aircraft from aircraft. Together with antiaircraft fire from the Japanese ships, the smoky fog broke squadrons apart into flights, and flights into individual aircraft; mid-air collisions were a real risk. The gunners aboard the defending Japanese ships, for their part, had to take care not to hit each other as they fired on the wave-topping B-25s.

The attack quickly became incoherent. Darting from skeins of phosphorous fog into the clear, and back into the fog again, the B-25 crews released their

The objective of the November 2, 1943, attack on Rabaul was the shipping in Simpson Harbor. George's 499th Bomb Squadron was tasked to lay the smoke screen visible in the background. (USAAF)

bombs; some fell harmlessly into the water while others slammed into Japanese ships. Raymond Wilkins, the commander of the 3rd Attack Group's 8th Bomb Squadron, put a 1,000-pound bomb into the side of a destroyer, and shortly after stuffed another 1,000-pound bomb into a large transport ship. His aircraft, badly damaged, was nearly uncontrollable. Still, intent on drawing fire away from the other aircraft in his flight, he attacked a cruiser with his nose guns, swinging the hail of bullets back and forth across the big ship's deck. As he turned away, the cruiser's guns caught him in the underside. Wilkins's aircraft was blasted to pieces and he and his crew smashed into the water.

George's flight was well clear of Rabaul by the time that the last B-25s of the other two groups left Simpson Harbor. Although the engines on both Parke's aircraft and Jack George's seemed to be running smoothly, he was nevertheless careful to fly in a way that would not stress them, and he kept a close eye on both during the return home. The crews aboard all three B-25s breathed easier as Dobodura hove into view.

"I landed first," said George. "Jack George had declared an emergency because his landing gear would not come down—his hydraulics had been shot out. And he had wounded men aboard. We needed to get on the ground in front of him in case he clobbered the runway when he landed. Bill Parke came in behind me and landed with no problem. As it happened, Jack made a good belly landing and they were able to get everyone safely out of the aircraft."

The mission was over at the cost of eight B-25s and nine P-38s, and virtually all the men that crewed them. Despite the losses that were endured over Rabaul that day, the mission was hailed as a great success, and the story was trumpeted by Allied newspapers across the globe. In Adelaide, Australia, *The Advertiser* repeated the pronouncement from MacArthur's headquarters that Simpson Harbor had been, "practically swept clean." And the *Los Angeles Times* declared, "Rabaul Staggers Under Assault by MacArthur's Planes." It wrote that the "harbor at Rabaul is ablaze after raid by American bombers."

The damage that was actually inflicted is open to debate. The Fifth Air Force tallied a total of three destroyers and eight cargo vessels sunk, along with a collection of smaller craft. Heavy damage to two cruisers was also claimed. And the combined scores of both the P-38 pilots and the B-25 crews against enemy aircraft—on the ground and in the air—was 82.

The Fifth Air Force, in a tacit acknowledgement that the initial results were somewhat optimistic, later stated that the destroyers it declared had been sunk, had only been damaged, and that the numbers and sizes of the cargo vessels it believed it had destroyed were also not as great. Still, although no major warships were destroyed, the loss of so much transport shipping—together with the damage dealt to the cruisers, the destroyers and to the smaller combatants—was a stinging blow to the Japanese. And the enemy pilots that were killed in air combat were not easily replaced. Ultimately, if the raid had not been a spectacular triumph, it had still been a success.

Indeed, the Japanese were being inexorably ground down. But it wasn't apparent to at least some of them that day. Tameichi Hara, the commander of the Japanese Imperial Navy's Destroyer Division 27, recorded that the morale of his crew was indicative of men who had prevailed in battle, rather than lost. "Considering the size of his effort, the enemy achieved very poor results with that raid," he noted. "Gunfire from surface ships is usually of little effect on fast airplanes. But it was quite different that day. The enemy planes practically flew right into our gunfire. I saw at least five planes knocked down by *Shigure* [his ship]." Hara observed that, after the battle, "Every man of the crews was justifiably proud and jubilant … Officers and men alike were able to joke and laugh again."[2]

The mission disturbed several of the 345th's men. "Jack George was so shaken by the experience that he asked to be removed from combat duty," George recalled. Aside from having just been nearly shot out of the sky over Rabaul on November 2, his aircraft had almost been knocked down on the mission to Salamaua on July 13—the same mission during which Alden Thompson and his crew crashed into the sea. The command honored Jack George's request. Combat flying was only done on a voluntary basis, and it was apparent that his luck had nearly run out. If he felt unfit for fighting, it was reasonable. Moreover, it was unwise to force an airman into combat. Not only would he be a danger to himself and his crew, but also to the successful execution of the mission.

"The same thing happened to William Cabell," said George. "He sometimes flew on my wing, but also developed severe anxiety before each mission—he didn't eat for fear of vomiting. I tried to convince him to request relief from combat just as Jack had done, but he refused. He said that his apprehension usually subsided once he got airborne."

George wondered at his own character—if perhaps he was different or missing something inside. "I don't recall ever being nervous before a mission, although I knew that some of the others were." he said. "I did feel a certain tenseness within myself and the rest of the crew while we waited to start the engines. But that tension seemed to go away once we were settled in the cockpit and the engines were running. We really didn't talk about it much, and I often was a little curious about what the other guys felt."

"In fact, most of the time I was eager to get on with it. That's what we were there for." George felt this way despite the fact that his original flight was in tatters. Alden Thompson's crew, after being shot down once, had gone back into combat and been killed in a horrific crash. Jack George had been badly shot up twice and was taken off combat operations at his own request. William Parke's aircraft had been so severely damaged on two different occasions that it was remarkable he was still flying.

"I'm not sure why I didn't get upset, or dwell on the possibility of getting killed," George recalled. "I guess I felt that I knew enough and had seen enough to keep myself out of trouble. I was here today, so I figured I'd be here tomorrow. Of course, my common sense told me that I could be killed on any given day. I can't explain why or how I felt what I felt."

\*\*\*

When George returned from Dobodura to Schwimmer the following day, he didn't write to Betty about the mission to Rabaul, or even allude to it. He couldn't. Instead he wrote of their little family. "Cilla will be half a year old when you get this. It will be fun to give her a birthday party. Then there will be Christmas to get her presents and watch her open them." His next sentence reflected his surety that he would survive: "We will have many happy years ahead."

\*\*\*

George sat on his cot on the morning of November 9, when he heard the screams.

"Coop! Coop! Come help me, Coop!"

George sprang up and dashed out of the tent. The tenor of the cries was terrifying. He knew that it was Bill Parke but couldn't figure out why he was shrieking. A short distance away he spotted flames and several squadron mates standing over a smoking figure.

"Bill had been making a fire to heat water for his laundry," George said. "He soaked a bunch of wood with gasoline and got a little careless when he lit it. The gas can exploded and spattered him with burning fuel. His shorts caught fire and his arm and leg were burned raw as were several parts of his body."

Parke quaked with shock, but recognized George. "I burned myself, Coop. I burned myself." He was in real danger and George and a couple of the others lifted him to his feet and half-carried him toward the squadron dispensary.

There, the medics administered first aid while transport to the main hospital was coordinated. "He was very much in pain and asked me to go to the hospital with him," George said. "He was talking and shaking like a child and it made me feel peculiar to see such a change in him."

"All the way to the hospital he kept telling me how much he thought of me and how he wanted to fly on my wing. He talked about his wife and of the wrong acts he had committed in his life. He asked me to write her and to take care of myself. I believe it was the morphine that loosened his tongue that way."

The hospital staff went to work on Parke immediately after he arrived. When George returned to visit him that night, he found him in a drug-induced coma. "The surgeon," George recalled, "said he would recover in about ten days, and would be comfortable inside of three."

The following day, Parke's condition startled George. "That morphine seems to make a baby of the person it is administered to," he wrote to Betty. "Parke every now and then just rambles and changes the subject every few seconds." Still George made regular trips to the hospital and was relieved as Parke—just as the surgeon promised—started to recover.

Bill Parke was recuperating safely when George wrote to Betty on November 16. He had woken up late that morning—after a big night at the officers' club—and treated himself to a breakfast of crackers and chocolate in his tent. He had gotten up too late to make it to morning chow. In his letter he described how a group of bombardiers and pilots had gotten into a booze-fueled quarrel the previous night after a couple of pilots had stated that bombardiers were useless. "They got around to arguing about who was the best and worst pilot," George wrote, "and each bombardier stuck up for his own pilot. They all ran [Oren] Loverin down, though, and rated him the worst." Their declaration was especially humorous to George because Loverin was part of the group doing the arguing.

***

The next day, November 17, aboard the submarine USS *Drum*, Lieutenant Commander Delbert Williamson studied the enemy ships.[3] He and his crew had been stalking them for almost two hours. The small convoy was made up of five vessels—two sub chasers and three large transports. They were 12 miles to the east, and zig-zagged on a course generally to the north. He guessed they were sailing from Rabaul to the Japanese stronghold of Truk, about 500 miles to the northeast.

Williamson also suspected that the largest of the ships was the same one he had unsuccessfully attacked almost a week earlier on November 11 when it was southbound. For their trouble that day, he and his crew had been run off and forced to endure an expertly delivered depth-charge attack. Fortunately for them, the attack had not been expert enough.

Anxious not to fail again, Williamson gave orders to submerge, and to move *Drum* between the enemy escorts and the larger ships they were protecting. There was nothing tricky or unique about the attack he planned; it was a normal approach that he and his crew had practiced many times. Still, he was wary of the sub chasers.

An hour later *Drum* was positioned just less than a mile from its target—confirmed as the same large transport the crew had attacked the previous week. At 1440, calculations complete, Williamson ordered four torpedoes fired in quick succession from the submarine's bow tubes. Once those were away, *Drum* dove deep and commenced evasive action. Almost immediately, the noise of a distant explosion reached the crew. One of their torpedoes had found their mark.

There was no time to celebrate as *Drum* was rocked by three sharp explosions. One of the sub chaser's crews had fixed their location and was doing its best to kill them. Pieces of sound-deadening cork and flakes of paint broke loose from the submarine's interior and fell onto the crew. Reflexively hunkered down against the depth-charge attack, the men brushed the debris out of their hair and off their shoulders. A string of 12 more depth charges shook the submarine during the next 15 minutes, but none detonated close enough to do real harm. *Drum* and her crew survived the attack.

But they didn't leave. "At periscope depth," recorded the submarine's diary, just more than an hour after firing its torpedoes, "sighted the damaged ship, bearing 075 degrees true, distant 12,000 yards, listed about 20 degrees to port; one escort between us and the ship; and two columns of smoke to the northward. Commenced closing for kill. Another maru [transport ship] and the second escort are lying to near the damaged ship, range 9,000 yards. Apparently, they plan to tow the damaged ship, or to remove personnel should she sink."

The damaged Japanese ship broadcast a message that was intercepted: "… received one torpedo hit in No. 3 hold; No. 2 and No. 3 holds flooded. At present no danger of sinking." The ship sank a couple of hours later, as Williamson and his crew worked unsuccessfully to position *Drum* for a second attack.

So ended the career of the *Hie Maru*, the passenger ship that had brought George to the United States three years earlier. She had been converted into a submarine tender and pressed into military service in 1942. That service had put her on the ocean floor.

\*\*\*

Despite the rigors of combat, and all the flying a man could stand, George still thrilled at opportunities to flex his flying mettle. By this time, several months after his first combat mission, his reputation as a daredevil was well established and he was considered the 499th's hottest pilot. "I had a routine whereby I returned to base by flying up the runway, props barely above the steel matting, as fast and as low as I could go. Some of the men swore that my propeller tips occasionally brushed the matting and sent up a shower of sparks."

"Then, at the far end of the runway," he said, "I pulled the nose up and chandelled sharply into a climbing turn to the left. Almost immediately, I brought the aircraft hard back around in the opposite direction, leveling off at about 500 feet. At that point I lowered my flaps and landing gear as I continued in a left turn and started a descent."

"I continued to lose altitude in a tight turn," he said. "And then, just before the wheels touched down, I leveled the wings and let *Jayhawk* settle very gently onto the runway. The ground crews loved to watch those sorts of landings. They argued amongst themselves as to who had flown the lowest or tightest, or who had gotten on the ground the quickest."

George got away with those sorts of stunts because the squadron's leadership let him; he was as good a pilot as any of them, aggressive almost to a fault, and had seen as much or more combat than just about any pilot in the entire group. Max Ferguson, the 499th's communications officer, recalled an instance when George gave the squadron area a demonstration. "He was only five foot six, or five foot seven," Ferguson said of Cooper, "but his flying skills, his muscular coordination, and visual acuity were so good, he believed he could stretch the performance of the old B-25 to the very limit."[4]

The 499th's camp was located at the base of a double-peaked mountain. Ferguson's tent was staked out just below the gap between the two peaks. "One morning," Ferguson recalled, "I heard the roar of a B-25 and looked out to see Coop and *Jayhawk* lower than our tent. He swooped down over the mess hall and up toward the notch between the two mountains. Never in my life have I had a few seconds so tense as I mentally pushed *Jayhawk* up the mountain to keep it from mushing into the ground. They barely made it through the notch."

George had flown the stunt in response to a dare, and his recollection of how close he came to crashing coincided with Ferguson's. "I thought for a moment that I wouldn't get over the mountain. The plane felt like it was about to stall, and at the last moment, just when the nose of the plane cleared the peak, I shoved the control yoke forward to kick the tail up and over. It was much the same as a high jumper does when he brings his feet up as his body clears the bar. It was too close for me or anyone else to try that again."

"In truth," George said, "the risks to which I exposed myself and the aircraft—and especially the crew—were irresponsible. I needlessly put men and equipment in danger. Yet no one in my crew ever expressed any concerns or showed any reluctance to fly with me. They always seemed to share in the excitement of a challenge." Indeed, George's crew probably took pride in being able to declare they had been aboard the aircraft that had flown the latest showboating exploit about which everyone was talking.

Much of the flying George did in New Guinea was not in combat. He flew training missions, of course, and also courier runs and maintenance check flights. It was on one of these latter flights that he had a very close call. "One of *Jayhawk*'s engines was changed and I took it up to 'slow time' the new engine. In other words, I operated the engine at low power settings to help break it in—to make certain that all the seals and gaskets and such seated properly before operating it at high power settings."

George taxied onto the runway and applied power to both engines, watching the associated gauges as he did so. At the same time he visually checked the new engine to be sure that it wasn't leaking, or throwing parts or showing any other signs of failure. No problems were indicated and he released the aircraft's brakes and continued to keep an eye on the new engine. It wasn't until *Jayhawk* was accelerating down the runway that he noted the airspeed indicator had failed.

"I didn't abort the takeoff," George said. "I knew the aircraft well enough and felt that I could estimate the airspeed pretty well with the RPM and manifold gauges—and through feel." Indeed, *Jayhawk* got airborne with no problem and George climbed and turned to the west of Schwimmer on what should have been little more than a relaxed local sightseeing flight.

"We had been flying for about an hour," George said, "when we spotted a C-47 down in the swamp. There were two people waving at us from atop the fuselage. I was able to raise base operations on the radio and give them the aircraft's location. They acknowledged my call but advised that it might be a day or more before they could get a rescue team in the area. Except with a boat, the area was nearly impenetrable."

"I was worried about how they might get along until they were rescued," George said, "and decided to drop our aircraft's emergency kit. It had rations and other survival equipment. I opened the bomb bay doors and my flight engineer, Henry Jepson, positioned himself with the kit so that he could throw it out on my command."

George descended as low over the trees as he dared and pointed *Jayhawk* at the downed C-47. "Using the engine instruments and feel, I slowed down to what I felt was about 20 miles per hour above stall speed," George said. "Just as we were about to fly over the other airplane I shouted at Jepson to dump the rations." George banked slightly and saw the package splash down next to the C-47.

"When I turned around I saw that we were going to run into the trees. I applied full power but it was too late." A ripsaw roar vibrated through the B-25 as it mowed its way through a long swath of treetops before George was able to pull it clear. "Luckily, it still flew alright," he said. "Mostly, I was struck by the very strong smell of fresh-cut lumber that permeated the aircraft. On landing, we had to pull branches from the engine nacelles and other parts of the aircraft, but other than a need for some minor sheet metal repair, *Jayhawk* was just fine.

The C-47 that George and Jepson had found was *The Amazon* from the 317th Troop Carrier Group. It experienced a double engine failure while en route to Port Moresby from Townsville on December 1, 1943, and went down west of Port Moresby. With the information George provided, a rescue party was sent out the following day. Traveling first via motor launch, and then by foot, the rescuers found the crew and brought them safely to Port Moresby.[5]

***

Although George most eagerly watched for mail from Betty, he did also stay in touch with a wide variety of family and friends. He heard occasionally from his older brother Marion who served aboard the aircraft carrier *Yorktown* until he was released on a medical discharge. Marion subsequently worked as a draftsman and engineer. Older sister Helen lived in Palo Alto, California, where her husband served in the Army as a lawyer. Younger brother Lester was heard from only very infrequently. He was an engineer in the Merchant Marine. One of his ships had been attacked and sunk by a U-boat off the coast of Brazil; happily, he survived. And George and Betty both stayed in close touch with Aunt Gertrude in Peabody, Kansas. George was especially attentive and frequently asked Betty to send her money so that she might be more comfortable.

\*\*\*

The Japanese were pushed out of, or had abandoned, most of their bases in eastern New Guinea and retreated west and north as the end of 1943 approached. Consequently, based out of the airfield complex at Port Moresby, the 345th's four squadrons were hard pressed to reach important targets. Indeed, the three attacks the group made against Rabaul required the squadrons to stage themselves through Dobodura near the north coast of New Guinea. Consequently, in order to bring more targets into range, and to ease logistics and personnel burdens, the decision was made to move the group to Dobodura.

The move was made over a period of a couple of weeks during December, and combat operations continued more or less uninterrupted. It was of no great concern to George or most of the other men as they occupied a camp that had been built by a unit that had moved further forward. And it included an already-constructed officers' club that was at least the equal of the one they had left behind, minus the well-painted nude on the wall. George particularly liked that his tent was sited near a cool, clear stream that was large enough so that he could bathe.

But a lot of the move happened while George was away. He had flown enough missions to merit another period of down time in Sydney. He really liked the town but had mixed feelings about leaving the squadron. "I no sooner get down here," he wrote to Betty, "when I want to go back again. Not that I don't appreciate Sydney and the relaxation I get here, but it means missing out on missions which bring me closer to home."

Still, he had a good time. He met with friends from the 345th and other units, and he spent time with an Australian family that befriended him and other American servicemen. He and Bill Parke—whose burn wounds were fading from purple to something lighter—went dancing, to the movies and to a play. But when it was time to go back to New Guinea, he was ready. The more missions he flew, the closer he was to going home.

## CHAPTER 11

# "It Was a Bit of a Shock"

It was a rainy midmorning on December 19, 1943, when Richard Gale, the head stockman at Canal Creek Station, toed a piece of wreckage with his boot. He kicked it over for no reason and then scanned the trees and scrub around him. Small fires—some of them bodies—illuminated the grayness. The skin was torn away from part of an aircraft fuselage. Its structural members—bent and skewed and scorched—creaked and popped as they cooled in the misty morning. A wing, nearly intact, laid on the ground a short distance away. The foliage was hung with grisly bits of clothing and bodies and pieces of blown-apart aircraft. The air stank of burning fuel, metal and meat.

He had been on the veranda of the house, about 30 miles north of Rockhampton, when he first spotted the aircraft.[1] It was a USAAF C-47 transport and it spun out of a low layer of clouds through a thin drizzle. It was whole but smoking and obviously doomed. And then, only an instant before smashing into the ground, it blew apart. Seconds later, the cracking rumble of the explosion rattled his chest.

He hurried inside the house to telephone the authorities, but the telephone exchange was fussy and he could not make a connection. He left that task with his wife, jumped into his truck and bumped across the countryside to the crash site. He almost wished he hadn't.

The aircraft, from the 374th Troop Carrier Group, had left Townsville for Brisbane earlier that morning. There were 31 passengers aboard. The 499th's Orlen Loverin, his copilot, William Graham, and navigator George Snyder were among them. They had been bound for Sydney where they planned to spend Christmas.

"It was a bit of a shock, and sad, that they were killed not in combat, but on their way to get some rest and relaxation," said George. "But there was nothing really for us to do, other than to keep doing what we were already doing. I don't know if we had just gotten tough, or numb, but there was no mourning. They were simply gone, just like others were."

George, cautious of the censor, shared no details of the 499th's casualties with Betty. In his first letter following his return from Australia he simply wrote, "Loverin joined Bryant and Thompson. They have a squadron of their own now."

"I don't see any prospects for a Christmas celebration," he said in his closing paragraph. "Not even a Christmas dinner, but we are just as happy. Raids on Japs are celebration enough."

If that was the case, then George and his comrades must have done much celebrating as they hit Japanese positions at Cape Gloucester, on New Britain Island, through most of December. Those missions reached their apex on December 26, 1943, in conjunction with a highly successful amphibious assault by Marines of the First Infantry Division. An indicator of the confidence that the 345th's leadership had in George was the fact that, immediately upon his return from Australia, he was assigned to lead the 499th "Bats Outta Hell" against targets at Cape Gloucester on three successive days—December 24, 25, and 26. In fact, of the 19 missions the group flew during that 30-day period, George led the squadron on nine of them. The lead assignments for the other remaining ten missions were split between five other men.

\*\*\*

"How's my favorite captain?" asked Betty in her letter of January 6, 1944. George had been promoted the previous month, and Betty and her family were very proud. "The kids all had to tell their teachers about their brother-in-law." The promotion reflected the service's confidence in George's ability, and with that confidence came more responsibility in the air and on the ground. Of course, it also came with an increase in pay.

"I saw the sweetest sight the other day," she continued. "A second lieutenant and his wife; he was pushing a baby carriage. And he didn't care who saw him. I guess he was too proud to care. It made tears come because I could see you in his place." Betty reflected on the fact that she would never see George push Pris in a baby carriage. "Pris will be able to walk with us by the time you come home."

The next day, Betty stepped in from the gray, cold Wisconsin morning—a letter clutched tightly in her hand. She studied it again. It was from George, but the writing on the envelope was not his. What did it mean? Was he sick and unable to write in his own hand? Had he been injured? Or worse, had he been killed? Did the envelope hold an unfinished letter that one of George's friends had forwarded? But if that was true, wouldn't there have been a telegram notifying her of his death?

She didn't want to but, heart pounding, she finally tore the envelope open. She unfolded the pages and found one of George's usual letters. As always, he found a way to tell her how much he loved her, but there was no explanation as to why someone else had addressed the letter. She didn't care—it wasn't important so long that he was alive.

That same month, Betty wrote to George, obviously disturbed at the loss of so many 499th men she had known. "I still can't believe that Cliff [Bryant] and Alden [Thompson] are gone, and now [Orlen] Loverin. It isn't right. This war must end very soon." Betty wrote that she could endure much, but not the loss of George. "Do be careful," she begged. "You and Pris are all I have and I love you both with all my heart."

Betty's plea to George was still being sorted in the post office when George wrote on January 13 that he would likely reach the 50-mission mark the following week. To that point, 50 missions had been the magic mark for the completion of a combat tour. It wasn't officially codified as a policy or a regulation, but was the point at which most men could ask to be "recommended" for return to the States. In truth, most of them were worn out physically and mentally by the time they had flown 50 combat missions and needed to be sent home anyway.

But after months of the practice, Fifth Air Force headquarters was concerned that too many experienced men were going home too quickly. Rumors spread that the policy might change, and those rumors had obviously reached George. "I seriously believe I will have something more like 70 missions before I go home. I suppose it really doesn't matter," he wrote with resignation, "because I will be back eventually, even if I do not get home soon."

Consistent with his new captaincy and demonstrated competency, George was made the 499th's operations officer during January 1944. The assignment was not only a reflection of his abilities and the respect that the 345th's leadership had for his abilities, but also the realities of war. So many men senior to him in rank had been killed or sent away, that the survivors—George included—moved up in the squadron hierarchy. "So many of the first-string boys have gone home or been killed," he wrote to Betty, "that we have started on our second string for leaders. Really though, our second-string pilots are as good as, or better than our original first pilots."

Indeed, half a year of combat had taken a toll on George's original flight and crew. Of course, Thompson was dead, and after several near-catastrophes,

Captain George Cooper, January 1944, Dobodura, New Guinea. (George Cooper)

Jack George was relieved from combat. And of George's original crew, only he and his trusty, sharpshooting flight engineer, Henry Jepson, were still flying together. Stevens had been sent to a B-24 unit, Parke had his own crew, and his steadfast and reliable radioman, Harvey Green, had already completed his combat tour and was sent back to the States. And early on he had lost his original gunner, Alston Bivins, when he was badly burned while assigned to a mosquito abatement project.

George was different. "Really, I have come to enjoy these missions," he wrote to Betty. "And even now that I have all I need to be recommended to go home, I hate to miss out on going along. I have kept on flying and will continue to do so until the month is over. Even then, I can say nothing definite on when I might be back." Certainly, Betty must have been unsettled by George's seemingly nonchalant attitude.

\*\*\*

The Japanese were deadly to be sure, but foul weather could be just as lethal. The weather was always a consideration during the air campaign that ultimately ground Japanese forces there to bits. New Guinea had plenty of it, and it could be of the very worst sort—thick, heavy and violent. Surviving it took skill or luck, and sometimes both.

"I was sent down to Brisbane, Australia, to pick up a new crew—the Bob Spears crew," George said. "On the way back to New Guinea, I had Bob sit in the copilot's seat. He was curious and asked why we didn't have a navigator for the long overwater flight. I told him we didn't need one."

In truth, George could navigate well enough using his gyro compass and the aircraft's drift meter. With it, the aircraft's drift was estimated by measuring the ocean's waves, their size and their direction. But his ace in the hole was the towering set of cumulus clouds that virtually always towered over Port Moresby.

"Of course," George said, "We hit Port Moresby on the nose. Bob was amazed." After a quick refueling they were soon on their way to Dobodura. George wanted to fly the direct route through the mountains which rose in places to 12,000 feet. However, the way was blocked by heavy clouds. The alternative route would take them around the eastern part of New Guinea and would take much longer.

"I knew of a pass through the mountains," George said, "because I had flown it many times before. I decided to fly through that pass, even if we had to punch through the clouds on instruments." When Spears questioned George about navigating through the cloud-shrouded mountains—a practice that was generally discouraged—he had a mixture of curiosity and concern in his voice.

George climbed to 7,000 feet, well above the floor of the valley through which he intended to fly. A short time later visibility decreased to nothing as the weather closed around them. "It wasn't long," George said, "before I sensed that something was wrong. I held my course and applied full climb power as I brought the nose up. I willed *Jayhawk* to climb as quickly as possible. We finally broke out of the clouds at about 10,000 feet, with a mountain just off to our left side."

Spears exclaimed to God out loud—and with a great deal of vigor—and asked George if he had seen the mountain. "I answered calmly that I had," said George, "and told him that was why we had climbed so steeply. I have no idea what made me fly the aircraft as I did. Some would say God was with me. Bob Spears later used to claim that I could see through clouds."

\*\*\*

On January 16, 1944, George led a three-ship flight to the vicinity of Wide Bay, only about 50 miles south of Rabaul on New Britain Island, and to

Pacquinot Bay which was located another 50 miles to the southwest. It seemed somewhat ironic to him that only three months earlier he had been part of three multi-group attacks against Rabaul—often with heavy fighter cover. Now he was leading a tiny flight to the same vicinity with no fighter protection whatever.

"We were looking for shipping," George said. The flight from Dobodura to New Britain offered them nothing in the way of targets. Nearing New Britain, George descended the flight down to a few hundred feet and then, upon reaching Wide Bay, he turned generally southward to follow the coastline. The aircraft on his wing were flown by two of his good friends, Jack Snyder and Norman Hyder.

The weather was dreary with low gray clouds and thin drizzle. And the hunting was poor. The three olive-drab B-25s cruised purposefully over the dark water, occasionally banking through the mist toward the shore to better investigate potential targets. Notwithstanding their careful search, the coastline was either devoid of enemy vessels, or the vessels were too well camouflaged for them to spot. Finding nothing worthwhile at Wide Bay, George continued down the coastline to Pacquinot Bay.

There, at Palmalmal Plantation, a barge was snugged up to a dock. Uniformed figures moved supplies from the craft onto the shore. The three B-25s immediately turned to attack. Jack Snyder went first, as he was the closest, and he ripped the dock, the barge and the surrounding area with his machine-gun fire. George followed Snyder. As he closed the range he could see no one on the barge, the dock or the shore—they had all gone to ground. Seconds later he mashed down on the firing button and watched the bullets from *Jayhawk*'s guns tear into the barge. He gently stepped on one rudder, then the other, and watched the spray of his gunfire move back and forth as he let the aircraft's nose track across the rest of the target area. Chunks of Japanese material flew through the air in front of him and he was gratified.

Very close to the dock, George stopped firing and hauled the aircraft around in a hard, left turn to follow Snyder back out over the water. With Snyder in sight, he looked over his shoulder and saw Hyder finish his firing run. The dock area was a shambles and the barge—hard hit by the guns from the three B-25s—started to burn.

"I didn't drop any of my bombs," George said, "because I wanted to save them in case we found a real ship—something other than a barge." He watched his friend Jack Snyder maneuver to set up another attack from a different direction. Making more than one pass against a target was always risky as the enemy defenders, if they hadn't been ready and alert during the initial attack, certainly were afterward.

Snyder weighed the risks and decided they were in his favor. George watched the olive-green form of his aircraft, *Snatch*, work its way inland before turning back toward the barge. Just above the treetops, Snyder's guns lashed the target area with streams of bullets. A shot of flame erupted from the right engine as the aircraft passed the dock. And then, rather than turning hard away, the B-25 suddenly seemed to go limp. Its nose lifted, and then it rolled slowly to the right.

The roll continued and the nose dropped and Snyder and his crew were killed in a spectacular, gasoline- and bomb-fed explosion. "It was misty, and perhaps because of that, none of us saw where the gunfire that hit him came from," said George. Wary of what had seemed an innocuous target—especially because the location of the enemy guns was unknown—George made a decision. "I called Hyder and told him to join me. We were going home. If the enemy gunners could hit Snyder, they could hit us too. And that barge and those supplies weren't worth what it had already cost."

The flight back to Dobodura was a solemn one. None of the men aboard the two remaining B-25s was used to receiving worse than they gave. Snyder's loss was not only personal to George but ominous. "There were four of us from my advanced training class at Victoria, Texas, who went to the 499th 'Bats Outta Hell.' It was me, Cliff Bryant, Jack Snyder and Owen Hawver. I was the only one still alive." Several months earlier, Owen Hawver, like Orlen Loverin, had been killed in the crash of a C-47.

"I had a wonderful dream toward morning," Betty wrote to George four days later. You were really home, but you looked so different—you were much heavier. I could see you on the couch holding Pris. She was much older. I suppose she will be a lot older before you see her."

Certainly, she wasn't getting shot at or sleeping under mosquito netting, but Betty—like millions of other military wives—wasn't living an easy life. Housing was scarce and women were often compelled to live with family or other women in similar situations. And they were raising children on their own. "Our little girl is a sick chick," Betty wrote. "I called the doctor in tonight and she has the flu. Her fever is 102 degrees. I try not to worry, but she is so tiny and can't tell me if it hurts."

And then there were the maddeningly mundane but necessary tasks they were stuck with. "I made a mistake on the amount we still owe on the 1942 taxes," Betty wrote to George. "The total was $118.40. The balance due is half, or $59.20. Do I figure the 1943 taxes on your base pay, or total salary?"

But probably most difficult for the wives was not knowing if their man was well or not. All of them dreaded the notion of a policeman, uniformed serviceman or telegram delivery boy approaching their house. All of them silently imagined the horror of learning their loved one had perished.

\*\*\*

Following the completion of his 50th mission—the end of his combat tour—George was happily surprised by the return of an old friend. "Ralph Stevens came back to the 345th after doing a stint with one of the B-24 units," he said. "It was good to see him and we talked of the 'old days' of just a couple of months prior. He was anxious to go home, but was five missions short of the 50 that were required."

Stevens made a request of George that drew upon the very heart of their friendship. "He asked me to fly another five missions so that he could go with me and reach the 50-mission mark," said George. George pointed out the obvious; there were any number of other crews that Stevens could fly with. "But he didn't want to go with anyone else," George said. "He wanted to fly with me. It wasn't that he thought the other crews were bad or incompetent, but he said he just knew somehow that I would always get him back safely. It was a feeling he had."

Stevens's request was additionally problematic because, as a bombardier, he didn't have much of a role to play. "Our missions were almost entirely low-level strafing," George said. "There was no need for a bombardier whatsoever. When we were bombing from higher altitudes, he was absolutely critical to our success, but that was no longer the case. Certainly, it was good to have another set of eyes in the aircraft, and Stevens was experienced and was good company, but he wasn't an essential part of the crew at that point. Having him aboard during a mission would do nothing other than get him one more notch on his mission count." Of course, from Stevens' viewpoint it was essential to get those notches so that he could go home.

George knew that he would be tempting fate should he agree to Stevens's request. Many of his friends were already dead for no reason other than bad luck. And it only took one mission to get killed. "I'm not sure why I agreed to do it," George remembered. "I guess I did it because Stevens was my friend and I felt an obligation toward him. On the other hand, I also had an obligation to Betty and Pris and to myself."

Despite his conflicted introspection, his letter to Betty on January 22 sounded almost breezy. "I have been informed that it will not be necessary for me to fly any more missions as I have my quota. However, I will continue to fly every now and then until they send me home." The words must have felt like ice on her heart.

On January 24, 1945, he led the squadron on an attack to Los Negros and Manus Islands—part of the Admiralty Islands Archipelago—where he shot up a trio of barges and scored a direct bomb hit on a stockpile of supplies. And he went back to the same area the very next day. The airfields at Momote and Lorengau and their supporting infrastructure were the primary focus, as was any ship or barge traffic that might be laying offshore. Yet, anything that might be of value to the Japanese—buildings, bridges, jetties, etc.—was still considered fair game.

Rather than leading the squadron as he had the day prior, George was assigned to lead the 499th's third flight. Flying with him, and the sole reason for his participation on the mission, was his old friend and bombardier, Ralph Stevens.

It was a big effort as the 345th was joined by the 38th Bomb Group, making a total of 64 B-25s. An escort of three P-38 squadrons added muscle and

A close up of war-worn *Jayhawk*'s nose. Its gun barrels are covered to keep out dirt, water and small creatures. (USAAF)

protection. The two bomb groups took off from Dobodura at midmorning and rendezvoused overhead with the 345th in the lead, before turning northwest to pick up the P-38s over Finschafen. The entire force then motored north for the Admiralties.

The 275-mile overwater flight was unopposed and unremarkable. As the islands came into view, the 345th's squadrons, with the 500th at their head, dropped down toward the sea and arranged themselves into a trail formation, as did each flight within those squadrons. The formation leader, Glenn Taylor, angled east and then turned west over Pak Island, which was ten miles east of Manus Island. During the turn, the 499th's formation went momentarily akimbo behind the 500th's, and George eased his flight into the second position as the squadron patched itself back together. Ultimately, the stream of B-25s stretched back more than two miles. So then, with plenty of room to bomb and strafe, the 345th's crews, together with the 38th's threw themselves against the enemy.

If the flight to the Admiralties was unremarkable, the reception prepared by the Japanese that day was not. The defenders laced the sky with medium- and small-caliber antiaircraft fire. Bright orange flashes punctuated the positions of the antiaircraft guns, and gray-black explosions smudged the sky. The 345th's B-25s raced low through the maelstrom from east to west across Los Negros and then immediately over Manus. Their bombs and machine-gun fire further corrupted what had minutes earlier been a peaceful tropical island-scape.

The plan called for the group to bomb and strafe along Manus Island's northern coast. The crews were then to make a left-hand turn to reverse course and attack targets ashore while flying from west to east. The intervals between squadrons and flights gave the B-25 crews time and room to employ their weapons—per the plan—without the need to worry about the aircraft in front of, and behind them. But those intervals also gave the Japanese antiaircraft gunners time to zero in on the 345th's crews, fire at them and reload. And the fact that the attacks were coming from the same direction further eased their task.

"I saw a big, bright explosion almost immediately in front of me as one of our B-25s was hit," said George. "And then, two other balls of fire, probably pieces of the same airplane. What was left of it fell to the ground and exploded again in a swampy area near Papitalai Harbor, in between Los Negros and Manus. I immediately regretted my decision to fly extra missions for Ralph. I might be killed on any one of them." For his part, Ralph Stevens, who was sitting behind George and taking in the same deadly panorama, also probably regretted his decision to keep flying.

The aircraft that was knocked down was flown by Jack McLean of the 500th Bomb Squadron. He was leading the squadron's third flight when his aircraft was hit hard by 20-millimeter cannon fire. The left engine, bomb bay and a fuel tank absorbed the brunt of the fusillade and the aircraft instantly burst into flames. The secondary explosions when he hit the ground were likely caused by his remaining bombs.

George turned his attention from the burning wreckage that had been McLean's aircraft and concentrated instead on the task at hand. Skimming low over the waves, he led his flight past a barge that was engulfed in flames. Ahead, he saw bombs exploding and small geysers as machine-gun rounds skipped across the wave tops. He pointed *Jayhawk* at a jetty stacked with supplies and dropped one of the five 500-pound bombs he carried. Seconds after he flashed over the jetty, the bomb slammed home, exploded, and sent a column of debris and water and mud skyward.

Continuing low and fast over Seeadler Harbor, George pointed toward a little islet, Pityilu, and sprayed a collection of shacks with his machine guns. To his left, thin streams of antiaircraft fire reached out from Lorengau Airfield but fell harmlessly short into the water. Past Lorengau he reversed course in a left-hand turn, flew toward a bridge that straddled a ravine and mashed down twice on the bomb release button. He felt only a single mild jolt. One bomb, rather than two, fell clear, went a few yards long and exploded between the bridge and a building.

The remaining three bombs that *Jayhawk* carried would not release. It frustrated George that everything that had been done to get the aircraft over the target—making it mechanically ready, and loading it with fuel and bombs, and actually taking the risk to put it in harm's way—was largely negated by the fact that it could not drop even half of its bombs. He turned south across Manus Island toward the rendezvous point and fired desultory bursts of machine-gun fire at fleeting targets of no great value.

Behind him, his friend Ken McClure was busy getting himself in trouble. Jack McLean had been McClure's friend, and when McLean went down, McClure sought to avenge him. He wracked his aircraft into a hard turn toward the point where his friend's aircraft fell to earth. As he cleared a small ridge he was startled by a barrage of heavy antiaircraft fire. He tried to turn away but was caught by the enemy shells. His crew recalled that the sound was as if someone had thrown a handful of stones against the side of the aircraft.

Stung, but undeterred, McClure made a complete circle and dumped all his bombs into the area where he believed the antiaircraft guns were located. That done, and with his left engine failing, he turned for home. Meanwhile,

George and his two wingmen joined Taylor's flight at the rendezvous point. The radio was clobbered with chatter and believing that McClure and his flight were clear of the target—and with fuel becoming a concern—the two flights started for home. Behind them, smoke and fire evidenced the success of their attacks.

Smoke and fire were also issuing from McClure's left engine. If he and his men were shaken by their close encounter with death, so certainly must have been McClure's dog, "Flaps," whom he had brought along on the mission. The dog had been a gift from Major General Donald Wilson, a friend of McClure's mother and the chief of staff for Kenney's Fifth Air Force. At that moment, as McClure pointed the aircraft south and tried in vain to extinguish the growing flames in a deck of clouds, Flaps was clutched by Jim Mahaffey, the crew's navigator.

The aircraft could not be saved. A crew from the 38th Bomb Group shepherded McClure and his crew away from the Admiralties as they descended inescapably toward the sea. It wasn't long though before the 38th crew departed, probably low on fuel. When McClure's burning B-25 finally met the grasping waves, it hit hard. The crewmen were thrown violently against their harnesses and were momentarily stunned as the aircraft was snatched to a halt and settled in the water.

Seconds later, with the ocean rushing over them, the crewmen recovered their senses and sprang to action. McClure clambered clear and after some difficulty inflated a life raft before slipping back into the aircraft to help pull his copilot from where he sat, still in shock. Mahaffey spent precious moments splashing around inside the aircraft looking for McClure's dog, Flaps, who was torn from his grasp when the aircraft struck the water. The dog was nowhere to be found and Mahaffey, exhausted and in danger of sinking with the bomber, finally pushed himself away. Chagrined upon learning that his dog was missing, McClure went back into the aircraft in a last-ditch rescue attempt. Ultimately, like Mahaffey, he was unsuccessful.

Crews from the 501st, who had trailed the 499th over the target, circled the downed men and dropped rescue kits and rafts. Much of the material was lost or damaged, but McClure and all his men were safely aboard two rafts by the time the 501st's men winged away. It was the same time that the sharks started to circle.

The waterlogged men readied their pistols and watched the sharks as they paddled south, away from the smudge on the horizon that was Manus Island. They also cast their eyes skyward, hoping to spot the rescue force they were certain their squadron mates must have called.

They looked for several hours. And then looked some more. The sharks left them alone, but that was small solace against the fact that they were drifting into oblivion. They all knew that the longer they remained adrift, the odds grew greater that they would remain so. Over the course of only a couple of days, winds and currents could carry the men so far that the size of the search area would exceed the capabilities of the search and rescue resources.

Finally, as dusk approached, the men spotted five distant specks which quickly grew to be recognizable as four fighters and a larger aircraft. McClure and his crew—fearing the Japanese more than the sharks—made ready to slip into the water and pull the blue-painted bottoms of the life rafts over their heads. During the next few minutes they alternately scanned the water around them and focused on determining the identities of the aircraft.

Happily, they were American. It was a flight of four P-47s and a Navy PBY amphibious boat. They had been searching a badly plotted location and were nearly out of fuel and preparing to give up the search. Someone in the rafts fired a pair of flares which immediately caught the attention of the rescue aircraft. The PBY was soon overhead and it circled once before setting down on the water and pulling McClure's crew—minus Flaps the dog—aboard. They were back at Dobodura the following day.

George shared the story of Flaps' demise with Betty shortly afterward. "However, we have a new mascot, a police dog named, 'Strafer.' He has not yet been initiated in combat." George described how, when it was decided to take Strafer on a short-notice mission to "one of the Jap hot spots," the dog slipped away and wasn't found until the end of the day.

CHAPTER 12

# "I Would Have Stayed"

*Kill them all, kill them all,*
*From Wewak right down to Rabaul,*
*Kill all the slant-eyes and set their suns,*
*Hold down the trigger 'til their yellow blood runs,*
*Because the 499th's on the ball,*
*We'll strafe 'til we see them all fall,*
*There'll be no more Zeroes or Japanese heroes,*
*For the Bats outa Hell killed them all!*

—FIGHT SONG, 499TH BOMB SQUADRON

On the morning of February 3, 1944, George watched the 498th's B-25s skip over the jungled ridge and disappear down the other side. Antiaircraft fire, protecting the eastern approach to Dagua airfield, exploded harmlessly above them. Farther ahead an aircraft trailed flames and fell earthward. High above, P-38s and P-40s tangled with a smaller hodge-podge force of Japanese fighters.

The Japanese had lately been rebuilding their air power at the Wewak airfield complex and the Fifth Air Force was anxious to smash it down, just as it had done several times during the previous months. An hour previously, a force of B-24s and their fighter escorts had hit Wewak and But airfields, and now the 345th was tearing into the airfield at Dagua.

As the 498th had done a minute earlier, the 499th's crews hopped the ridge east of Dagua and dropped to the deck on a westward heading. And just as the Japanese antiaircraft gunners had fired too high above the 498th, they did so with the 499th. George, with Ralph Stevens looking over his shoulder, let *Jayhawk* settle just a few dozen feet above the ground and set a course that would take his flight down the center of the airfield. Already, fires burned from the 498th's attacks, and smoke drifted across the airfield. However, notwithstanding the 498th's excellent work, many targets remained.

Parafragmentation bombs were especially effective against "soft-skinned" targets such as aircraft. Here, they are about to touch ground and explode at Dagua—part of the Wewak airfield complex. (USAAF)

George dipped the nose of his B-25 and fired at a set of light antiaircraft guns. His bullets covered the positions, tearing up great clods of earth. Only a few scant seconds before passing over the enemy guns, he dropped several parafrags which fell away from *Jayhawk's* belly and drifted down on the hapless Japanese gunners.

Streaking across the airfield, George alternately fired his guns and dropped strings of parafrags. Japanese aircraft were parked all over the airfield, many of them with their engines running. Fuel trucks serviced several of them, and George sent a burst of gunfire after one which exploded into spectacular orange flames. Bill Parke flew to George's right and dropped a string of parafrags onto a long warehouse-type structure. Seconds later the roof flew off the building.

It was all over in less than a minute. George turned *Jayhawk* north over the water, collected his two wingmen, and adjusted his heading and power to rendezvous with the rest of the squadron. Behind them, fire and flames

By the time George flew his last mission in New Guinea—an attack against once-mighty Wewak on February 3, 1944—the Japanese forces there were a shambles. (USAAF)

blanketed Dagua as the 345th's other two squadrons, the 500th and 501st, finished the destruction.

Wewak and its airfields would never again present a serious threat. During the next weeks the Japanese collected most of what was worthwhile, abandoned the rest and retreated westward along New Guinea's coast. It was fitting, as it was also George's last sortie with the 345th—he had gotten Ralph Stevens to the magic 50-mission mark.

Knowing that George was nearing the end of his combat tour, Betty wrote to him the following day. "Over and over again, I keep saying and thinking, Georgie is coming home! Pris, Daddy is coming home! We're so awfully anxious, darling. Please don't keep us waiting too much longer."

"I was approached at that point by the group's leadership," George said. "They asked if I would stay to serve as the group assistant operations officer—a major's billet. It was a fantastic opportunity and a quick route to promotion. And I'd still get to fly combat missions if I wanted, although not at the same pace."

"If I had been single, I would have stayed," George said. "But I could not come up with an explanation that would have convinced Betty. There was

George's last mission was to Dagua, on February 3, 1944. (USAAF)

no good way to declare that I chose to continue flying combat—and run the very real risk of being killed—rather than coming home to her and our new baby. Besides, I did want desperately to be home with her and Pris."

George was pleased that the group thought well enough of him to offer such a position, but he respectfully declined it. He consequently received orders back to the States toward the end of February. "I flew *Jayhawk* for the last time on the flight to Brisbane," he recalled, "from where I was to catch a ship home." With George was Ken McClure who had recently been shot down, and who had lost his dog, Flaps.

George and McClure were accompanied to the battle-worn aircraft by a cadre of well-wishing comrades with whom they exchanged farewells, back slaps and handshakes before climbing into the aircraft. George, as he always had, sat in the left seat—the pilot's seat. There, he took a long last look at the airfield and the 499th's other aircraft and the jungle and his friends.

Even then, George knew that there would never again be a time in his life during which he would feel such camaraderie—such a sense of closeness and duty and trust. He knew that some of the faces that smiled up at him and McClure would never make that same flight. And that despite the intimacy that he felt for the other men, and that they felt for him, life would take them separate ways, and he would never see some of them again even if they survived. He felt a momentary sadness at this. And for the friends he lost and would lose, he felt a greater sadness that he knew would always be a part of him.

"It was a typical Cooper takeoff," remembered Max Ferguson, one of George's friends. "He held the plane on the runway to the very end, gained all the speed he could, then roared into the air."[1]

George turned south and pointed *Jayhawk* skyward. Max Ferguson turned to another of George's friends, Martin Wood, and bet him that George, against form, would continue on his way without giving the squadron a show. Wood took the bet. As *Jayhawk* receded into the sky during the next minute or so, Ferguson began to believe he had won.

"I decided to give the ground crews one last goodbye," said George. He pulled the aircraft around in a steep, descending, left-hand turn and thundered toward the 499th's squadron area. "Down, down he came as the wings began to release a peculiar whine," said Ferguson. "I prayed all the rivets and bolts were good ones as the roar of the engines increased." George pulled out of the dive only just barely above the ground and stood the aircraft up on one wing in order to pass between two stands of trees.

"He disappeared below the treetops," Ferguson recalled, "and for an instant I had a sinking feeling—he's not going to make it." An instant later, *Jayhawk* roared up from the jungle, flashed across the camp in a hat-lifting low pass, and leapt skyward once more. George was on his way home.

After arriving at Brisbane, George and Ken McClure were ordered to Major General Donald Wilson's office where he presented them both with Oak Leaf Clusters to their Air Medals. Wilson was a friend of McClure's family—he had given the doomed dog Flaps to McClure—and he invited the two young flyers to lunch with him in his office.

"While we waited," said George, "he stepped out for a moment and came back with a pair of Martinis for me and Ken. When he left again, I told Ken that I couldn't drink mine. He finished his in a hurry and gulped mine down as well. When General Wilson returned, he noted that our glasses were empty and had them quickly refilled. We fiddled with them a bit and when the general left the office again, Ken told me he couldn't drink any more. We poured them into a potted plant. It was still upright when we left."

\*\*\*

"They put me on a Liberty ship that zig-zagged all the way back to the States," George remembered. "Nothing memorable happened except that as we approached San Francisco, they wouldn't let us into the harbor—the fog was so thick that it would have been dangerous. So, there we sat, unable to sail the last couple of miles after having come so far."

While George sat on the ship waiting to step on American soil for the first time in nearly a year, William Cabell, his oft-times wingman, was part of a strike on March 5, 1944. The 499th was tasked to bomb and strafe enemy positions as Army units came ashore near Saidor on the northern coast of New Guinea. Cabell had continued to get nerve-sick prior to each mission and refused to eat beforehand lest he puked. But he nevertheless reached deep each time. "In a way," George said, "his bravery was exceptional. He flew, even though he got physically ill at the thought of doing so. I had urged him to stop flying combat—just as Jack George had done—but he refused. He was determined to complete his combat tour."

For no reason that anyone discovered, Cabell's aircraft fell slowly out of formation on the way to the target area. He dropped out of sight and nothing was ever found of him or his crew.

\*\*\*

The first monthly recap the 345th Bomb Group wrote was for the last month of George's service in the group—February 1944. It closed with the following declaration which does much to capture the unit's spirit during that time.

> We hate to see the older crews going home. Many "Fifty-Mission-ers" have left already, others await orders. New lads are coming in—many strange faces in the mess hall. Those of us still here are trying to give them something of the tradition of the 345th, and hope to imbue them with the fine esprit de corps that has distinguished this unit ever since training days. We expect a lot of them as our older boys were "tops," but they all come through when their turn comes ... And the group will have more experiences, more ships destroyed, more enemy planes downed and more damage to enemy stores and installations, for it is a good group.

As the 345th grew to become one of the USAAF's most lauded units during the coming campaigns, discussions sometimes turned to the unit's early days when the crews flew missions from Port Moresby and Dobodura. Men talked with an almost hushed reverence of brutal missions to Rabaul and Wewak, and of the old hands who flew them. George and his comrades—those that survived—took special pride at having introduced a unit to combat which earned a reputation for aggressiveness and effectiveness that was second to none.

## CHAPTER 13

# "I Opened the Door"

"I had asked Betty to meet me at my Aunt Gertrude's house in Peabody," George said. "My cousin, Virginia Cooper, picked me up at the train station and took me back to the house." There, George was almost overwhelmed at seeing his young wife again. She was lovelier than ever and holding her was like a dream—the sight, the feel, the smell of her. When they finally came out of their embrace, Betty pulled him to the bedroom where Priscilla had been sleeping.

"I opened the door, and there she was, standing in her crib," George said. "She held the rails and looked at me, curious. I could tell she was wondering who I was, but she wasn't afraid and didn't cry. It was almost as if she somehow knew who I was."

George stepped over and lifted her from her crib. "Again, she didn't cry," he said. "She seemed happy to be with me. I walked her through the house and out the front door. There was an elm in the front yard and I stood her up against it and grabbed my movie camera and shot several feet of film of her standing and looking at me."

*** 

"This is such a pretty place," George wrote to Betty from Santa Monica, California. "It would be perfect if you were with me. I feel sort of naked without you—as if I had left my shirt off."

Toward the end of April 1944, after a few weeks visiting with relatives and friends in Kansas and Wisconsin and Michigan, George had left Betty and Pris and reported to Santa Monica Army Air Force Redistribution Center No. 3, in California. It was one of four centers to which the Army Air Forces sent combat-stressed personnel to relax while they awaited orders to new units.

George was ecstatic to be home from his first combat tour, and to finally meet his new child, Pris. But he was anxious about his family who were still trapped by the Japanese in the Philippines. (George Cooper)

While there, they also underwent various medical and psychological evaluations to ascertain their fitness for follow-on duty, and what sort of duty it might be.

The redistribution center was nothing more than repurposed civilian infrastructure. The Army had taken charge of several hotels and beach houses in Santa Monica, as well as a number of other recreational facilities including a riding stable, skeet range and athletic fields. George was billeted near the beach at the upscale Shangri-La Hotel which had been built just before the war in the Streamline Moderne style which suggested the form of an imposing ocean liner.

As nice as it was, George didn't hole up in the Shangri-La, but rather took advantage of what the Army made available to him. "Yesterday I went horseback riding out by the Uplifter's Club," he wrote to Betty. "They were Army cavalry horses. This morning, I feel the results of the ride. I have a few aches about my body, and my legs are chapped and bruised from friction with the saddle."

The redistribution center was also the scene of many impromptu reunions as men crossed paths with others with whom they had trained or served in previous units. George was happy to see Glenn Taylor from the 499th, among others. From Taylor he learned that the 345th's loss rate seemed to be accelerating. "I sort of wish I could be with them," he wrote to Betty, "because only the new boys are left, and I believe it is partially because of their inexperience that our losses mount."

Others gave him more news. "I understand that Major [Julian] Baird is coming back. His flying got so poor that he was grounded. I imagine that [Richard] Reinbold will take over the squadron as he is the oldest member left." Reinbold had been George's green, excitable copilot during the 345th's last mission to Rabaul.

Little was required of the men and they were generally free to do as they wanted until such time as they were given orders to a new assignment. George visited his older brother Marion and his wife, and other friends such as Lionel Stagg, a schoolmate from Manila. "Dina is his wife," he told Betty. "She is French–Russian and rather startling in her thoughts and opinions. I like her, personally. She says she hates housework, but she is constantly moving around the house, making improvements. I have never seen her sit down for more than a minute. Dina is very blunt in her limited English and thinks nothing of discussing the very personal."

Lionel's father, Samuel, was a missionary who had been recruited by U.S. Navy intelligence just before the war. By the time George was visiting with Lionel, Samuel had been seized by the Japanese and interned at Santo Tomas. However, Lionel's mother Mary, an active humanitarian and supporter of the resistance, and his brother Samuel, had been arrested and tortured by the Japanese and were imprisoned at Fort Santiago from where few persons emerged alive.

George also entertained Billie—Bill Parke's wife—several times at local GI social events, and generally enjoyed the many attractions the area had to offer, to include a guided tour of the Warner Brothers film studios. "I did see a few stars including Hedy Lamar, Peter Lorre, Paul Henreid and John Ridgely." It was apparent from his letters that, if George was suffering from any sort of combat fatigue, his stay in Santa Monica was providing plenty of diversions.

In fact, he was smitten with the area. "This is the place I want to live," he declared to Betty. "It is just beautiful and living is comparatively cheap. With so much beauty, I cannot help but much regret that you are not here to share it."

And so, he bought a house. "Today you can mark as the start of a real beginning (or fall)," he announced to Betty. "I found a beautiful home in North Hollywood for $7,950. It sounds like quite an obligation, but trust me Pretty, it is a sound investment." George described the home, located at 6151 Simpson Avenue (and still extant), and how they might live in it, rent it or share it with family. He thought they could pay for it in three years, and he wanted to try to do it in two.

That the house was a sound investment was correct. It was in a nice neighborhood and housing was in short supply and would continue to remain so in that part of the nation. It could be resold or rented with little trouble.

But Betty was not as taken with the idea. She had no friends or family there, the house and surrounding area were far from her roots, and there was nothing about either that was familiar. Certainly, George was enthusiastic but the same things about which he was excited were not always exciting to her. And no doubt, it must have crossed her mind that if something were to happen to George, she would be a widow with a house she did not want or need. And finally, although she did not say so, there is a possibility that she was disappointed or resentful that—without consulting her—George had committed them to a considerable financial obligation.

In fact, two weeks later he was still waiting for her to share her opinion. "I have not yet received a letter from you," he wrote in early May 1944, "and the suspense of waiting on your comment on the house grows each day. You will get to see it some day and I believe that we can do just as well in California as anywhere else."

Notwithstanding all the attractions and distractions that George's stay at the redistribution center offered him—and the stress associated with the new house—Betty and Pris were always foremost on his mind. "I wonder what you and Pris are doing now. Has it been warm enough for her to go outside much? I wish that I could look out my window and see you and Pris walking in the park by the beach."

***

Betty and Pris met George at Greenville, South Carolina in mid-May 1944. There, he was assigned as a B-25 flight instructor at Greenville Army Air Base with the 330th Army Air Forces Base Unit. As part of a wave of returning combat-experienced pilots, his talents were especially valuable. From George, and others like him, the new pilots learned proven techniques and tactics, and would not have to "unlearn" outdated textbook nonsense when they were sent to their operational units. More importantly, the skills that George and his battle-experienced comrades imparted to the new men would save lives and help to better destroy the enemy.

"As an instructor I flew in the copilot's seat or stood behind the pilot," George said. "I taught tactical formation flying, bombing, and gunnery.

I also qualified pilots as aircraft commanders. It was interesting to see how the training had become more useful and realistic since my time."

Again, housing was tight. "We rented a single room that had a bathroom and a stove. Our kitchen sink was a pan that was filled and emptied from the bathtub." Happily, it wasn't long until they were able to rent a house. "It was the first real house we'd had since we were married. And it was there that Pris took her first steps and had her first birthday—I baked the cake."

***

George looked at the door of the house. Coming here, Morgantown, West Virginia, was something he had promised himself he would do when he returned to the States. But he wasn't sure he wanted to do it.

The house belonged to Alden Thompson's parents, and George had arranged to visit his mother—his father was in the Navy and stationed elsewhere. "I wanted to tell her about her son, what a fine pilot, officer and leader he was, and how much he was liked and respected. And I wanted her to know what a good friend he was and how much he meant to me. And I supposed she would want to know details about how he had been killed. I wanted to do all of this for Alden."

George walked up the steps to the door and knocked on it. Thompson's mother, who looked like any other mother, opened the door and smiled at George and ushered him into the kitchen where she had him sit down. "She was very nice," George said. "I shouldn't have been nervous. She thanked me over and over again for having taken the time to visit with her. I was glad that I came as she seemed to appreciate hearing about Alden from one of his close friends."

George shared what he came to share. "I was there for about half an hour, which seemed about the right amount of time to visit. And I could tell that, although she was very glad I came, the thought of Alden, and her love for him had made her sad. It was time to go." Thompson's mother accompanied him to the door, thanked him and said goodbye. Out in front of the house again, alone, George sighed, put on his hat and walked away.

***

George and Betty were happy enough in Greenville. "Some of our friends from the 345th, including Jack George and Claude Burger and their wives, and others, were there. And some from cadet days as well. We often met on the patio at the officers' club which overlooked the runway. From there we ate and drank while we watched aircraft take off and land. The Burgers had a girl, Nan Priscilla, who was the same age as Pris. They sometimes played together."

So, duty at Greenville was comfortable and familiar. George got to fly as much as he wanted, and it was as safe as was reasonable for a wartime training unit. And George and Betty likely could have stayed there until the war was over.

But there wasn't much about it that was very exciting. "After a couple of months at Greenville, I noticed a post on the bulletin board," George said. "It asked for volunteers to train as instructors on the new Douglas A-26," George said. "I put in for it and was given orders to report to Battle Creek, Michigan."

The Douglas A-26 was nicknamed the Invader. It was a bigger, faster, more capable successor to the same company's very good and much-liked A-20 Havoc. Typically crewed by a pilot and a gunner—with an extra seat next to

*Jayhawk* soldiered on after George left the 345th. Here, another crew poses proudly at its side. Although hit several times during 121 combat missions, *Jayhawk* was never knocked down by the Japanese and flew until October 1944 before being declared war weary and taken out of service. It was one of only two of the 499th's original aircraft still flying. (USAAF)

the pilot—its two R-2800 Pratt & Whitney radial engines powered it to a top speed of more than 350 miles per hour—on par with many fighters of the day. It also had excellent range and was capable of out-legging both the A-20 and the B-25 while also carrying more bombs and other weapons.

And as a strafer, it exceeded even the B-25 in the number of forward-firing .50-caliber machine guns it carried. The A-26B mounted eight guns in its nose and three in each wing. External gun packs that could be carried under the wings added to that number.

"Douglas ran a mobile training unit at Battle Creek," said George, "with provisions for classroom work, and aircraft system mockups for hands-on training. I was very impressed during my first orientation flight. The Douglas pilot explained to me that he wanted to demonstrate the aircraft's power and its ability to fly safely on one engine."

George sat next to the pilot in the observer's seat during the takeoff. Soon after getting airborne the pilot pulled the left engine to idle, feathered the propeller and continued to climb on one engine while turning left into the

A top-level view of the A-26 which George flew at the end of his combat career. This example is pictured over Europe. (USAAF)

traffic pattern. "It was always emphasized to us—a cardinal rule—that you never, ever turned into a bad engine for fear of falling into an unrecoverable stall. Yet, the A-26 obviously had more than enough power to do so. The pilot continued through the pattern and made a nice, single-engine landing with no fuss at all."

Finding the A-26 fun and easy to fly, George embraced his training at Battle Creek and soon had the aircraft mastered. He was especially taken with the aircraft's range when he took his operations officer to Pecos, Texas. "It was about 1,300 miles to Pecos, beyond what we would have tried in the B-25," said George. During the flight, he leaned the engine mixtures and made other adjustments to easily make the flight to Pecos without refueling—and at a faster airspeed than he could have flown the B-25. "It was clear to me that the range of this aircraft with normal fuel tanks was more than 2,000 miles—far better than that of the B-25," George said.

As enamored as George was with the A-26, he was more so with Betty and Pris. "We rented an apartment on Gull Lake," he said, "which came with a small rowboat. During the evenings when it was warm, we sometimes paddled around the lake with the little boat. And Pris made friends with an older girl in an adjacent apartment. We weren't there long enough to have much of a social life, but Betty and I were happy and content with Pris at the center of our lives.

## CHAPTER 14

# "I Got Plowed in the Skull"

Once George finished training on the A-26, he was sent away to instruct. The A-26 far outshadowed its predecessors and the USAAF was anxious to get it into service. Just as he had been valued as a combat-experienced veteran at Greenville, he would be equally valued at Marianna, Florida, to where the service sent him as an instructor with the 381st Base Unit. He, Betty and Pris made the trip by car in the heat of the summer, and made a home at Malloy's Auto Court, an iconic business establishment in the little city.

George and Betty were content with the new assignment and their living arrangements where they quickly made friends with several other young couples. George liked the A-26 and was glad that Betty and Priscilla had adjusted so well to the move. For her part, Betty was happy at the notion that their little family would be in one place, together, for at least a few months. Still, it was wartime and they both knew that some of their friends were far from being so well situated—the war was happening to them all in varying degrees.

One of those friends was George's boyhood pal, George Wightman. The two of them, together with George's little brother, Lester, had been nearly inseparable. George had lost track of Wightman since he had left the Philippines, but guessed that he might be in an internment camp somewhere. It was in fact a guess as there was little information from the Philippines about anyone or anything that was directly connected to him.

It is difficult to guess at George's reaction had he any idea of what his dear boyhood friend endured.

The reality was that, although he was technically a British citizen, Wightman volunteered to serve in the U.S. Army in the Philippines. He had lived his entire life there and it was what he knew and loved. The Americans accepted him as a second lieutenant and his commission was pending even as he

For a short time during 1944, George and Betty and Pris were a family. (George Cooper)

participated in the ill-fated defense of the Philippines. A fellow officer recalled his value, "Wightman had lived in the islands all his life. He knew the native psychology and their ways."[1]

That Wightman "knew the native psychology" was especially appreciated as he ultimately ended up with the Visayan Force on Cebu Island under the command of Brigadier General Bradford Chynoweth. The Visayan Force was an under-equipped organization led by American army officers but made up largely of Filipino soldiers who had received very little training. There, Wightman served as a supply officer. He scrounged and allocated what little resources were available during the desperate and hopeless fighting that followed the Japanese invasion.

When American and Filipino military personnel were ordered by General Jonathan Wainwright to surrender in May 1942, Wightman was made a prisoner of war. At this time, George was still going through flight training and wooing Betty via the mail. Half a world away, Wightman was eventually taken to the POW camp—a converted prewar penal colony near Davao, on Mindanao Island. There, the nearly 2,000 prisoners were forced to harvest lumber from the surrounding jungles, plant crops and perform other grueling labor. They were not treated as POWs, rather they were abused as slave laborers. All the men grew steadily weaker from insufficient diet, overwork and illness; among other diseases, essentially everyone at Davao suffered from malaria.

And they were beaten by their guards—often savagely and senselessly. The slightest provocation or smallest mistake often provoked crippling attacks. Many of the prisoners never fully recovered from the mistreatment and abuse they endured, and some were killed outright. Neutral Swiss representatives made a wartime report on the Japanese cruelties at Davao which included the following statement:

> Sergeant McFee was shot and killed by a Japanese guard after catching a canteen full of water which had been thrown to him by another prisoner on the opposite side of a fence. The Japanese authorities attempted to explain this shooting as an effort to prevent escape. However, the guard shot the sergeant several times and, in addition, shot into the barracks on the opposite side of the fence toward the prisoner who had thrown the canteen. At about the same time and place an officer returning from a work detail tried to bring back some sugarcane for the men in the hospital. For this he was tied to a stake for 24 hours and severely beaten.[2]

On March 2, 1944, while George Cooper was making his way home from New Guinea—and to Betty and Priscilla—Wightman was moved a short distance, along with hundreds of others, to Lasang. There, he and the other prisoners were put to work building an airfield. Conditions at Lasang were as miserable as they had been at Davao, and the condition of the men continued to deteriorate. However, their spirits were lifted when American aircraft attacked the airfield on August 17. It was ironic that the men were so happy to see the results of their backbreaking labor bombed to bits. Aside from the obvious fact that it would be a while before the airfield would be useable by the Japanese, the raid was an indication that the Allies were resurgent. The war was coming back to the Philippines, and with it the possibility of liberation.

The POWs at Lasang were not put back to work. Instead, in the predawn darkness of August 20, 1944, they were tied together at their waists and marched barefoot 20 miles to a pier that reached into the Davao Gulf.[3] There, they were literally—at bayonet point—crammed into the holds of a Japanese ship. There was no room to move and the men took turns standing so that others could sit to rest. The ship set sail that same day.

The holds of the ship soon turned into hot, stinking, human-cooking cauldrons. The buckets the Japanese lowered to the men were inadequate to handle their waste, and the men soon wallowed in feces, urine and vomit. There was no ventilation and the heat became insufferable. The dirty handfuls of rice that the men received were inedible. Worse, the water barely measured a pint per man per day and was sent down into the holds in the same buckets that carried their waste topside.

The ship arrived at Zamboanga, on the other side of Mindanao, four days later. There, the men—George Wightman among them—were kept in the blistering holds for ten, soul-crushing days. Uncharacteristically, the Japanese allowed the men on two occasions to climb to the main deck and pass under a spray of sea water. These expedient showers might have been refreshing but they were little more. The prisoners were forced back down into the holds each time and were once more covered with filth. Deprived of food, water, fresh air and even the most basic hygiene needs, some of the men collapsed in fits of insanity.

Finally, they were ordered out of the ship and onto another that was moored alongside. This new ship was the *Shinyō Maru*. It had two holds and 500 POWs were forced into one, while 250 were crammed into the other. The ship had been built and launched in Scotland in 1894, exactly 50 years earlier, as the *Clan MacKay*. During the five decades since, it had been sold, resold and renamed many times until the Japanese seized it in Hong Kong at the end of 1941.

Regardless of its history, the Japanese turned it into a floating perdition. They sent it to sea on September 5, 1944, as part of Convoy 076 with 750 American POWs onboard. The convoy turned north for Manila and hugged the coast, while overhead, Japanese aircraft watched for American submarines.

And they watched for good reason. An American submarine, *Paddle* (SS-263), was two weeks into its fifth war patrol during the early morning hours of September 7, 1944. Its crew had seen no action up to that point and the captain, Byron Nowell, was hopeful. New orders, based on updated intelligence, had changed the area he was to patrol. Based on those updated orders, Nowell and his crew expected to find good hunting close to Mindanao's coastline. Accordingly, he positioned his boat ten miles north of Sindangan point at 0520 and waited.[4]

*Paddle*'s crew kept watch for most of the day without seeing anything remarkable. Finally, late in the afternoon, Nowell spotted smoke to the west. A few minutes later, he also caught sight of a float plane patrolling ahead of the enemy convoy. The aircraft evidently did not spot the Americans as it continued its search circuit without deviating.

At 1613, *Paddle* recorded the convoy's composition as a medium-sized tanker, a small tanker, two medium-sized cargo ships—one of those being the *Shinyō Maru*—two small cargo ships, and two destroyer escort (DE) vessels.

The USS *Paddle* torpedoed and sank the *Shinyō Maru*, a hell ship which was transporting Allied POWs, including George Wightman. (U.S. Navy)

The sea was calm and *Paddle* moved at just a few knots to intercept the Japanese ships. The periscope was used only fleetingly so as not to give the submarine's position away; the sea was almost glassy and some of the enemy vessels were on course to pass very closely. Nowell had to do very little other than let the enemy convoy come to him and his crew. He held his course—and his breath—as one of the Japanese escort ships motored past *Paddle*'s bow less than 300 yards away.

And then, Nowell and his men made their final preparations for the attack. "The approach was made on the tanker since it was the most valuable ship of the convoy," he said. Finally, at a range of 1,875 yards, Nowell ordered four torpedoes launched from the boat's bow tubes. Once the "fish" were away, attention was turned to another of the ships which was only 1,350 yards away. That ship was the *Shinyō Maru*, and Nowell sent two torpedoes after it.

Almost immediately after firing on the *Shinyō Maru*, an explosion reverberated through the water and reached *Paddle*'s crew. The blast indicated that one of the first four torpedoes had struck the tanker. A second detonation, 14 seconds later, was evidence that another of the torpedoes had found its mark.

Nowell spent no time watching the stricken tanker through the periscope. "Two torpedo wakes were seen headed for [*Shinyō Maru*]," he noted, "as [the] periscope was turned toward [a] DE. Escort on starboard beam seen to have turned directly toward [us] so the order was given to go deep." During this time, two more explosions were heard as torpedoes slammed into the *Shinyō Maru*.

Only seconds before the torpedoes hit the *Shinyō Maru*, a bugler topside sounded the alert. "In the process of blowing it he trailed off," recalled one of George Wightman's fellow POWs, Onnie Clem. "He just pooped out—hit some sour notes."[5] At the same time, the Japanese soldiers tore back the hatches covering the holds and dropped hand grenades on the stunned Americans. Machine-gun fire followed.

"The only thing that I remember was that I saw a flash, and everything turned an orange-colored red," said Clem. "No feeling, no nothing. Everything just turned a solid color. I don't know if the grenades went off first or the torpedo because it all meshed together ... The next think I knew, I was kind of flying, just twisting and turning, and there were clouds of smoke all around me. I couldn't see anything but these billowy forms like pillows."

Clem thought he was dead. Water rushed into the hold and stirred mangled bodies and pieces of bodies into a vortex. His wits returned to a degree and he realized that the "pillows" were bodies suspended in the water that was rapidly filling the ship. Thinking that he was fated to drown, he opened his mouth to hurry the inevitable. "I found that my head was above water," he said, "and I was just gulping air. I looked up, and I could see light coming through this open hatch."

Clem chose life over death and swam for the light that shone through the opening. He and his comrades—abused, starved and dehumanized for more than two years—fought each other to survive as the ship started to sink. "Everybody was clawing at each other, trying to get to the hatch. You'd pull one person out of the way, to get a little closer to the hatch."

He and two other men pulled themselves through the opening together. A volley of machine-gun fire knocked all three of them back down. "I got plowed in the skull," Clem said. "Another bullet chipped out my chin." When he clambered back onto the deck, the Japanese gunner was dead, splayed out on the deck. Together with other survivors, Clem jumped into the sea and started for the shoreline, two or three miles distant.

He was surprised to see that the *Shinyō Maru* had been part of a convoy. "The other ships had put out lifeboats to pick up the Japanese," he said, "but they were shooting all the Americans. They were shooting them, or some of the officers were taking swipes at their heads with sabers." About 20 Americans were plucked from the water and executed aboard one of the boats for, "attempting to escape." Overhead, the patrol aircraft dived on pockets of Americans and strafed them. Between the aircraft and the Japanese in the lifeboats and other ships, Clem was shot two more times.

Not far away, deep underneath the surface, *Paddle*'s crew wondered at the damage they had done while simultaneously readying for the depth charges they knew the enemy destroyer escorts would soon be dropping into the water. "Loud, characteristic, breaking-up noises were heard almost immediately, however, and continued for some time after depth charging began."

Those "breaking-up noises" were made by the *Shinyō Maru* as it came apart and slid under the surface of the sea. They masked the screams and cries and drowning spasms that were the dying noises being made by 667 fellow Americans, including George Wightman, an American at heart if not

George Wightman, who perished when the Japanese hell ship *Shinyō Maru* was torpedoed by the USS *Paddle* on September 7, 1944. (George Cooper)

by birth. Having no idea who or what had been aboard the *Shinyō Maru*, Nowell and the rest of *Paddle*'s crew endured a barrage of 45 depth charges before sneaking away to safety.

Only 83 of the 750 American POWs made it to shore where they were collected and nursed by Philippine guerillas. Of that number, one died of his wounds. The remainder were taken away under cover of night by the submarine *Narwhal* on September 29, 1944.

\*\*\*

As it developed, the tanker that *Paddle* torpedoed was run aground by its captain to save it from sinking. And aboard *Shinyō Maru*, George Wightman had actually been one of four British citizens among the 750 POWs. The others, like him, had volunteered to serve in the American army and one of them, James Gardner, survived.[6]

\*\*\*

"So, you are trying to get back over here," wrote an old 499th squadron mate in a letter to George. The letter was dated September 25, 1944. The letter was evidence that George was keenly interested, since at least the month prior, in getting back into the fight. He had only been home for about four months. It was apparent that George's friend wasn't particularly taken with the idea: "I can understand that, and still, without a great search of my brain I can find many reasons to stay back there."

\*\*\*

By the middle of September 1944, Lawrence Cooper and his fellow internees at Santo Tomas had endured more than two-and-a-half years of maltreatment at the hands of the Japanese. Captivity and poor living conditions aside, they had little news of the outside world, or of how the war was progressing. Certainly, their jailers regularly trumpeted the latest propaganda, but they knew there was little truth in what the Japanese wanted them to believe, and the best they could do was read between the lines of what they were being told.

But the grand spectacle that was presented to them on the morning of September 21 required no reading between the lines. The Japanese could not represent what they saw as anything other than what it was. It gave the internees great encouragement.

Lawrence noted that gray puffy clouds floated languidly in the sky over Manila, and that Japanese planes likewise circled lazily, seemingly on no important mission. Japanese antiaircraft guns boomed occasionally, probably shooting registration rounds. But there was nothing to indicate that this was going to be a special morning. The internees had seen all of this before.

And then the antiaircraft guns began booming in earnest. Someone cried out, "Look, they are shooting at their own planes!" But the Japanese were not shooting at their own aircraft. "A thrill of joy, subdued but audible, ran through the camp," said Lawrence. "They were our boys, our bombers up there. Tears trickled down cheeks. People grasped hands and pressed heartily. They laughed—almost hysterically."

"The Jap antiaircraft clattered at them but they flew on steadily to their tasks," said Lawrence. The aircraft, on reaching their targets seemingly paused in midair, then plummeted almost straight down with their bombs. Shrieks went up from the onlookers at Santo Tomas. Unfamiliar with the concept of dive bombing, many of the internees believed the American aircraft had been shot down. "The cries soon stopped," Lawrence recalled. "With every dive, a bomb dropped true to the mark and explosions were followed by bursts of smoke until the eastern and southern skies were murky. Pride and joy filled our hearts; our boys, our children, skillful and daring ..."

The internees were treated to further grand performances that afternoon when more waves of American aircraft were spotted among the persistent gray clouds. "Our planes sported through them like porpoises in a choppy sea," Lawrence remembered. "Again they dived through a spray of enemy fire. The most spectacular hit of the afternoon was a large deposit of gasoline to the southeast of us. The flames leapt out and vied with the smoke in climbing to the sky. At nightfall, the holocaust was still belching."

The next three days treated the internees to additional excitement. Although they were more distant, it was obvious that the American flyers were hitting targets at will—the Japanese were wholly incapable of stopping them. The harbor in particular, ships and supply stores alike, was savaged and there were no vessels of consequence remaining afloat by the end of September 24. The vast fuel storage complex burned for days afterward. It seemed to Lawrence and everyone else at Santo Tomas that their fortunes were on the verge of changing.

George's sister Dorothy remembered those same bombing raids: "Up to that point, my mother and I didn't have any idea how the war was going. According to the Japs, they were always winning. But when we saw the American bombers come back for several days in a row, we knew they were lying."

Aside from the fact that the Japanese were liars and had taken her father, there was much else about them that she disliked. She was angry that they had stolen many of the family's possessions, but there was more. "The Jap troops were filthy," Dorothy said. "They defecated and urinated in the field behind our house."

*\*\**

George picked his way around the smoking wreck. He was working in his new capacity as the flying safety officer for the 381st Base Unit, the A-26 training organization at Marianna, Florida. The pilot had lost an engine on takeoff and failed to clear the trees at the end of the runway. Debris was scattered everywhere and several small fires still burned. George stopped, bent down and inspected the object at his feet. It was one of the pilot's arms.

He stood up when he heard the flight surgeon call out. Approaching the other man, his nostrils involuntarily pinched at the smell of burnt flesh. George saw the flight surgeon kneeling next to the pilot's body which was badly burned and dressed only in tatters of charred uniform. The flight surgeon rested his clipboard on the corpse and calmly made notations. It seemed curious, or even callous to George, but he considered the fact that the pilot was dead and likely wouldn't have minded anyway.

"Aside from my flight instructor duties," George said, "they made me the group's safety officer. This was something totally new to me, and a position that the USAAF had ordered to be created in each unit. We didn't have a safety officer in the 345th, and I certainly had not had any training. The instructions from higher headquarters took up only a single page. But I figured that I was about as qualified as anyone, so I set about seeing how we could make things happen better and safer. The biggest problem was that, even that far along into the war, everyone was still new at their job. I was considered to be quite experienced, and yet it hadn't even been three years since I began cadet training."

With the permission of his commanding officer, Colonel Marvin Zipp, George convened his first meeting during which safety-related aspects of flying the A-26 were discussed. "We talked about equipment failures, emergency procedures and safe flying practices. And we went over recent incidents that caused, or could have caused a mishap. It was ironic that, considering my aerobatic antics back in New Guinea—which were decidedly unsafe—I was put in charge of safety."

"During the meeting, a pilot lost an engine on takeoff and was unable to maintain flying speed," George said. "He crashed and plowed through a stand of trees which tore off both wings and broke the fuselage in half. The wreck came to a stop in a clearing and then caught fire. The pilot got out but the gunner was trapped in the plane. The pilot went back to try to get him out, but was unable. The gunner burned to death and the pilot was hospitalized with severe burns."

Engine failures continued to be an issue. The situation vexed George. "The engines were generally very reliable, and even if one failed, the aircraft flew quite nicely. At our next safety meeting, an A-26 lost an engine during takeoff and the pilot couldn't stop it in time. The aircraft ended up in a ditch but, fortunately, no one was killed."

"Colonel Zipp called me into his office and was concerned that somehow my meetings were hexing the unit. He made it very clear that, although I should continue to perform my duties, he did not want any more unit safety meetings."

George kept after his duties. "Shortly after that last accident," he said, "another pilot had an engine failure. He feathered the propeller and was able to make a safe landing. The report came in to me as soon as the pilot declared an emergency on the radio. I immediately went out to meet him as he taxied in."

The aircraft's crew chief met George at the plane. The two of them put their heads together and tried to determine what the problem might be. Finally, George climbed into the cockpit and started the bad engine. "I unfeathered the propeller, and ran the engine up, checking all the instruments and making a magneto check. Neither I nor the crew chief found anything wrong."

George told the crew chief that he was going to take the aircraft on a test flight and the man volunteered to go with him. "We taxied out," he said, "and checked both engines again before calling for takeoff. The tower cleared us and I advanced the throttles. Both engines were generating full power as we sped down the runway."

Just as George was about to lift off, the bad engine started to backfire. There wasn't enough runway left to abort so he coaxed the A-26 airborne. "I eased back on the throttle of the bad engine once I got to a safe altitude," he said, "and the backfiring stopped about halfway back. It was still producing power, but not very much."

Even with one sick engine the aircraft was producing plenty of power. George quickly brought it back around and landed with no problem. "It was apparent that the engine problems had something to do with the air mixture to the carburetor," he said. After close inspection it was discovered that the neoprene boot in the air duct which led to the engine's carburetor was split, or torn. Consequently, as the airspeed increased during takeoff, the force of the airstream blew a portion of the torn boot back, which choked off much of the airflow to the carburetor. This essentially made the fuel mixture too rich, and the engine backfired and lost power. "When I had pulled power to the bad engine it reduced the amount of fuel going into the carburetor such that the air that was getting through the torn boot was enough."

As a result of George's investigation, all of the group's aircraft were grounded until the neoprene boots were replaced on every engine. The rash of engine failures stopped, and the information was shared with other units which operated the A-26. "The unit's maintenance engineer got really mad at what I did," George said. "He didn't like that I had flown that test flight without his knowledge. But at that point no one cared whether he was angry or not. Fixing the problem had been the priority, and we had done just that."

Safety duties aside, George had fun flying the A-26. "There was a P-51 training unit at Hurlburt Field, south of us," he recalled. "With permission, they often flew mock attacks against us as part of their training. On one occasion, I received a phone call from Hurlburt. The P-51 instructor wanted to lead his students on some practice gunnery runs against a flight that I was scheduled to lead. I agreed but briefed my students that when the P-51s started after us we would apply maximum power and go into a very shallow dive."

George and his two student wingmen took off as scheduled. When he spotted the P-51s diving on the flight he gently tipped his aircraft over into a barely perceptible dive and advanced his throttles to METO—Maximum Except for Takeoff. The fighters were frustrated as they weren't able to catch the A-26s. "When he called me afterward," George said, "the P-51 instructor was quite frustrated. I told him that I just didn't know what to say; we were simply motoring along at our normal cruise speed."

\*\*\*

George, just starting to instruct other pilots on the A-26, still had no idea as to the welfare of his family in the Philippines. There were always rumors, but they were just that. He still had absolutely no information indicating whether they were alive or dead.

But they were alive indeed. And Lawrence, still interned at Santo Tomas, was taking heart at developments that were taking place literally over and around him. During September 1944, in preparation for MacArthur's upcoming invasion of the Philippines—planned for October—Fifth Air Force units and Navy carrier strike groups started hitting targets in and around Manila. He and the other internees celebrated as much as they could without antagonizing their Japanese jailers.

There followed a lull that lasted about two weeks. After becoming near-euphoric at the sight of the American warplanes, Lawrence noted that many of the internees fell into a state of near depression, while others held out hope: "The pessimists renewed their applications of salt to self-made wounds," he wrote. "The optimists held their renewed faith and waited hopefully. The majority of the internees had already adapted themselves to the climaxes and anti-climaxes of Santo Tomas existence."

And then, just when it started to seem that the series of air strikes the previous month might have been an isolated episode, the American flyers returned on October 15, 1944. "Our own planes again dived out of the clouds in great numbers," Lawrence said. "They combed the perimeter of Manila with intense machine-gun fire. Some planes dropped heavy bombs in the vicinity of Mariquina. The day was as spectacular as any experienced previously."

Additional attacks made on October 19 were particularly impressive to the internees at Santo Tomas. "The heaviest bombs yet were used," said Lawrence. "The concussions were almost deafening, even though sometimes distant. Buildings vibrated as if from earthquake tremors."

In fact, the air activity was part of the colossal milieu of air, ground and naval preparations being made to retake the Philippines. The first American fighting men waded ashore at Leyte—followed by MacArthur and dozens of press men—on October 20, 1944, thus beginning a campaign that lasted, essentially, to the end of the war. But that was almost a year and many bloody battles away. And those bloody battles were almost always prefaced with air action.

The sky over Manila continued to serve as a combat arena. Lawrence described October 29 as the day of, "another glorious occasion. Our planes came in on top of the clouds. It was a complete surprise." He described how, "wave after wave of our planes" dived on Japanese positions with scarcely any interval between them. Here, finally, were the great formations of American aircraft that he had so mistakenly expected during the days following the start of the war.

Following these October raids, and the passage of a typhoon that punctuated the end of the month, Lawrence noted that in Santo Tomas, "Spirits were buoyant. What would be the next move? What might tomorrow have in store?"

What tomorrow and the next few months actually had in store for Lawrence and his fellow internees was increasing hardship and deprivation. The Japanese Army had taken over the administration of Santo Tomas from

Japanese government officials earlier in the year. That takeover resulted in harsher treatment and shrinking rations. The availability of medicine and health care also diminished. Some of this was due to the dire war situation for the Japanese, but most of it was attributable to vindictive, small-minded racism. Regardless of the causes, the internees at Santo Tomas—George's father among them—grew thinner, sicker and more desperate.

\*\*\*

At about the same time that American forces waded ashore at Leyte on October 20, 1944, George asked for orders back overseas. He wrote to his old commander, Jarred Crabb, and asked to be reassigned to the 345th. He knew that his old bomb group would be in the thick of the fight, and that the fight would eventually reach Manila. There, he hoped to find his parents and sister.

Betty didn't want him to go, but she also understood how much he loved his family and how badly he needed to find and help them. She did not try to stop him, and George took heart knowing that she knew how conflicted he was. "I was just getting to know my wife again," he said, "and my dear little girl for the first time. In fact, I was worried that she would forget me. And, I was not just going to leave them after less than a year at home, but I was also putting myself back in harm's way. There was a chance that I might be killed. In a way, I felt like what I was doing was a little bit selfish."

\*\*\*

Prisca had been running her little school for almost three years by early January 1945. During all that time, she had never been discovered by the Japanese. Now, with the Americans ashore at Leyte, and landing at Lingayen in northern Luzon, her luck changed. "One day a Japanese petty officer chanced by while my class was in session. He may have heard us singing. He came in without warning."

The Japanese man, clearly agitated, stomped through the children and stopped in front of Prisca. "I was startled," Prisca said, "and my heart pounded furiously so that I could hardly utter a word." Her fear was justified. There was a real possibility that she might be taken to prison. People had been executed for much less than running an illicit grade school.

"He asked if the school was authorized and approved by the Japanese imperial government," Prisca said. "I tried to tell him that it was not a school—that the children were having a party. He took my name and address and said that he would report the matter to the colonel who was in charge of the schools. He warned me that I would be called in to explain to the colonel."

The order to report to the authorities never reached Prisca, most likely because she was forced from the house. A group of officers arrived during the next couple of days and told her to leave the house as they intended to occupy it. "The officers made their quarters in our house," she recalled, "and our beautiful yard of fruit and shade trees was filled with drums of gasoline and oil, and some trucks." Prisca took Dorothy to a neighbor's house where they settled in to wait for what came next.

Prisca Cooper's school was out of session, never to reopen.

CHAPTER 15

# "Roll Out the Barrel"

As January 1945 turned into February, George waited at Hamilton Field for transportation overseas. He and Betty had packed their 1938 Chevrolet earlier that month and, with Pris in tow, headed west. Their route took them across the south and the desert southwest. "There was little traffic," George said, "partly because of gasoline rationing, but also because population was thin through the western states. We were warned to take along a supply of water while traveling through the desert regions in case our car broke down. It could be a long wait for help as service stations were far apart."

In California they had enough time to visit some of George's friends in and around Los Angeles before heading north to see his brother Marion and his wife Marge, who had moved to the San Francisco area. George left Betty and Pris there, and reported to Hamilton Field for transportation to the Philippines. It had been from Hamilton that he and Bill Parke had left for New Guinea in 1943.

While he waited there, he kept a keen eye on the Army's advance toward Manila. It had been almost five, often lonely years since he had seen his father, mother and Dorothy. And it had been three, long and angst-filled years since he had heard from them. Those few years felt like 20 when he remembered the day he had hugged and kissed his mother goodbye in 1940.

Now, the maps in the newspapers showed arrows—American army units—converging on Manila. It wouldn't be long until he knew his family's fate. And knowing the capacity of the Japanese for cruelty, he was powerfully worried about what that fate might be.

\*\*\*

At that very moment, MacArthur was demanding action that would determine the fate of George's father, and thousands of other internees. On January 30,

1945, a daring raid by Army Rangers and Filipino guerillas liberated more than 500 American and Allied POWs from the camp at Cabanatuan, 60 miles north of Manila. On that same day, MacArthur, full of enthusiasm at the raid's success, ordered a similar foray to be sent south to Santo Tomas. Just as he had been worried about Cabanatuan, he was justifiably apprehensive that the Japanese would slaughter the internees at Santo Tomas. Only the month prior, Japanese soldiers had crowded 150 American POWs into dugout shelters on Palawan Island. Then, they drenched them with gasoline, set them afire and cooked them alive.

"Go to Manila," MacArthur exhorted the commander of the 1st Calvary Division. "Go 'round the Nips, bounce off the Nips, but go to Manila. Free the internees at Santo Tomas." Accordingly, just after midnight on February 1, a "flying column" started racing south toward Manila. Divided into three elements, it was made up of nearly 2,000 men riding aboard hundreds of armed jeeps and trucks, as well as 16 Sherman tanks.[1]

As darkness gave way to dawn, Marine Corps flyers at the controls of nearly obsolescent SBD Dauntless dive bombers, arrived overhead. The Marine Corps had made a commitment to maintain a continuous, nine aircraft, close air support umbrella over the column during the daylight hours. They covered the flanks and rear of the column, and reconnoitered the route ahead.

A small detachment of seven, radio-equipped Marines rode with the Army men and coordinated the advance with the Dauntless pilots. When the pilots spotted danger, they called it out to the men below. Likewise, when the men on the ground encountered trouble, they reported it to the flyers. If the threat was imminent, the dive bombers attacked it. The men in the column watched with a mixture of reassurance and wonderment when the Marine aircraft plummeted almost vertically earthward to strafe and drop bombs on Japanese positions. Smoke and dust from the attacks rose ahead and to either side of the column.

But the Marine pilots could not neutralize every threat. As the different elements of the flying column penetrated south and continued deep into enemy territory, they were ambushed several times and forced to dismount and fight pitched battles against Japanese patrols and outposts. Yet the Japanese were thrown back each time and the men climbed back aboard their vehicles and continued the run to Santo Tomas. It was a daring and dangerous mission as they were far ahead of any other friendly units, and the Japanese lines closed behind them as they sprinted south.

Fighting aside, the men in the flying column were also periodically slowed by the need to ford or ferry the different rivers that ran across their path. The

Japanese had destroyed many of the bridges, and each makeshift crossing took time and left the column vulnerable to attack. Still the speed at which the Americans advanced was stunning.

And that speed caught the Japanese off guard. On one occasion, a small convoy of four Japanese trucks, loaded with men and supplies, edged onto the highway directly in the path of one of the American elements. The American drivers waved them off, just as they would back home in the States. Dumbfounded, and at a loss of what else to do, the enemy drivers stayed out of the way. The men aboard the column's succeeding vehicles swung their weapons around and opened fire. By the time the column passed, the four enemy trucks were ripped to ribbons. The pieces that remained blazed brightly, and dead Japanese soldiers burned atop and around them.

In stark contrast to the minor holocaust that had been the enemy convoy, was the frantic joyfulness of the Filipinos. The nightmare of the Japanese occupation was ending and they rushed roadside to cheer the advancing Americans on their way. They waved and flashed victory signs, they jumped for joy, threw flowers and handed off food. "I never did figure out what to do with a live chicken or a raw egg," remembered one member of the column, "but I knew it was given from their hearts. Frankly, we loved all this attention and it made what we were doing a little more worthwhile."[2]

\*\*\*

On February 3, internees at Santo Tomas shaded their eyes and watched the little speck drop out of the sky and arc toward them. On and down it came, at rooftop level. It sped at them, closer and closer and then roared across the camp, wagged its wings and pulled up and away. It was a Marine Corps SBD Dauntless and the white stars on its wings and fuselage were clearly visible. Children and adults alike jumped up and down, cheered and clapped their hands. For just a moment none of them—scarecrow-like as they were—was hungry.

The guards, to save face, looked away from the American aircraft. If they refused to look at it, it didn't exist. So, they missed what a few of the sharper-eyed internees saw; a small object fell from the Dauntless and settled onto the northeast courtyard of the main building. It was quickly snatched up and spirited away. Out of sight of the guards, the internees examined it and discovered that it was a pair of flying goggles with a note attached. It read: "Roll out the barrel. Santa Claus is coming Sunday or Monday."[3]

\*\*\*

That same day, less than two days since starting, one of the flying column's elements stopped just short of the steep-sided Tuliahan River where it was crossed by the Novaliches Bridge, about ten miles north of Manila. The Japanese had rigged the bridge for demolition and lit the fuze just as the Americans arrived. If the bridge went down, the race into Manila would be stalled for a day or more. The Japanese wouldn't need that long to kill the internees.

The two sides started shooting at each other and heavy sniper fire kept the Americans hunkered down. Knowing that time was running out, James Patrick Sutton, a bomb disposal expert on loan from the Navy, dashed down the highway and onto the bridge at great disregard for his own life. Bullets whizzed past his face and ricocheted off the pavement around his feet. Finally, atop the bridge, out of breath and still taking fire, he cut the fuze and tossed several mines into the river below. The way to Manila was clear.[4]

That was, in fact, actually the case. Aside from isolated pockets and patrols, the Japanese had ordered the greater part of their units deeper into the city where they planned to make a concerted, bloody, last-ditch stand. Although the Americans ran into light resistance, the close-quarter street melee that they expected did not materialize. They were primarily harried by enemy snipers, mortars and scattered patrols to which they replied with blasts from the main guns of the escorting tanks. So, with no serious resistance, the column pushed south toward Santo Tomas.

As least, they thought they were proceeding toward Santo Tomas. Dusk turned to night as the lines of American trucks and jeeps and tanks turned first one way and then another. Their maps did little more than confuse them, and progress was fitful as it was difficult to get the force turned around and moving in the right direction once it had started in the wrong direction.

But help came from a welcome source. Just as they had since the day MacArthur stepped ashore with his massive invasion force at Leyte almost four months earlier, Filipino guerillas came out of seemingly nowhere to aid the Americans. Manuel Colayco and Diosdado Guytingco, intimately familiar with the city, met the column and set it on the right path.[5] Tracer rounds cut brilliant lines through the dark streets as the vehicles rolled purposefully past the one- and two-story buildings typical of Manila's northern suburbs.

Above them, the protective screen of Marine dive bombers was gone as it was too dark for the flyers to see well enough to do any good. Devoid of aircraft, the smoky sky pulsed orange–black as it reflected the fires that burned here and there within the city. Periodically, flares rocketed upward and left trails of sparks before detonating and bathing the streets below with a ghostly, chemical light.

As was every internee in Santo Tomas, George's father, Lawrence Cooper, was almost sick with anxiety as he wondered at the distant clamor. At first it was a faint, ill-defined murmur, but the unique parts that made the whole of the noise soon became distinguishable. Trucks roared, gunfire barked and tanks grumbled and clanked. That it grew louder could mean only one thing—whoever was making the racket was coming closer.

There were scarcely any internees at Santo Tomas who were not feverish at the thought that the commotion belied the approach of their liberators. But those emotions were checked at the notion that it might be a Japanese force coming to spirit them away, or worse, annihilate them. The rumors that they might be murdered en masse had not been refuted by any competent authority. And whether the internees were aware of it or not, the Japanese were certainly capable of such a grotesquerie. Indeed, just a few days before, the Japanese had murdered three of their leaders. Regardless, Lawrence and everyone else in Santo Tomas sensed that, for better or worse, their lives were on the cusp of a dramatic change.

Then, just before 2100, the head of the flying column, including six tanks and a number of trucks and jeeps, hove into view and rumbled up to the main gate. From the guard house, a Japanese soldier heaved a grenade at the Americans. Shots rang out and the Japanese soldier was shot dead. Among the wounded was Manuel Colayco, the Filipino guerilla.

One of the Sherman tanks crashed through the gate and others followed. Headlights illuminating their path, the tanks clanked up to the camp's main building where a pair of Japanese civilians surrendered themselves. Next, Lieutenant Nanakazu Abaki, dressed in jodhpurs, boots and a sword, stepped up to the Americans. When he reached for a hand grenade the American soldiers shot him down. Several internees—men and women—recognizing the wounded man as a long-time tormentor, rushed to him and beat and kicked him. One of them drew Abaki's sword and tried to slash away his ear. Ultimately, they were pushed away and Abaki was taken to be treated for his wounds.[6]

Where Lawrence Cooper was when the Americans arrived is uncertain, but it is quite possible he was confined to the Education Building to where most of the Japanese—about 70 men—had retreated. There, they held more than 200 internees, primarily men and boys that they intended to use as hostages. The Americans, unaware that there were internees in the building, opened fire with machine guns and tank cannons. There were casualties among both the internees and the Japanese.

Desultory volleys of gunfire were exchanged by the two sides throughout the night. The Japanese refused to surrender, and the Americans couldn't kill

The men liberated from Santo Tomas during early February 1945, were in danger of dying of starvation. When George's father crept home through the wreckage that was Manila, his wife and daughter barely recognized him. (National Archives)

them or force them out of the building without hurting the internees being held at gunpoint. As February 4 dawned, away from the Education Building, the internees continued to celebrate their liberation. One recalled, "Huge tanks, giant-sized soldiers and ecstatic internees. The soldiers were as overwhelmed at seeing women and children as we were at seeing them."[7] Another noted in his diary that the Americans, "Have everything well under control, but the Japs are still holed up in the Education Building. Our forces are withholding fire and are trying to get them out by negotiation." He additionally observed, "What a sight they are to us—tanned, healthy, young Americans, covered with dirt and grime from their rough trip."[8]

The hostage situation was brought to a close the following day, February 5. There had been nothing like it in the war to that point. The Japanese in the Education Building, rather than killing all their captives and fighting to the death, or committing suicide, agreed to an arrangement whereby they would leave Santo Tomas with their rifles, pistols and other personal weapons, under American escort. The Americans were to accompany them a short distance towards Japanese-held positions before returning to Santo Tomas. As it developed, the Japanese asked to be taken toward a location that was actually under American control. It is believed that Filipino guerillas dispatched them soon after the Americans turned back.

So then, Santo Tomas was completely under American control. Nevertheless, neither Lawrence Cooper nor anyone else was going anywhere. In fact, the situation was somewhat precarious as the Japanese had returned to the Novaliches Bridge, re-rigged the explosives that had been overlooked by the Americans when they crossed it on February 3, and blew it up. Consequently, the American forces in Manila were isolated for the next day or so until the Tuliahan River could be crossed again. Anxious about the possibility of a Japanese counterattack, the American commanders moved much of the flying column into defensive positions behind the walls of Santo Tomas.

At that point, the Americans had no good idea what the situation in Manila actually was. Japanese resistance was light, ineffective and seemingly ill-coordinated. Elements of the flying column had already captured the nearby prison camp at Bilibid, Malacañang Palace and the Legislative Building, and

Newly liberated Santo Tomas, early February 1945. (National Archives)

MacArthur himself was on his way. In fact, he already believed that Manila was liberated. He couldn't have been more wrong.

He still wasn't aware of that when he visited Santo Tomas on February 6, and was received almost as a demigod. The internees crowded around and called out to him; they pressed forward to get a close look at him and stretched their arms out to touch him. It was, to a degree, unnerving. A member of his staff recalled: "The scene was far different from anything I could have imagined. We watched in horrified silence when we saw, coming toward us, emaciated men and women dressed in torn, limp clothes. Hoarse cries came from their throats. Tears flowed down their cheeks."[9]

The Japanese were hard at the destruction of Manila by February 7. Explosions rocked the city and smoke clouds rose skyward as they triggered demolition charges. At the same time, the Americans moved a number of artillery guns into Santo Tomas and used the clock tower as an observation post. Japanese artillerymen lobbed shells into the campus on that day as recorded by an internee: "This afternoon and evening the Japs fired into the Main Building and killed ten people and injured 50 more."[10] The irony of being killed by the Japanese only days after being liberated was not lost on many in the camp.

The fight for Manila was brutal. Here, American soldiers clamber up the banks of the Pasig River, down which George, his friend, and his brother sailed in their handmade boat many years earlier. (National Archives)

## CHAPTER 16

# "They All Lined Up and Marched Away"

George's sister Dorothy looked down on Manila and watched the battle unfold as more Americans approached the city, fast on the heels of the 1st Cavalry's successful dash to Santo Tomas. "The airplanes buzzed around and dived and dropped bombs, just like the Japs did when they bombed the city right after the sneak attack on Pearl Harbor. We had known that we were winning the war because there had been bombing raids for several months before."

More exciting developments followed. "We could tell something was going on because the Japs were running around all over the neighborhood," Dorothy said, "and then, one day, they all lined up and marched away." When the Japanese moved out of the neighborhood and down into the city, the Cooper family home stood empty.

After a time, certain that the Japanese troops were not coming back anytime soon, Prisca and Dorothy approached the house in the company of a few of their neighbors. Its exterior hadn't been painted or otherwise cared for, and the lawn and landscaping were overgrown, and parts of the fence were torn up, but structurally the house was undamaged. They looked through the windows and, finding it empty, stepped through the door.

"It was a mess," Dorothy said. There was dirt and dust and trash. And most of the furniture was missing. Our servants were so good to us; they scoured the neighborhood and all the other houses that the Japs had taken over. We were fortunate that they found and brought back almost all our furniture. And it all had stickers on it that said: 'Property of the Imperial Japanese Government.'"

It was apparent that the Cooper house had been used as a headquarters of some sort. "There were papers tacked to the walls and, for some reason, nails pounded into the floors. And some beautiful carved furniture was missing. Worse, was my father's extensive book collection which had been burned in a pit in the yard."

Such was not the case in Manila, only a few miles below them. MacArthur had declared it an open city before the Japanese occupied it on January 2, 1942; he knew that defending it would be near impossible, and that trying to do so would destroy it and cause the deaths of thousands of civilians. Now, three years later, as his troops prepared to complete Manila's liberation, the Japanese army had already evacuated it for many of the same reasons.

The commander of the Imperial Japanese Army forces in the Philippines, General Tomoyuki Yamashita, had more than a quarter million troops under his command on Luzon. Although he did not declare Manila an open city, he ordered his commanders there to destroy the bridges, and to block the highways as best they could. That done, they were to withdraw north into the hills where Yamashita planned a coordinated defense designed to bleed the Americans dry, and to delay their advance on the Japanese home islands.

This, Yamashita's Army units in Manila did. However, Rear Admiral Sanji Iwabuchi, who commanded a force of more than 10,000 sailors and naval infantry troops, and nearly 5,000 Army troops, refused to obey Yamashita's orders. Instead, he directed his units to defend the city to the last man, declaring, "We will daringly engage the enemy. Banzai to the Emperor! We are determined to fight to the last man."[1] Much to Yamashita's frustration, Iwabuchi was backed by the Navy's leadership in Japan.

Beginning on February 3, as they engaged the Americans advancing on Santo Tomas, the Japanese also began to systematically—and senselessly—demolish and burn virtually everything that could be demolished and burned. Particularly tragic was the mindless destruction they wrought upon the churches, convents, monasteries and other religious buildings inside the walls of Intramuros, the old, walled city at the heart of Manila. Artifacts were stolen and entire libraries were burned. When the Japanese turned what was left into fighting positions, American artillery and air units necessarily reduced it to rubble.

But the very worst—the most grotesquely evil—acts of which the Japanese were capable, were committed against Manila's people. Father Francis Cosgrave was part of a group of 70 religious men and laypeople—about half of whom were women and children—who had taken refuge in De LaSalle College. Since the start of the fighting, they were forbidden by the Japanese to go outside, or even to look through the windows.[2]

Then, on the early afternoon of February 12, a Japanese officer came and took away two house boys. "Five minutes later," said Cosgrave, "they returned these two boys whom they had wounded. Then, the officer gave a command and all at once the soldiers began bayonetting all of the men, women and

children." Shrieks and shouts and screams echoed through the chambers as
the Japanese lunged and stabbed indiscriminately. Pistol shots punctuated the
bedlam as the officer dispatched the most troublesome victims.

"Some of the children were only two or three years old," Cosgrave said. "A
few were even younger. These were given the same treatment as their elders.
When the Japanese had finished bayonetting us, they dragged the bodies and
threw them in a heap at the foot of the stairs, the dead being thrown upon
the living."

What followed simply underscored the depravity of the Japanese.
"The soldiers retired," Cosgrave recalled, "and we heard them later drinking
outside. Frequently during the afternoon, they came in to watch us, and
laughed and mocked at the suffering of their victims. We remained there all
the afternoon, during which time many who had been wounded had already
died."

Cosgrave crawled out from under the pile of bodies and ministered to
those that still lived. Corpses laid in pools of congealed blood. The wounded
and dying whimpered and sobbed—murdered loved ones sprawled in
incongruous forms all around them. Cosgrave was deeply moved when he
witnessed, "Some of them actually praying to God to forgive those who had
put them to death."

The degeneracy of the Japanese knew no end. They neither tended to the
wounded, nor did they put them out of their misery. "Sometimes," Cosgrave
said, "the Japanese soldiers came in and tried to violate the young girls who
were actually alive." So then, with the battle for Manila reaching its height,
the Japanese defenders—dissolute cowards—butchered and raped defenseless
civilians rather than fighting on the battlefield.

A few days later, during the night of February 19—after weeks of captivity
and abuse—Father Belarmino De Celis was marched to a bomb shelter
dug out in front of the Manila Cathedral.[3] An Augustinian priest and a
Spaniard, he was forced into the stuffy bunker along with more than 80
other men. There, in the dusty blackness of the tightly constrained space,
the men shuffled and shrugged against each other and tried to find room
to rest.

"In about half an hour," said De Celis, "the Japanese began to throw hand
grenades in through the air holes." Blinding, concussive blasts shook the
captives to their cores; hot shrapnel sliced into their bodies. "We were all
very badly wounded. We ran to the door in order to go out and a group of
soldiers received us with a volley; and what is worse, they laughed while they
were doing it."

The Japanese rolled large stones and dirt-filled gasoline barrels and soil against the door to the shelter, and blocked the air vents. "They covered the entrance as best they could so that we were being suffocated," De Celis said. "We were, in reality, buried alive." In fact, as most of them were already dead, they were simply buried.

Rocks, dirt and other debris dropped continuously on the corpses and on those few men still living. De Celis was badly wounded, but nevertheless resolved not to die in that stinking hole. Already, after only hours, flies covered the wounded and the bodies began to decompose. "I went up to the door," he said, "and scratched and dug in the earth until I was able to open a hole to breathe through." The next morning a Japanese soldier spotted the hole, stuck his rifle through it and fired several shots before covering it again. De Celis was not hit. "After a while, I opened it and no more Japanese came by that way."

Ultimately, De Celis clawed his way through the small fissure and into the open. "I had a companion near me, Mr. Rocamora, who was the only one I was able to save." Several more days of misery and dangerous encounters

Filipino civilians fleeing the Japanese during the fight for Manila, February 1945. (National Archives)

followed until De Celis encountered an American patrol and was taken to a hospital.

By that time, George had finally left the States. He penned a letter home on February 19 from Nadzab, New Guinea. It was the same night during which the Japanese stuffed Belarmino De Celis and more than 80 other men into the shelter. "Without a doubt I was crazy to have left you a second time," George wrote to Betty. "It will take a little while to get used to it, but I'll always keep wishing that I could come bursting in on you, to take you and that little rascal into my arms again."

While George wanted to burst in on his wife and child and clutch them in a loving embrace, Japanese troops were bursting into Filipino homes with rifles and bayonets. Carolina Coruna, a nurse, was staying with the Veles family on Anda Street during the fight for Manila.[4] The Japanese had already seized Mr. Veles, leaving his wife, their baby, his wife's sister and Miss Coruna on their own.

The baby was crying one night when a Japanese soldier came to the house and asked if there were any men inside. "I came outside and told the sentry there were only women inside. He told me to return and see that the baby kept quiet." Coruna turned and walked back toward the house. "I had only taken a few steps when this same Japanese sentry opened fire on me with his automatic weapon. I fell to the ground, shot in the legs and paralyzed from the waist down."

Her eyes wide open and unmoving, Coruna pretended to be dead as the man stepped over her. "The Japanese soldier advanced with his gun and bayonet fixed, and thrust the blade into the head of the child," she said. "Mrs. Veles screamed and the soldier opened fire with his rifle and killed her instantly. He then turned on Mrs. Veles's sister and likewise shot and killed her. Immediately thereafter, he left the shelter, walking by me as I lay crumpled on the ground, still feigning death."

George's air war, although it was dangerous and sometimes staggeringly violent, was generally not a close-quarter fight where he and his fellow airmen came face to face with the horrors of which men are capable. It contrasted mightily with what his comrades fighting in Manila encountered at every turn. Major Gilbert Ayers went into a government building that had just been seized.[5] After descending a set of crude, partly burned stairs he turned to look into a room which measured about 20-feet square. In it were an estimated 75 bodies. "There was a powerful odor of ammonia," he testified, "and considerable heat was evolved from the decomposition of the bodies."

American soldiers protect Filipino civilians as they flee the Japanese in Manila in February 1945. (National Archives)

Evidence indicated that the people had been barricaded inside and, "met their death through thirst, suffocation or violence."

And it wasn't just the fighting men who stumbled onto these horrors. Army medical personnel were presented with the worst of the Japanese atrocities—and were compelled by compassion and duty to treat them. Captain John Amesse recounted a partial list which included, "One girl of about 10 years, and one 2-year-old boy, exhibited amputation, complete, of left forearm," and, "Five teenage girls exhibited bilateral amputated nipples and areolae, with penetrating bayonet wounds in both chest and abdomen."[6]

Less than five miles away, and around the clock, George's 12-year-old sister Dorothy, and his mother Prisca, were rocked by the din of the battle. When it seemed especially threatening, they hid behind Dorothy's piano. But they could not escape the loud crack of the artillery, and the deep booms of the aerial bombs. And the staccato snapping of rifle shots, backdropped by the ripping sound of machine-gun fire, were a fainter but virtually continuous presence.

But mercifully, they could not hear the screaming.

***

Surely, although most evidence indicates otherwise, it is not possible that every Japanese soldier behaved like a vicious, less than animal. Certainly, there were isolated instances of kindness, or pity or mercy. Father Joaquin Garcia Sanchez, a Franciscan, described an act which, if it was not overtly empathetic, was at least disinterested.[7] For weeks, Sanchez had been marched at bayonet point from place to place as a part of various large groups of imprisoned religious men and laypeople. The Japanese tormented them mercilessly. They took special glee in throwing hand grenades down onto the huddled captives during artillery bombardments, declaring that they were actually American shells.

Then, inexplicably, the prisoners were told they could leave on February 22. "First," Sanchez said, "the Japanese would point out one exit, and then they would close it. Then, another. 'No, not that one, this one. No, that one.'" The Japanese continued to toy with them until an officer came and asked them if they wanted to leave. "We said yes," Sanchez recalled, "but that the door was shut and that he should open the door for us." Finally, the officer ordered a door opened and the group went into the streets waving a white flag. Minutes later, they were safely in American hands.

Notwithstanding such isolated episodes of indifference, the almost countless instances of butchery, of the slaying of innocent men, women and children—to include babies—are what best characterize the Japanese actions at Manila. They burned people alive. They mowed massive groups of them down with machine guns. They staged big bayonet orgies. They locked them up and left them to die of thirst. Their lack of humanity, put on a scale, measured below bestial.

They destroyed the heart and soul of George's boyhood world.

Ultimately, conservative estimates of the number of civilians killed during the fight for Manila exceed 100,000. Certainly, many of these were unintentionally killed by American bombs and artillery, but those numbers would have been minimal had the Japanese allowed the citizens to evacuate or had declared Manila an open city. But they didn't. Rather, they killed innocents for fun and sport.

Such was the enemy that George had fought and would fight again.

In early 1945 the Japanese refused to declare Manila an open city as Douglas MacArthur had in 1941. The consequent fighting destroyed nearly four centuries of precious architecture and history. (USAAF)

Because the Japanese refused to declare it an open city, as MacArthur had done in 1941, Manila was destroyed during February 1945. An estimated 100,000 civilians perished. The city in which George had grown up was gone. (USAAF)

## CHAPTER 17

# "We Watched Daily for His Return"

Lawrence Cooper, greatly weakened by years of privation, carried two small bags and set out from Santo Tomas on February 26, 1945. Manila had yet to be secured and the Japanese were still murdering civilians. It was not safe for him to go out on his own, and the Army refused to provide him transportation. He was permitted to leave only at his own risk. At Santo Tomas he could be kept relatively safe. In the city, he could not. Yet, his leaving was not unique as other internees—chafing after more than three years of confinement—also took their chances outside the university.

All through February Lawrence had watched and listened as Manila was reduced to rocks and ashes. He grew accustomed to the sounds of battle, and towering clouds of smoke and dust were typical. Yet, he still was not prepared for what he saw as he picked his way warily through the debris. The beautiful, old city that he had known and loved for almost 40 years was gone.

The destruction dazed and disoriented him. Landmarks had disappeared and buildings that were once beautiful monuments to the city's history were little more than piles of broken masonry. The expanded horizon—no longer blocked by centuries-old architecture—made him feel vulnerable and out of place. What had once been intimately familiar was foreign.

And it stank. Here and there, bodies and parts of bodies laid in the streets or stuck out at awkward angles from the battle-trash. Flies buzzed him. Dirt and mud and rubbish covered his route. And already, weeds grew from what were once proud and distinguished buildings. He had done business here … he thought. And wasn't that his old friend's home? And there was the bank he had first used when he had moved the family to Manila. Or was it?

Lawrence was still grossly malnourished even though he had been eating good, American rations for three weeks. And he was weak. And, as much as he might want to believe otherwise, he was getting old—61 wasn't old, but it was well on its way to being so.

He didn't run—he couldn't. But he stepped quickly from mounds of debris to the jagged teeth of mostly destroyed structures, to bomb craters and then out again. He did not want to make himself an easy target for Japanese snipers. Although as thin as he was, he made a poor target indeed.

Lawrence was stymied when he arrived—still unmolested—at the San Juan River. The beautiful, strong bridge of the same name that once spanned the river did so no longer. Rather, it rested in chunks below the current. Only a water main reached from one bank to the other. He walked to where it met the near side and shoved at it with his foot. It was solid and would no doubt bear his weight and more.

He turned around, scanned the rubble-scape and considered his chances. Out on the conduit he would be exposed—helpless. Everyone who watched the river would see him. And he would have nowhere to hide should he come under fire. His only chance would be to drop into the river, and in his weakened state he wasn't sure he could swim to safety.

*** 

"I had gotten word from Santo Tomas that my husband was alive and well and would return home as soon as the fighting in Manila was finished," recalled Prisca Cooper, George's mother. "As the roar of battle became less and less, we watched daily for his return. One afternoon we caught sight of an old, gray-haired man plodding up the slope behind our house. He carried a bundle in each hand."

Several of the family's servants had already returned and one of them rushed out to meet the man and take his bundles. "It was my husband," said Prisca. "He had walked six miles from Santo Tomas—he crawled across the San Juan River on a water pipe that had not been destroyed. He had summoned up the strength for his half-starved body of 96 pounds to carry him home."

Of the reunion with her father, Dorothy recalled her mother, "Crying and crying for joy. I did too." Prisca and Lawrence would never again be separated.

***

George sweated his way across the Pacific until he reached Leyte in the Philippines. There, he was stunned by what he saw at the airfield at Tacloban. "There was debris everywhere," he said. "Wrecked aircraft were bulldozed to the perimeter, and destroyed military vehicles were pushed off both sides of the roads."

Those roads were grudgingly yielding quagmires; it had rained terrifically and the military traffic—trucks and jeeps and tanks—had churned them into knee-deep mud. "At one point," George said, "I saw two black soldiers arguing in the middle of a road. One hit the other a solid blow to the head and he fell flat into the mud. No one went to his aid, nor was the one who had hit him arrested. At that point, black soldiers served primarily in the support units and were considered inferior to white soldiers."

A few days later George let his A-20 settle onto the runway at recently recaptured Clark Field. The date was February 27, 1945. Less than two months earlier his old bomb group, the 345th, and his new bomb group, the 3rd, had dealt Clark a killing blow during the Fifth Air Force's biggest mission of the war to that point. Once the crown jewel of the old Army Air Corps in the Far East, the airbase had been captured by the Japanese soon after the attack on Pearl Harbor. Just as it had been a major base for the United States, it served Japanese army and naval air units similarly. Indeed, especially as the Americans advanced on the Philippines, it was used as a base for the deadly kamikaze attacks that had killed so many men.

George was alone in the aircraft. He needed no gunner as there had been little chance that he might be jumped by Japanese fighters on the quick trip from Mindoro. And he needed no company for what he had planned for the next day or two.

As he slowed and taxied clear of the runway, George was struck by what he saw. Bulldozed clear of the runways, taxiways and parking ramps, were the wrecks of Japanese aircraft of all types. Broken Betty bombers and burned-out Zero and Tony fighters—and many other models he didn't even recognize—littered the airfield.

Moreover, bomb craters filled with festering water remained unrepaired. And many structures were little more than shot-up hulks. Weeds grew haphazardly and piles of debris dotted the area waiting to be buried or carted away. Clark had seen much action during the previous three years.

But now it was as lively as any airfield in the Pacific. In contrast to the already rusting Japanese junk, hundreds of newly arrived American aircraft were parked in well-ordered rows. A line of them taxied for takeoff while overhead a four-ship of fighters separated in a hard turn and arced around to land. Jeeps and trucks raced back and forth carrying men and equipment and parts. Fuel bowsers replenished empty gas tanks and loaders lifted explosives into bomber bellies. The fruit of the nation's industrial might—and the energy and commitment of its citizens—was evident everywhere. And with it, the

Americans had reclaimed Clark and were using it as a base from which to hammer the Japanese forces still alive in the Philippines.

As much war as he had fought, and as much war-making material and equipment as he had seen, George still couldn't help but be at least a little awed by what he saw. He taxied toward where a ground crewman waved, and then he stepped on one of the aircraft's wheel brakes to swing it around until he was directed to taxi forward. When the man on the ground clenched his fists over his head, George stepped on both brakes and brought the aircraft to a halt. The other man, careful of the propeller, ran under the left wing with a pair of wheel chocks. He kicked them into place and reappeared. George ran the engines up momentarily to clear any pooled oil, and then abruptly shut them down.

The hot engines made a slow ticking sound as they cooled. George peeled the sweat-stained helmet from his head, double checked that the myriad of switches, levers and knobs were configured as they should have been, and then pushed back the hatch that covered the cockpit and much of the top of the fuselage. He grabbed his small bag and, like a cliff-dweller, used the various

George was assigned to the 3rd Bomb Group during February 1945. It had been using the A-20 with great success since the early part of the war. (USAAF)

covered hand- and footholds to climb down from the wing and fuselage and onto the ground. After greeting the ground crewman and passing instructions for his aircraft, George was on his way.

"I caught a ride to the motor pool and didn't have any problem getting a jeep—especially after I told them where I was going and what I was doing. From there," George said, "I found a field mess and they were happy to give me a stack of 10-in-one rations. Each was intended to feed ten people for a day. At that point I didn't even know if my folks were alive, but I figured that if they were, they could probably use the food."

George started for Manila, his jeep loaded with a spare can of gasoline together with his bag and the cartons of rations. "Before I left," he said, "I was told to watch out for sniper fire, but that was something I could do nothing about." He drove away from Clark and noted adjacent Fort Stotsenburg. There, a world war and many years earlier, he had picnicked with family and friends and taken part in Fourth of July celebrations on the massive grass parade ground. He recalled casual food, games, fireworks and the traditional parade. "My favorite was the cavalry—they rode beautiful horses and wore their dress uniforms with gold braid, and scabbards with gleaming swords. It was quite a spectacle, and something to aspire to as a young boy." The dichotomy between the bangle-bedecked cavalrymen of his boyhood and the oil- and gas-stained aerial warhorse he had just flown into Clark could not have been greater.

"The trip to Manila went slowly because of military traffic moving in both directions," George said. "There were also a lot of Filipinos moving back to their homes or getting away from the fighting that was going on elsewhere. The countryside looked almost normal, and except for a few burned-out wrecks and some damaged buildings, there didn't seem to have been much fighting along the route I was traveling." Notwithstanding the traffic, George made decent time and covered the 40-some miles to the outskirts of Manila in just a few hours. There, the scene changed dramatically.

The wreckage before him was barely recognizable as the city in which he grew up. "I couldn't believe it," George said. "Everything was ruined—blown to bits or knocked down or burned up. Many of the landmarks were gone. It was mind-numbing." Although there was no doubt that the Americans controlled most of the city, fighting continued. The sound of artillery fire rumbled across the ruins occasionally, as did rifle shots and machine-gun fire from scattered patrols and snipers.

After several missed turns and detours he rolled up to the main gate at Santo Tomas. "I told them who I was and what I was doing," George said. He listened as the public address system was keyed and his name echoed over and around the shabby campus: "Captain George Cooper is looking for his father, Lawrence Cooper."

"Almost immediately, Stanton Turner, a man of Dad's age and a friend of the family, arrived and told me Dad had left camp the day before to return to the family home. Soon, people crowded around me," George said. "It was like a reunion with a good portion of the people I had known while growing up. It didn't occur to me until then that the last they had known of me, I was just a playmate, or the son of my father and mother. Now, I was a captain in the Army Air Forces—a decorated combat pilot. It was exciting for them, and a little gratifying for me."

"There were old school friends, and family friends. And there were people I didn't recognize for a moment or two—they had changed so much. They all looked like stick people. Like scarecrows. Charles Armstrong, a boyhood friend, was there. He had joined the guerrilla forces in the Philippines and happened to be at Santa Tomas—just as I was—looking for friends and relatives. He had found his father, who I also saw. And then there were people that I didn't know, or only barely knew, but who knew my father and wanted to see me. It was quite emotional."

In fact, the visit was like a roll call of his youth. There was, he wrote to Betty, "Jean George, Josephine Hemminway Wilson, Mr. Turner, Dr. Beuley, Jimmy Farnes and a boy by the name of Bowman. I also visited Bob and Marian Russell, and saw Francis Salmon Black, and Tom Chapman. Mr. Carmen was killed [just a few days earlier] when Santo Tomas was shelled. Mrs. Carmen lost an arm. Mrs. Stagg had been in the camp for a while but was taken out, possibly to Fort Santiago, where executions were made. Sam Boyd is well."

In fact, "Mrs. Stagg" was the mother of Lionel Stagg with whom George had visited during his time in Santa Monica. And she was dead. Having worked with the resistance, she was betrayed by a Filipino double agent and brutally tortured by the Japanese at Fort Santiago. At the end of August 1944, she was taken with three other women and a man to the Cemeterio del Norte where they were all beheaded.

There was no recent news of his mother and little sister, Dorothy. But he learned of friends and schoolmates that were gone. George recalled that, "Mr. Turner's son, Stanton Jr., had left the Philippines before the Japanese invasion, entered the Army and was killed during the landings in France. Jimmy Young died in the Bataan Death March. Tony Saiz was caught and accused of being a spy. The Japanese cut his hands off and then executed him. Betty Gewald, a schoolmate, had died at Santo Tomas only a couple of months earlier. She had been an attractive girl, the daughter of an Army officer, and very popular."

These were among many others who were gone. George was peppered with questions and he likewise made inquiries. But it seemed that every answer generated many more questions, and time was passing. As happy as he was to see old friends after so many years, George was anxious to start for San Juan, the neighborhood in which he had grown up. And to the house where, God willing, his father, mother and little sister were—at that very moment—putting the pieces of their lives back together.

"Jean George, a school friend, came out to meet me. She wanted to go with me to help find my family," George said. "She had always been a very chatty girl, and still was. I thought it might be useful to have her with me to help me find my way home. The city was a wreck and I wasn't sure that I'd be able to get there."

George and Jean bid goodbye to their friends and left Santo Tomas. Together, they bounced through the wrecked streets. They pointed out demolished buildings or other sites to each other that once meant something to them. "I did find Santa Mesa Street which took us to where the San Juan Bridge—which crossed the San Juan River—used to be. It had been destroyed, but some Army troops directed me a couple of miles away to a pontoon bridge that had been thrown up by their engineers."

George felt some relief as he wheeled the jeep through San Juan, his old neighborhood. Although the roads had gone to pieces and the yards were overgrown with weeds and the houses were in disrepair, everything was largely unscathed. And it was familiar. Here was the main street on which he and his friends had ridden their bikes on their way to one or another adventures. There was the big old tree up which he had climbed so many times. That was the Wightman house where his friend George and his missionary parents had lived. Memory upon memory flooded back and he barely noticed Jean's happy chit chat.

\*\*\*

George's little sister, Dorothy, now 12, looked up from where she sat on the front porch. A jeep clattered to a halt on the other side of the iron gate that guarded the house. A man in uniform was at the wheel, and a young woman sat at his side. He was familiar. Dorothy skipped down the steps and ran toward the gate and stopped just short—her attention focused on the man.

George smiled at Dorothy who immediately burst into happily confused, sputtering tears, spun around and dashed toward the house. She screamed the joyous news at the top of her lungs: "Brother George is here! Brother George is here!"

"She didn't even open the gate for me," George said.

He stepped from the jeep, opened the gate and drove up to the house. His parents rushed out and there followed a tearful reunion. After years of anxiety, worry and simply not knowing, he was overwhelmed by relief and happiness. It was almost as if a physical burden fell from his body. He considered his family: "In view of all that she had gone through, mother looked good, but tired and thin," he said. "I recognized Dorothy, of course, despite the fact that she had grown tremendously during the five years since I had seen her. But Dad looked terrible. He was literally nothing but skin and bones and probably weighed no more than 90 pounds."

Lawrence and Prisca and Dorothy wanted to know everything about everyone. Although they had known that George joined the Army Air Forces, they were not aware that he had married, or had a child—or anything of his recent life. Likewise, they wanted news of the other children: Helen and Marion and Lester. There was so much to talk about.

Jean George's presence as a talkative outsider, through no fault of her own, was awkward. Naturally, the Coopers were emotionally charged and primarily interested in catching up on family events. Yet, Lawrence and Prisca felt compelled to treat her as a guest—to direct some of their attention to her although they knew her only as one of George's schoolmates. "I realized then," George said, "that bringing her along hadn't been a good idea."

Neither George, nor his parents nor Jean knew it at that time, but Jean's fiancé, Walter O'Brien, had been made a POW early in the war and was subsequently killed aboard the *Shinyō Maru*, just as George Wightman had been.

Dorothy made quite an impression on George as he wrote to Betty the following day. "She is quite a grown girl and as smart as they come. Dad showed me a piece she composed when she was eight, and she plays the piano as well as I have ever heard [older sister] Helen play—maybe better." This was high praise indeed, as Helen was well regarded as a highly accomplished pianist. "She has been studying right along. Her attachment for me made me feel as though I was the one that liberated them. I have had no one exhibit as much pride in being with me."

Neighbors stopped by to visit. "I saw the Alicantes," George said. "Catherine died of sickness a year ago because of lack of doctors and medical supplies. Feliche Araneta married and has a boy, nine months old. Mrs. Araneta died, and the house was sold." From the neighbors he learned that, "George Wightman joined our forces at Bataan and though he was taken prisoner, his whereabouts now are not known."

That evening, things did not return to what they had been before the war—they couldn't. And they wouldn't ever. Aside from the sorts of changes that happened to every family as the children reached adulthood and set out on their own, the Japanese had destroyed everything around them. And they had stolen several years from their lives.

Still, there was a happy feeling in the house, even as artillery and machine-gun fire boomed and rattled in the distance. "My father cornered me in quiet conversation," George said. "He was just as alert and outspoken as ever. All the years since I had seen him, and all his time in Santo Tomas, hadn't really changed him; he was still a man of energy and thoughts. We talked of just about everything. He had ideas on the reasons for the war, how it had been conducted and how it should be fought from that point forward. We talked about what the United States ought to do with Japan after the war, and everything in between. We talked about what sort of business he might go into, or if he would go back to his previous employer. And of course, we talked about family."

George wanted Lawrence, Prisca and Dorothy to go to the United States as quickly as possible. Manila and its businesses were in ruins. Moreover, the war was still ongoing, and even if it ended soon there was no way of knowing what would happen in the Philippines. It was to be granted independence very soon; what life would be like after the American authorities departed was unknown. If they went to the United States the family would be reunited if not in one location, then at least in the same country.

George spent the night in his boyhood home. It felt different in a way, and not just because the enemy had occupied it. Certainly, it had changed to some degree in the years since he had been there, but he had changed more. He had matured into manhood and become a husband and a father. He was not the same person who left the house in 1940.

He wrote to Betty, "There is still fighting in and around. The explosions of cannon fire shook the house and rattled the windows all night long. Machine-gun fire can still be heard. The Jap atrocities of the past days are a repetition of [the grotesque, massive-scale murders] at Nanking. I talked to some that had lost relatives or friends, and the stories of killings were the same." He wondered at the possibility of a punishment that would ultimately never be levied on the Japanese. "It may not be hard to tell what will become of the Jap nation, now."

George and Jean ate breakfast with his family the following morning. George then started the difficult task of saying goodbye. He still had a war to fight and his mother and father knew that they might still lose him in that fight. It was a sad but necessary farewell, and after a short time he and Jean stepped back into the jeep and bumped their way back into Manila.

\*\*\*

Following George's departure, his father Lawrence considered what he might do. Like George, the U.S. authorities urged all American civilians to evacuate back to the States. But Lawrence wasn't sure he wanted to leave. The Philippines had been his home for nearly 40 years. It was what he knew and loved. And Prisca and Dorothy likewise were uncertain. Neither had ever known a home outside the Philippines. All their memories—their happiest moments and their sourest—had been made there.

But Manila would never again be as they knew it. Aside from the destruction, the soon-to-be-granted mantle of independence that the Filipino people would assume, carried a degree of risk that was unknown. The government would change and so would the relationships between well-to-do Americans like the Coopers, and the Filipinos who had been their friends, their servants, their relatives and so much more. Lawrence considered all of this and decided to leave with his wife and daughter.

"Army trucks came to the neighborhood and picked us up, along with several other American families" said Dorothy. Each person was allowed one bag or trunk. My parents didn't know it, but I packed a small bomb that I found in the ground after the Japs had left. It was interesting to me and I wanted it."

Dorothy's emotions were mixed. The idea of leaving home and everything she had ever known was sad. But she was also thrilled to some extent at the thought of going to the United States. It was the most powerful and exciting nation on earth and the home of her father; she looked forward to seeing all its wonders and to meeting family she had never known.

There was, however, one aspect of leaving that tore at the very center of her heart. "When I was small, George had a dog named Spot. When she had puppies, I was allowed to keep one of them; I named her Bowser." Through most of what she could remember of her life, Dorothy had loved her constant companion. Bowser had been faithful during peace and during war. She had shared the family's joys and heartbreaks, and had been a wonderful friend when it wasn't safe for other friends to visit. "I loved that dog," Dorothy said.

But Bowser couldn't go with her. Army regulations—for many reasons— forbad the transport of household pets. Dorothy buried her face in Bowser's fur and cried goodbye. Bowser would move down the hill to the barrio where she would be cared for by the family's friends and former servants, but Dorothy could have no hope of ever seeing her dear companion again.

## CHAPTER 18

# "It Almost Felt Like Two Different Wars"

George arced his A-20 around the column of smoke that rose from the valley. Stark white against the shadowy darkness of the jungle, the smoke came from a phosphorous-filled artillery round that had been fired by an American unit to mark the area where they wanted the 90th Bomb Squadron's crews to drop their bombs. Those crews—including George—circled overhead in a lazy circle.

Hands and feet working automatically, George peered intently down into the trees that blanketed the valley. But their multiple layers were too dense and he saw no sign of the Japanese troops that hid below them. So long as he released his bombs as directed, he didn't need to see them to kill them.

The radio crackled. It was George's turn. The man on the ground who was attached to the nearby friendly unit, and who controlled the squadron's attacks, called out the heading he wanted George to fly. George repeated the man's instructions. Attacking from a different direction might endanger the American troops on the ground.

George opened his A-20's bomb bay and let the nose drop down into the valley. As the aircraft accelerated, he checked the mountains around him; he wanted to be certain did not put himself into a canyon out of which he could not fly. In range, he mashed down on the firing button and watched tracers from his machine guns drop down into the target area. A few seconds later he felt the aircraft jump slightly as he released his load of parachute demolition bombs.

Once he was certain the bombs were clear of his aircraft, he pulled skyward and banked into a hard, left turn just in time to see them settle into the jungle. Seconds later he saw flashes as the bombs exploded. At the same time, concentric concussion rings raced outward as the moist air was pressed outward by the bomb blasts.

A call came over the radio, "Good bombs!"

*****

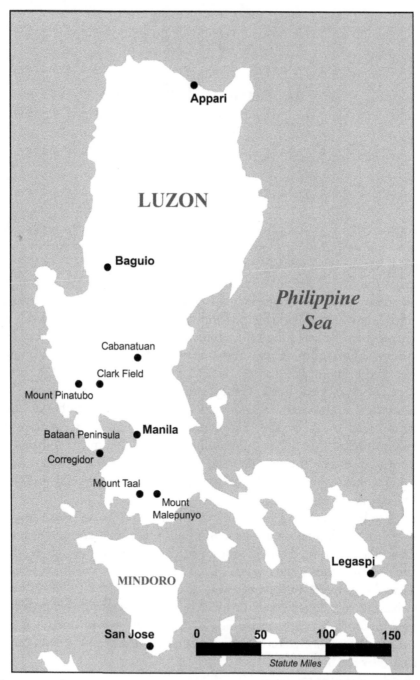

The majority of Cooper's second combat tour was concentrated in the Philippines from February to July 1945.

Most of the missions George and the 3rd Bomb Group flew in the Philippines were in direct support of U.S. Army ground units. (U.S. Army)

"When I went overseas the first time," George said, "the attitude was, 'Let's get the Japs—they bombed Pearl Harbor!' And most of us were eager to do just that. But when I went into combat the second time, the attitude was completely different. It was, 'Let's just finish them off so we can go home.' It almost felt like two different wars."

For his part, George felt almost downcast. He had pulled a big string to get back to the Philippines so that he could find his mother, father and sister. He had been anxious to do whatever was necessary to ensure they were safe—if he found them still alive. To his great joy they were very much alive, and he was confident they would remain so.

He wrote to Betty, who had moved to Tacoma, Washington, to live with her mother's sister. "Now that I know the folks are alright," he wrote, "I wish that I could get back to you. If I could only be back by next Christmas, it would be the best Christmas that we have ever had. Tell Pris not to forget her daddy."

In short, he had accomplished his personal objectives within just the first few weeks of his arrival in the combat theater. But now he was obligated to stay and complete the combat tour he had asked for, however long that might be. Indeed, assuming he lived, it could be a year or more before he saw his beloved Betty and Pris again.

The thought was gut wrenching, and he almost wished that he hadn't sought a second combat tour. His assignment did little to salve his melancholy. "I naturally thought that I would go back to the 345th," he said. "It made sense to me, and I learned that the 345th had requested me when they learned that I was coming back to the Pacific. But Fifth Air Force's Bomber Command—headed by Colonel Jarred Crabb—sent me to the 3rd Bomb Group instead. They were based in the Philippines at McGuire Field, on the island of Mindoro." Indeed, McGuire was one of four airfields situated near the town of San Jose. The area was a hub of air activity.

The 3rd Bomb Group, which had only a year earlier been known as the 3rd Attack Group, was the oldest unit in the Fifth Air Force. Its lineage dated back to 1919, and it had been in the war since it had started—long before George's first unit, the 345th Bomb Group. And its men had performed well, especially during the early days when stopping the Japanese advance toward Australia was not a foregone conclusion. They had done so with a grab bag of limited equipment, too few men and spotty support. When the 345th had arrived in New Guinea, just as the tide was turning in America's favor, the two groups became natural competitors.

And the newcomer 345th Bomb Group, George's unit, seemed a head-line-grabbing overmatch for the 3rd. It was fully equipped with aircraft and the well-trained men necessary to fly and maintain them. Whereas the 3rd had variously operated the A-24 (the same aircraft as the Navy's Dauntless dive bomber, except in Army livery), the A-20 and the B-25, the 345th's four squadrons all flew the rugged and reliable B-25. When the 3rd converted in its entirety to the shorter-legged A-20 during early 1944, the 345th began to outrange it with its B-25s. It achieved notable results wherever it went.

George was assigned to the 3rd Bomb Group's 90th Bomb Squadron; the others being the 8th, 13th and 89th. "For the most part, everyone was cordial and professional, but as a former 345th guy I was definitely an outsider. When I was with the 345th, we had flown the same missions to Rabaul, Wewak and other targets, along with the 3rd and 38th Bomb Groups. There had always been a little competitiveness between the three units." Because of that competitiveness, George occasionally felt an undercurrent of resentment from some of his new comrades.

And that was reflected by what was done with him after he reported to the 3rd at the end of February. Despite his tremendous experience, he was essentially left to languish, and had little to do. Still, he tried to make the best of it. "I have no job yet," he wrote to Betty. "I am just one of the squadron [pilots] which is only natural since I am new in this outfit. There are no openings and they don't know my capabilities. Advancement will come however, if I apply myself and bide my time. I will be running missions, but they should be few, and not hazardous."

George did check out on the A-20H, a model of the A-20 which the group was flying at that point. "Getting qualified," George remembered, "consisted of reading the manual, studying the cockpit arrangement with all of its controls and switches and instruments, and then simply starting the engines, taxiing to the runway and taking off. On my first flight, an enlisted airman came up just as I was about to climb into the cockpit. He asked if he could go along in the gunner's seat. I told him that he was welcome to come along, but I also told him that it was the first time I had flown the A-20. He looked a little hesitant. He looked at me, and then the airplane, and then back at me. He broke out in a big grin and said, 'That's alright, Sir!'"

The other man climbed aboard and George had the aircraft airborne a few minutes later. "It was a delight to fly," George said, "and handled almost like a fighter. And it cruised at 220 miles per hour with a bomb load of 2,000 pounds. But it didn't have the same range or bomb payload as the B-25, and consequently couldn't reach a lot of important targets."

But for the first few weeks he had little to do other than to put a few hours of A-20 time under his belt. He made a couple of exploratory sojourns into the nearby scrub and jungle with his tent mate and new friend, Herman Pancher. They carried a carbine in the event they came across wild game such as feral hogs. The firearm might also prove handy if they stumbled upon Japanese soldiers that had refused to surrender. As it developed, they found no game and no enemy. In truth, these little adventures were very much like the ones he had made as a boy with his friend George Wightman, and his brother Lester.

He also played cards—poker and bridge—read, wrote letters, went to the movies and discussed all manner of topics with his new friends. In fact, he was rather more frank with his descriptions of Betty than she might have liked. "I'm always ready to tell about you," he wrote, "your best points and your failings. I tell them how sweet you can be, what a good mother you are, and then I tell them how my wife may turn so cold it would seem that she caught me necking with the woman next door. However, after the discussion is over, I always feel that the others envy me to a smaller or greater degree." Betty's reaction to George's forthrightness is not recorded in her letters.

"A former occupant of this tent," George wrote to Betty, "tacked up numerous pictures of the 'body beautiful,' posing in some artistic manner completely divested of clothing. Looking at them, I can only think of my own beautiful wife."

The missions the 3rd Bomb Group flew at that time were unremarkable. Whereas, his original unit, the 345th, was sending formations out to the farthest reaches of the South China Sea, or to Formosa, or China or Indochina, the 3rd primarily flew missions in support of army operations in the Philippines. The group did occasionally hit more distant targets, but because the A-20 could not fly as far as the B-25, it had to stage out of other airfields—such as Lingayen—that were closer to those more far-flung objectives.

During March of 1945 the 3rd supported Army ground operations across the Philippines, to include amphibious landings on Mindanao, Negros Island and Cebu. The group also bombed ahead of Army units as they advanced across northern Luzon. Additionally tasked to hit Japanese lines of communications and logistics dumps, the group chased the Japanese as they retreated along the limited road systems, and as they paused in towns along the way.

"It seems in their determined effort to keep in the fight," the group's monthly narrative noted, "the Japanese have hidden ammunition, troops and supplies in native shacks and churches and it has been necessary to bomb and destroy them." Indeed, a review of the group's missions during March showed the Japanese did not hesitate to occupy churches, and the 3rd did not hesitate to attack those same churches, or any other place the enemy occupied.

The attack on the town of Cuenca in the vicinity of Lake Taal on March 17 was typical: "All assigned planes reached the designated target and dropped their bombs and strafed the place thoroughly. The church on the east end of town was destroyed. Several large buildings in the center of town were destroyed, and one building burned fiercely. The schoolhouse in the west side of town was demolished. The entire area was well strafed and many buildings were hit and destroyed."

George felt a sense of irony during this time. "I saw more of the Philippines during these missions—and from an obviously different perspective—than I had ever seen during the time I grew up. It was strange to attack towns and cities I had studied or been to in my youth, such as Legaspi, Cabanatuan, Appari, and Corregidor. In fact," he remembered, "we flew a lot of missions to places where my family had vacationed. For instance, we made several trips to Lake Taal when I was a boy; it was a beautiful area. I recall that my brothers and I came upon a very old church that had been almost buried by volcanic ash many years before when Mount Taal erupted. My older brother Marion climbed into the bell tower, and all the way down into the main part of the building while Lester and I waited above."

Also, during March and the months that followed, the 3rd flew missions in support of American troops who were directly engaged with the enemy. "For the most part we flew out to a particular area and contacted the army unit we were supposed to help that day" George said. "If they needed us to drop bombs, they fired a smoke round with their artillery, and then used that as a reference to tell us where to bomb. Sometimes a liaison aircraft—they used all types—marked the target with a bomb or a rocket. It was all jungle and we couldn't see the Japanese, or whatever we were supposed to be hitting. We bombed and strafed, and when we finished, the army unit thanked us and we went home."

Close air support for ground units was evolving during that time, and procedures were being developed to keep nearby friendly units safe, while still killing as many Japanese as possible. One rule was that an aircraft did not fly over or toward the line of American troops while making a bomb run. The danger was that a bomb dropped long or short might fall on the troops that were supposed to be supported. So then, the pilots were given attack headings that were parallel to the line of friendly troops. Bombs dropped long or short would then fall harmlessly to the front of the supported units.

But over featureless jungle terrain, it could still be confusing, even for a veteran as experienced as George. "I was startled on one mission," he remembered. "I made my bombing run, and almost immediately the controller came up on the radio and shouted for me to stop—I was on the wrong heading and was in danger of hitting our own troops. Fortunately, no one was hurt, but I paid extra attention from that point on."

Enough mistakes were made—particularly against friendly guerillas—that Fifth Air Force Headquarters put out a directive regarding such incidents. Especially those considered to be willfully negligent. "In the future, all reported or suspected attacks upon friendly forces will be investigated at once by the Air Force unit concerned, and a written report of the event, the circumstances, and the findings forwarded to this headquarters."[1]

"We knew that the missions were important to the soldier on the ground, and we were happy to help," said George. "But it wasn't the same as hitting enemy shipping, or airfields or that sort of thing." Indeed, the group's monthly narrative described the missions as, "delivering the daily 4th-class mail to the Nips." "In fact," George said, "the main hazards were from rifle and machine-gun fire, and from the terrain. Many missions were flown in mountainous country where even a slight misjudgment could cost you your life."

But the missions served exactly the purpose for which they were intended. For instance, the commander of the 38th Division, Major General William Chase, sent a message commending the 3rd's efforts around Mount Pinatubo, and additionally confirming their effectiveness. "600 to 800 dead Japs have been found for which the commanding general feels the air arm is for the most part responsible. Decomposed Japs found west of Fort Stotsenburg in Mount Borut area, apparently killed by air strikes."[2]

Jarred Crabb, the commander of Fifth Bomber Command, appreciated the recognition. "It is indeed gratifying to receive such confirmation of the results achieved in our air strikes in direct support of ground operations: especially since the pilots and crew members usually have no way of determining the destruction caused to the enemy."

And Edward Lahti, the commander of the 511th Parachute Infantry Regiment, sent a message to the 3rd which commended and thanked the group for the support it had provided during the regiment's actions in the vicinity of Mt. Malepunyo as it destroyed the Fuji Heidan command which was one of the last coherent Japanese units in southern Luzon.[3]

In fact, the Japanese were deeply entrenched in caves and tunnels. "No assault could be made," the 511th declared, "without first neutralizing the enemy and his positions. The air strike closed many caves and tunnels and demolished the prepared positions. Our troops, following your bombing so closely that the concussion caused bloody noses among the men, occupied each hill without opposition. On each objective, the Japs were found dazed and dead from concussion, and the remnants were easily annihilated. Our success was due to the excellent support rendered by your group."

The correspondence closed with a line that belied what everyone knew—and feared—about future operations. "On behalf of the men and officers of this regiment, I wish to extend our appreciation. We hope that such support will be forthcoming in Japan in the near future."

"By that time," George said, "everyone knew that the Japanese in the Philippines were defeated. It was more of a mopping up campaign. The big fight in the Japanese home islands was what everyone was considering. And everyone knew we were going to lose a lot of men on the ground and a lot of crews in the air. The fight for Okinawa was underway at that point and we were sustaining horrible losses. Okinawa, although on a much smaller scale, was an indicator of what was waiting for us in Japan. In a sense, even at that time, we were all getting ready for the invasion of Japan."

"We only lost two aircraft from my squadron while we were flying A-20s during that period," George said. "One boy flew himself into a box canyon and couldn't get out. He crashed and was killed. Another mismanaged the cross-feed valves on his fuel tanks, and his engines shut down."

In fact, one of George's closest brushes with death came while he was just outside his tent. "We had a baseball and a couple of gloves and I was playing catch with my tent mate, Herman Pancher." There was a distinct, whistling roar and both men looked up. It was a P-38 from a fighter group based at a nearby airfield. Quite often, out of boredom, the fighter pilots dived on the airfield, pulled out at very low level and then flashed across the tents at very high speed. "I had done the same thing many times," George said, "and most of the ground people got a big thrill out of a good buzz job. But if you got too low, some men would throw themselves to the ground for fear of being hit and curse you as you flew away."

"There was a cracking boom," George said, "and the aircraft came apart. The pilot's parachute opened and we could see pieces falling toward us. However, the main part of the aircraft was still high overhead and coming down in a tight spiral. It was unnerving to watch it fall, not knowing where it was going to hit. We didn't know to where we should run."

Unexploded ammunition spattered into the ground like heavy, metallic hail, and the ground literally shook when one of the P-38's engines slammed into the earth only ten feet from George's tent. "I dove for a shallow depression," he said, "thinking it would shield me if what was left of the aircraft exploded when it hit."

The corkscrewing wreck that was the P-38 finally came down atop a tent where an enlisted man slept. "It killed him," said George. "He had stood guard duty the night before and had been given the day off so that he could get some sleep." The event was senseless and tragic, but the "buzz jobs" continued as usual.

Melancholy and boredom sometimes chewed at George during this time. And he missed Betty terribly. In a letter he described how his friend Herman Pancher had lost faith in his wife. And then he reflected on his own behavior toward Betty: "I wonder sometimes if you know how much I do love you. I seldom have expressed my appreciation for the many things you do, have seldom told you how well you looked in a new dress, or how proud I am of you. Perhaps I take too much for granted." He wondered at his own nature and vowed to do better. And then he observed that, "Contact with others constantly assures me that I never chose wrong when I married you."

Some of George's dissatisfaction was with the 3rd Bomb Group. "It is not what it used to be, and is on the bottom of the list," he said. "If things don't break, I shall try to change the situation myself."

Salt in the wound came when he discovered that his camera, wallet and other articles had been stolen. He was especially upset at the loss of portraits of Betty and Pris, and a set of important papers. "I was not the only one who lost money or other articles," he wrote to Betty. "The thieves went through nearly all the officers' tents, and also the enlisted men's tents in the squadron next to us. I don't know whether they were Filipinos who did it, or G.I.s."

"I never felt like this in New Guinea," he noted. "I believe it was the whole outfit, including enlisted personnel, that kept a man sane there." Regardless, George kept going and did what was expected of him.

Following President Roosevelt's death in April, there was much discussion in George's unit about the new President, Harry Truman. "There has not been one man in this squadron that has expressed any faith in him," George said. "I hope that our impressions of him are wrong. I guess that every new man is questioned until he shows his worth."

George's tenure as a semi-autonomous pilot with little responsibility came to an end during May. "I was assigned as the operations officer of the 90th Squadron. As the operations officer I was charged with making crew assignments for each mission and ensuring that that the crews were well prepared to execute them. I typically received the target assignments from the group headquarters, and then personally briefed and debriefed the missions. On some occasions I also led the squadron. I was happy for the assignment as it gave me a greater sense of purpose, and a better understanding of what was going on from a big picture perspective."

As the operations officer for the 90th Bomb Squadron, George recalled his time in New Guinea and, "tried to create a more competitive flying spirit in the outfit, to put it back on the basis of what our groups used to have in New Guinea. I want to build up the flying reputation of the squadron, so that it will be a challenge to the others and a [source of] pride in our men."

Together with his commanding officer, he also quashed the riotous—often violent—behavior of the squadron's men when they had drinking parties. The men were still allowed to gather and drink, and George sometimes joined them, but rancorous misbehavior was not tolerated. Nevertheless, George emphasized with the men: "When I look about me and see men with three years overseas without having been home, I wonder how they have not cracked."

If the missions that George and the 3rd was flying weren't particularly exciting, the primary reason for that lack of excitement was that the American forces in the Pacific were absolutely and irrevocably dominant; the Japanese were utterly incapable of countering them in any meaningful way. In particular, the Japanese army and navy air forces were thoroughly defeated. Certainly, they mounted large kamikaze raids during the closing months of the war. And some of those raids killed many men, but no American capital ships were sunk, and they did little to deter the American advance on the home islands. In fact, the kamikaze attacks were desperate, last-gasp, death tremors which belied the fact that few skilled Japanese airmen remained alive.

Indeed, from February 1945 when George arrived, until the end of the war, no 3rd Bomb Group formations were intercepted by Japanese fighters. So, in short, if George and his comrades were bored, it was because they were winning. And that was good.

## CHAPTER 19

# "I Thought It Was Just Another Island"

Lawrence, Prisca and Dorothy, together with thousands of soldiers and former internees, made the best of life at sea. It was crowded and hot and generally miserable. Long lines for everything from the toilet, to the mess hall—and even to fresh air topside—marked their lives. Progress was slow as the ship and its escort of three destroyers carved a zigzag pattern through the ocean as they sailed first to Leyte, then to the Marianas and then to Honolulu. The war was still on and Japanese submarines were a very real threat. Although the zigzags slowed their progress, the continual course changes reduced the odds that a Japanese submarine captain might stuff a torpedo into their ship.

Nights were especially uncomfortable as everyone was pushed below decks where the men were separated from the women and children. That done, all the hatches were battened down. The ship became a great communal coffin within which the passengers sweated and tossed and turned as they sought sleep that was too slow to come.

Still, relative to what they had endured in the Philippines, the voyage aboard the *Admiral Eberle* presented no great hardships. Lawrence, always the writer, penned a multi-stanza poem. One of the stanzas was representative:

> The hatches are closed, not even a draft,
> From bottom to deck, from forward to aft,
> The toilets afloat, a saltwater bath,
> While long lines await with people a-wrath,
> But it's home boys, home. Home sweet home.

The ship reached San Pedro, California on May 3, 1945. Dorothy recalled how the children crowded the rails and watched for land. They wore heavy overcoats against the cold, California mists. "Very soon we began to see a faint line. I thought it was just another island, but when the fog began to clear and the tugboats began to appear around, with sailors yelling, 'Welcome home,' and no palm trees and sand, but houses, little red ones with smooth lawns that looked as if they had come out of a fairy tale, I began to think different."

"By this time, people began to crowd on deck," she said. "Many people wept, and by the time we got to the dock there was a regular sobbing chorus. A band played 'Star Spangled Banner,' and Red Cross ladies and sailors cheered."

George's family—all of it—was safe at last.

This, despite the small bomb that Dorothy had secreted in her luggage. "My parents were horrified when they found it," she said. "'They were not happy with me at all." It was subsequently discovered to be a small marking bomb that had already been spent.

\*\*\*

The reason for George's assignment to the 3rd Bomb Group rather than his original 345th Bomb Group became clear at the end of May 1945, soon after he took over as the 90th Bomb Squadron's operations officer. "We were told that the group was scheduled to transition from the A-20 to the A-26," George said. "General Crabb must have known this when he sent me to the 3rd. He recognized that my experience as an A-26 instructor would be valuable as the group made the transition. It was very exciting for me, but what was more exciting was that I was scheduled to take over as the commanding officer of the 8th Bomb Squadron."

The news came just in time as he had been asked by his earlier unit, the 345th Bomb Group, if he would take command of his original squadron, the 499th "Bats Outta Hell."

George considered the 345th's proposal and declined. He wanted to fly the A-26 in combat. That the 3rd offered him command of a squadron was smart. Firstly, it kept him and all of his experience in the group. And even though he was still a captain, George had shown himself to be an excellent leader. Moreover, he had been blooded in combat and had the piloting skills, intelligence and common sense necessary to perform effectively as a squadron commander. His background as an A-26 instructor was icing on the cake.

June of 1945 was a slow month for the 3rd Bomb Group. Together with Filipino guerillas, American forces had pushed most of what remained of the Japanese on Luzon into a pocket of territory on the northern part of the island. Aside from those ragged remnants there simply weren't many targets within range of the 3rd Bomb Group's A-20s. In fact, a total of only 211 sorties were flown during the entire month—an average of less than three sorties per pilot. This contrasted greatly with the 745 sorties flown the previous month.

This A-20 served in the 3rd Bomb Group's 90th Bomb Squadron—just as George did. (San Diego Air & Space Museum)

On the other hand, the group was embracing the new A-26 which it described as, "a superior ship over the A-20, having a longer range, and it can carry a large bomb load. There are many other improvements which qualify it as one of the fastest bomber planes in the world. It has 14 machine guns firing forward and is designed especially for low-level attacks. It is a much faster ship, and with the Pratt & Whitney engines, one can hardly hear the plane coming until it has passed."

The group started accepting new A-26s during June, and had 11 on hand by the end of the month. They were not flown in combat but were being used to transition the pilots from the A-20. "We had a lot of support from the Douglas Aircraft Company," said George. "They sent maintenance experts and pilots, and brought training material with them. Although it was fun and easy to fly, it was somewhat more complex than the A-20."

Indeed, although the A-26's potential was exciting, the changeover was also difficult as noted by the group's support section. "Our new A-26Bs began arriving this month with replacement crews, adding to our already many headaches. With much technical assistance from Douglas representatives, [we] began the task of modifications and technical order compliances."

As much-liked as it was, there were aspects about the A-26 that the 3rd's personnel found to be wanting. It was difficult to get at some of the radio equipment in order to service or replace it. And one of the lower antennas needed to be moved as it was positioned such that it might snag parafrags as they fell from the bomb bay.

***

George knocked on the door of his childhood home. He had been sent to Manila on official business and had time to stop by the house. His father Lawrence had written him with the information that the checks from the colonel who was renting the place had not cleared. A blonde woman answered the door—the colonel was not there. She didn't know anything about rent checks and had no time for George.

Stymied, and a bit affronted, George walked down the front steps that he had trod so many times through the time of his growing up. He turned and looked at the house, his house, then turned away. He would never see it again.

***

The 3rd—and George—saw even less action during July than it had during June. Only 82 combat sorties were flown which was an average of less than one per crew. "The Philippines campaign has just about come to a close," the group noted. "With the exception of a few scattered Japanese troops in the northern part of Luzon, there were practically no missions scheduled for the 3rd Group to fly."

However, the group did fly their A-26s in combat for the first time on July 6, and a few more times during the following week. "Using the A-26 Invader for the first time in combat," the group recorded, "we flew several bombing and strafing missions to Formosa [modern-day Taiwan]. Due to the increased range of the new bombing planes, they were able to fly there and back without landing in between for gas."

And the impressions the A-26 made on the pilots were very favorable. The 3rd's commander, Lieutenant Colonel Chuck Howe declared, "Boy, what an airplane! I can't wait until we hit the [Japanese] home islands. Never again do I want to fly any airplane other than the Invader."

George was also impressed by the type when he finally flew it into combat. After dropping his bombs into a railroad yard, he strafed a nearby building. "The building had a red tile roof," he said, "and when the rounds from the 14 .50 caliber-machine guns on my aircraft hit it, the tiles simply disintegrated into a cloud of red-colored dust. It was startling." His comments were echoed by Sam Frederick, who had been his commanding officer at the 90th Bomb

Squadron: "Strafing with all those forward-firing guns is like plowing—what an airplane!"

But other than the fact that they were reaching out to hit targets they had rarely attacked before, the missions were unremarkable. Again, this was good. The Japanese were so badly beaten that they were not only incapable of countering the A-26s with fighters, but they were likewise unable to defend themselves with effective antiaircraft fire.

On July 14, the 3rd stopped flying missions. Orders from higher headquarters directed the group to move to Okinawa, part of the Ryuku Islands, located just 400 miles from Kyushu, the southernmost of the Japanese home islands. Okinawa had only recently been declared secure after one of the bloodiest campaigns of the war, and it was from there that the 3rd and many other units would support the initial landings on Japan.

Bad weather and lack of transportation conspired to delay the group's movement until July 25, when most of the unit's men and equipment were loaded aboard LSTs and sent to join a convoy for the transit to the Ryukus. When July turned to August they were still en route.

## CHAPTER 20

# "Everyone Knew the End Was Very Near"

Futaba Kitayama was part of an all-women work party in Hiroshima, Japan, on the morning of August 6, 1945.[1] When one of her coworkers pointed to the sky, they all turned to study a bright silvery object. Almost immediately, a brilliant, shocking blast blinded and knocked them down. When Kitayama regained consciousness, she wiped at her face, her arms and her hands. Wherever she wiped, the skin came away in sheets. All over the city, thousands were dead and thousands more were going to die.

\*\*\*

Getting the 3rd situated at its new home, the air strips on Okinawa's Bolo Point, demanded hard work and ingenuity. "We desperately needed lumber to get our squadron area built," George said. "Knowing that liquor was a prized commodity, I procured some mission whiskey from the squadron's flight surgeon. This was given to us in shot glasses after we flew missions."

"With the whiskey," George said, "I then went out to where DUKW amphibious trucks were shuttling loads of lumber ashore from ships anchored not too far from the beach. I waved the bottle at the first driver that approached. He stopped, gave it a good look and asked, 'Where do you want it?' We had all the lumber we needed for the price of one bottle of booze."

"My crew chief wanted to name my plane during this time," George said. "I didn't want to name it *Jayhawk*, because that had been the B-25 that had served me so well in New Guinea. Instead, we named it after my wife and his, *Betty and Marjorie*.

\*\*\*

An A-26 of the 3rd Bomb Group on Okinawa. (USAAF)

An A-26 on Okinawa from another unit—this one, unpainted. (USAAF)

George leaned forward and looked to his left, and then to his right. His two wingmen in their heavily laden A-26s, and the two other flights making up his formation, were in position. It was the afternoon of August 11, 1945—only three days since the air echelon had arrived from the Philippines. The atomic bomb that was dropped on Hiroshima on August 6 had been followed by another at Nagasaki on August 9. Since then, rumors had been rife as to if, or when, the Japanese would surrender.

George was charged with leading the A-26s to Japan's inland sea on an anti-shipping sweep. From Okinawa it was a straight-line distance of more than 650 miles. The aircraft were carrying an unprecedented load of eight 500-pound bombs, and 14 5-inch rockets—seven under each wing—that weighed 134 pounds each. The drag the payload created was considerable, and the mission would stress the limits of their A-26s' range.

During the mission briefing George had emphasized the fact that fuel consumption might become critical. If any flight's fuel quantity approached 50 percent of capacity, the flight leader was to advise George and be prepared to reverse course, hit the alternate target near Kagoshima, and then return to Okinawa.

For his part, George was excited at the opportunity. The mission would take the formation to the heart of Japan's home islands where he was bound to find worthwhile targets. It wasn't going to be a forgettable strike against an unseen enemy hiding in an unnamed jungle. Instead, it was more akin to the missions he had flown out of New Guinea with the 345th earlier in the war. It was an opportunity to hit the Japanese hard—and on their own front porch.

Even though the route took George and the other crews past several enemy fighter fields, they remained unmolested. Nevertheless, the mission didn't go as planned. The formation was more than 100 miles from the inland sea when one of the flight leaders called over the radio and declared that his flight was low on fuel. George checked his own fuel state and noted that his aircraft had enough to complete the mission. Still, he knew that other members of the formation would have used more fuel in order to maintain the formation. But that fact notwithstanding, he was surprised that they had used so much fuel that they were unable to continue. He had no choice but to trust the other pilots. George ordered them home via the alternate target.

It wasn't much later when the other flight leader called and made the same declaration. George likewise released that flight. He continued northward with his two wingmen.

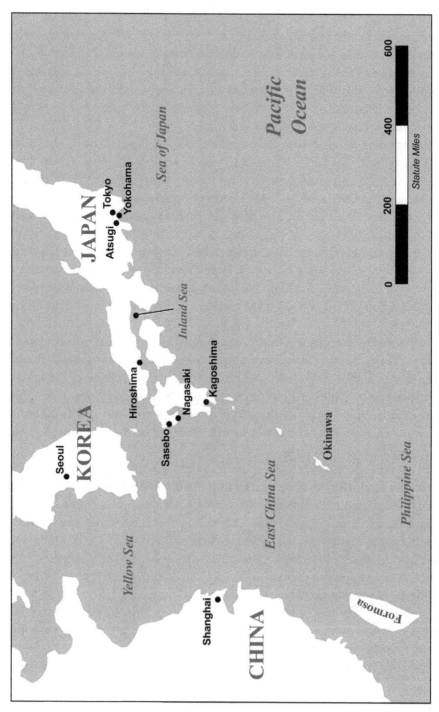

With the 3rd Bomb Group, Cooper flew from Okinawa against Japan in August 1945.

Low, scudding clouds and poor visibility met them when they reached the inland sea. It was not good hunting weather. Dropping down to just above the wave tops, George took his two wingmen into the wind-whipped mist, wary of the many rugged islands that rose from the water.

Finally, he spotted a small vessel and signaled his wingmen to drop back into trail as he circled to make the attack. He was anxious to try the rockets which he had never fired in actual combat. Yet, at low altitude in nearly level flight—targeting a wave-tossed ship—the shot was nearly impossible; the slightest deviation in bank angle or heading would send the rockets wild. George pressed the firing button and watched two rockets, one from each wing, streak from his wings. Their motors burned bright yellow against the dull gray, whereas the white-gray smoke they trailed blended almost perfectly.

The rockets missed. Yet, the flight's attack was successful as noted by the 3rd's monthly narrative: "A 70-foot barge, loaded with supplies was attacked with bombs, rockets and strafing. A near miss blew off the bow and the barge was left heavily damaged and possibly sinking."

One of George's wingmen called to report that his bomb bay doors would not close. George knew that if they remained open, the extra drag they created would cause the engines to work harder. In doing so they would burn fuel at a higher rate and the aircraft would go down in the water short of Okinawa. George terminated the mission, gathered his wingmen, and headed for home. Along the way, the balky doors closed and George led the flight in an attack on railroad yards and a set of factory buildings at Kagoshima. There, they expended the last of their bombs and rockets and returned to Okinawa without incident.

Although the idea made him uncomfortable, George considered that some of the other men in his formation—guessing that the war was near its end—might have sandbagged their way home in order to stay clear of danger. No one wanted to be the last casualty of the war. However, he had no proof of it and did not ask the question.

"I wonder how many prayers are being said back home for the peace that seems so imminent," George wrote to Betty the next day. "The strain at this point is much greater. It is like flying that last mission before being sent home on rotation. You think how bitter it would be to be killed just before the peace."

He described his new surroundings on Okinawa, where his unit was billeted in a "bombed out village," that he guessed had been "quaint" before being caught in the heart of the war. "There are no streets through it," he observed, "but lanes, flanked with ivy-grown stone walls. Hibiscus still grows thick in hedgerows. Just walking through the ruins of a simple village like this makes me realize so much more what a shame it is that this war had to happen."

George also told Betty of the mistaken celebration that took place all over Okinawa on the night of August 10 when it was mistakenly believed that the war had ended. On the island, men started firing weapons, large and small. Offshore, crews aboard hundreds of ships believed that a kamikaze attack was underway and fired their antiaircraft guns skyward. "The Navy, and ack-ack crews put out streams of tracers which laced the sky and turned the black of night to red," he wrote. At least six men were killed by shrapnel and falling rounds, and many more were injured.

"Several of our men," noted the group's monthly narrative, "had gone out to the landing strip to load our A-20s and A-26s with bombs and ammunition for the following day's mission. When the celebration started, they stopped their work for a while to join in and had to be persuaded that the war wasn't over just then, and that the mission would be carried out, regardless. It was a relief, nevertheless, to know that the Japanese were considering the terms and that in all probability, they would accept."

\*\*\*

On the evening of August 14, 1945, there was a general grumble during the mission briefing as the nature of the next day's strike became clear to the 3rd's aircrews. They were being sent to attack the Sasebo Naval Arsenal on the island of Kyushu. It was one of Japan's largest naval installations and was tucked into a protective ring of coastal mountains. Defended by a heavy concentration of antiaircraft guns, it was a formidable target notwithstanding the fact that it had been attacked several times previously.

But those previous strikes had been flown from high altitude. The 3rd was going in low. "We were scheduled to carry two 2,000-pound bombs," George said. "The plan called for us to come in from the north over a low mountain range, dive on the ships in the harbor, and then dash out through the mouth of the bay. When the intelligence officer pointed out all the known gun emplacements—pointing particularly at a concentration of antiaircraft guns at the mouth of the bay—there was a good deal of uneasiness among the men. Those guns would be pointing down on us if we survived long enough to get to that point."

"The war was supposed to be over by that time," George said, "and there were whispers among some of the men about refusing to go. Everyone knew the end was very near. It seemed wasteful, even nonsensical, to send men out on such a risky mission. I understood their perspective, but the war wasn't over and as far as I was concerned, I was going—and they were too."

George's gunner did not share his sense of duty. "He approached me and declared that he wasn't going to go," George said. "I told him that he didn't have to, but that I was going to bust him down to buck private—he didn't deserve to continue as a staff sergeant." Evidently, the gunner felt that being a live private was better than being a potentially dead staff sergeant.

Despite his commitment to fly the mission, George sympathized to a degree with the men who were reluctant to go. He longed for Betty and Pris and didn't want to risk his life any more than anyone else. He was a hardened veteran of more than 70 combat missions to some of the most heavily defended targets of the war. He knew all about dying and didn't want to do it—especially on a mission that would have virtually no impact on whether or not the war would end. That night he did considerable thinking as he tried to fall asleep.

A replacement gunner met George at the aircraft the next morning.

"We had synchronized our wristwatches the night before," George said, "and at 0545 precisely, I heard the whirring whine of engine starters followed by a coughing rumble as the first of those 18 Pratt & Whitney's roared to life. Within a minute, the growl of the engines was smooth and uninterrupted."

At the prescribed time, George taxied his A-26 from its hardstand. Checking behind him as he rolled toward the runway, he counted eight other A-26s falling into line. Before centering his aircraft on the runway he stopped and took a few seconds to run up the engines and perform his final takeoff checks. He pushed, pulled and rotated the control yoke to make sure his flight controls operated smoothly and freely. After checking the magnetos, oil and fuel pressures, and various temperatures, he double checked the flaps were in position and that the fuel boost pumps were on. And then, "I pushed the throttles forward and felt the aircraft surge. Another quick glance at the engine instruments told me that everything was as it should be, and I switched my focus to watch the airspeed build. The full load we were carrying required us to use almost the entire runway."

George lifted his aircraft skyward at the far end of the runway, raised the landing gear and flaps, and turned over the water. Behind him, he watched the rest of the squadron lift clear of the airfield and climb after him. Once he had the squadron joined, he fine-tuned his course for the group rendezvous point.

George and the rest of the 8th settled into position with the 3rd's other squadrons and headed north. No doubt, each man was gripped with some level of anxiety—apprehensive as to the state of the Japanese defenses at Sasebo, and to the cruel whimsies of which fate was capable. Most had never attacked such a target; it was a far cry from dropping bombs onto virtually undefended, unremarkable, jungle-veiled targets.

"We were about an hour from Sasebo," George said, "when a call came over our radio sets that we were to return to base. The war was over."

## CHAPTER 21

# "Instead of Brutality They Found Kindness"

"Soon after the war ended, the 3rd was moved to Atsugi, Japan, as part of the Army of Occupation," recalled George. "The organization was in tremendous flux as most of the old veterans were allowed to go home, and new men arrived. I had to stay as part of a contingent of essential personnel. We flew surveillance missions initially, and then transitioned to training missions to maintain our currency, but the emphasis was on our occupation duties. There was no more war to fight."

Aside from his squadron commander duties, George was put in charge of leading the repairs necessary to get the 3rd's formerly Japanese infrastructure in working order. This included heating, plumbing, electricity, and anything else that was remotely related. "I don't recall why I was assigned to supervise the reconstruction," he remembered. "I had no previous experience in construction, but I was eager to tackle the job."

In tackling that job, he and his team scrounged the area around Atsugi and on the airfield itself. "A lot of tools and material came from underground storehouses we found tunneled under the airfield. There was a complex of rooms for living, offices, eating, medical care and refrigeration units for food. And there were electrical power units to serve it all. We salvaged what we wanted and then filled in the entrances."

George was most surprised by the behavior of the Japanese; they were totally submissive—even gracious to the occupying Americans. It was difficult to reconcile them against the monsters of Manila. "Not long after we got to Atsugi," George said, "the local Japanese authorities came by to ask what they could do for us. Someone shouted—facetiously, of course—that we needed girls. The next night, a busload of girls arrived at the base. They were sent home."

On another occasion, George landed his aircraft at a Japanese airfield that had yet to be occupied by the Americans. During discussions with the base commander he mentioned that he was looking for wiring and switches and other electrical equipment. "He told me that he would help as best he could," George said. "When I got back to my aircraft a couple of hours later, the bomb bay was stuffed with all sorts of electrical equipment that had obviously just been torn out of a building."

When one of George's Japanese workers was hurt on the job, George ensured that he received medical care and then sent him home in a military vehicle. "The following day, a contingent of three Japanese from the village came to my office," he recalled. "They bowed and through my interpreter told me they wanted to thank me and give me gifts for the kindness I had shown the injured man. They said they were told by Japanese authorities that the Americans would rape their women, kill their men and steal their precious possessions. They were surprised and happy that instead of brutality they found kindness and respect."

Indeed, through the remainder of his time in Japan, George could not help but reflect on how the suppliant behavior of the defeated Japanese contrasted so starkly with the cold reception he had received as a young man when he was stuck in Yokohama with the *Laura Maersk* more than five years earlier.

\*\*\*

George was surprised and gratified to receive orders home in November. He left aboard a transport ship that, ironically, was berthed at Yokohama. Just as the *Hie Maru* was caught in a great Pacific storm when he sailed from Japan to the United States in 1940, so was the ship that took him from Japan to the United States at the end of 1945. Nevertheless, he was home for Christmas.

He was home for good.

# Epilogue

When George graduated from flight school, he and his classmates were asked to describe what they planned to do with their lives. Unlike most of his friends who described more tangible goals, George borrowed from Thomas Jefferson and declared, "Pursuit of happiness." That pursuit characterized the rest of his life.

George, Betty and Pris moved to Lawrence, Kansas in 1946 where George enrolled at Kansas University. In 1949 he realized his dream and graduated with a bachelor's degree in mechanical engineering. There followed a multi-decade stint in industry that culminated in his promotion to Vice President of Medical Gasses for Puritan Bennett. He retired in 1986 to his home outside Tonganoxie, Kansas, where he worked 160 acres to keep himself busy.

George continued his military service as part of the United States Air Force Reserve. Ultimately, he was promoted to colonel and put in command of the 935th Military Airlift Wing. He was recalled to active duty several times, and flew cargo and personnel into South Vietnam on many occasions. Additionally, when pay for military reservists came under fire during the 1960s, he advocated in many public venues for it to continue. He retired from the service in 1971.

At the same time, he and Betty—who later in life reverted to her birth name of Ruth—raised a family. Including Priscilla, they raised five girls and a son. Helping Betty to raise their children was a priority with George, as was educating them. Indeed, George helped one of his daughters—a third-grade teacher—in the classroom for 25 years. A beloved and reliable presence two days a week, he helped the students with reading and math.

Ruth Cooper, the love of George's life, passed in 2015 at age 93, after 73 years of marriage. At her side were George and four of her children. Aside from their six children they have been blessed with 14 grandchildren, 32 great-grandchildren and 4 great-great-grandchildren.

George still lives independently in his home outside Tonganoxie on part of his original 160 acres, near which reside two of his daughters.

Lawrence and Prisca settled happily in Burlingame, California, where Lawrence started another import and export business, and where Prisca did charity work and made many friends. Lawrence passed in 1968, Prisca followed in 1976.

George's little sister Dorothy assimilated into American schools immediately following the end of the war. With support from her parents she continued her piano studies and—as a teenage prodigy—won many awards. The summer after she graduated from high school she was the guest artist for Arthur Fiedler and the San Francisco Symphony Orchestra. Following the performance, Fiedler asked her to join him for a nationwide concert tour. She declined, attended university, married, raised two children and still lives a grand and colorful life. Among her dearest experiences was being an extremely active board member of the German Shepherd Dog Club of America. Still an ardent dog lover, she recalls with great fondness many of the champions she raised and trained. She lives in the San Francisco Bay area.

*Jayhawk*, George's original B-25D, serial number 41-30014, retained its name as it was passed on to several other crews in the 499th Bomb Squadron until the end of 1944. As it had done with George and his crew, it brought everyone home after every sortie until, after flying more than 120 missions, the loyal old bird was declared war weary and sent to a rear area. It was likely broken up and salvaged.

***

Bowser, the last of the Coopers in the Philippines, sniffed around the old house. Dorothy was long gone, but notwithstanding the arthritis that now inflamed her aged joints, Bowser regularly climbed the hill from the barrio to see if she had returned. On this day, as with every other day, Dorothy was not to be found. The old dog looked up and blinked into the sun, turned to gaze back down the hill, and then laid herself onto the lawn across which she had once played with her dear girl.

Bowser's nose filled with the sweet scent of the flowers and trees that had regrown since the end of the Japanese occupation. She sighed, fell asleep and was gone.

# Afterword by George Cooper: Reflections of a Centenarian

Having lived for more than a century, I have seen and done much. Among that seeing and doing were my experiences during World War II. They regularly offer me much to consider because my life prior to the war influenced how I behaved and acted during the war, and those actions consequently influenced what I did and who I became after the war.

There are two aspects about my wartime story that I believe offer special value—and neither of them is related to anything I did while flying combat; there were many pilots and crewmen who did much more. Firstly, I believe that better than most books about the war, this one—through my eyes and those of my friends and my family—describes what the war was really like. For the noncombatants it was hardship and boredom and sacrifice and worry and longing and sometimes death. For the combatants it was also hardship and boredom and sacrifice and worry and longing and sometimes death. Truly, virtually everyone was a participant to one degree or another.

The second aspect touches on the concepts of family, legacy and perseverance. To me, it has something to do with the spirit of *Jayhawk*—Kansas University, KU. Long before I was born, my grandmother watched it being built and pledged that her children would study there. My father did, and the imprint of the institution on him was such that it was also a part of my growing up from before the time I even knew what a university was. And because it was important to him, and because it helped to make him who he was, and because he loved it, I did too.

My father and mother created a home that was loving and nurturing, but at the same time, disciplined. There was an emphasis on education and hard work and the benefits that might be realized from them. When I left the Philippines in 1940 my only goal was to make enough money to study at

KU. I didn't know what I wanted to be—not with any sense of certainty. I just knew that I wanted to graduate from there as my father had, and as had my sister and my older brother.

Certainly, logic and my own experience tell me that other families enjoyed many of the same blessings without the benefit of higher education. And that same logic and experience further inform me that my father might have gone to another school and fallen just as emphatically in love with it. And that I might have named my aircraft—and this book—*Cornhusker*, or *Hawkeye* or *Boilermaker* or any one of many names. But he didn't, and I didn't. The love of my father and the rest of my family drove me to become a KU man.

And that drive stayed with me long after I earned my degree in 1949—four years after returning from the war. It propelled me to a career of nearly 30 years in uniform. And I rode it to the very top of my profession outside the military; after long decades in industry, I retired as a Vice President with Puritan–Bennett, a leader in respiratory health products.

That Kansas University drive was something that was recognized and appreciated by others. When I was promoted to colonel in 1964, I was very gratified to receive congratulations from my wartime commander, Clinton True. Together with others from the 345th Bomb Group, I—at the controls of *Jayhawk*—had followed him through a driving rainstorm to make a spectacularly successful attack on the Japanese fortress at Rabaul. It had been more than 20 years earlier. I like to think that my drive, my KU drive, had made an impression on that very brave man.

Just as my father and mother raised a happy and successful family, I take great pride in the family that my wife Betty and I created and raised. We started with Pris who was born while I was fighting the Japanese in New Guinea. And now, our legacy includes four great-great-grandchildren. And there are several among that legacy who proudly claim the title of *Jayhawk*.

Ultimately, I hope I can be forgiven for my pride at being recognized as the 2018 University of Kansas Mechanical Engineering Distinguished Alumnus. To me, it is evidence that my goal of becoming a true *Jayhawk*—first articulated when Calvin Coolidge was president—has been realized in full.

For that, and for all that I have been blessed with, I am a grateful, and undeniably old, man.

# Bibliography

379th Bombardment Group (H) World War II Association. *379th Bombardment Group (H) Anthology, November 1942–July 1945: A Textual, Statistical, and Photographic History of the 379 Bombardment Group*. Paducah, KY: Turner, 2000.

Badsey, Stephen. *The Hutchinson Atlas of World War II Battle Plans*. London: Routledge, 2016.

Craven, Wesley Frank, and James Lea Cate. *The Army Air Forces in World War II, Volume VI: Men and Planes*. Washington, DC: Office of Air Force History, 1984.

Darian-Smith, Kate. *On the Home Front: Melbourne in Wartime: 1939–1945*. Carlton, Vic.: Melbourne University Press, 2009.

Dielman, Gary. "The WWII Sinking of the 'Shinyo Maru': A Story of Loss and Survival of Two Baker POW's." Baker Library, 2015. https://www.bakerlib.org/files/archive/dielman-essays/2015-sinking-of-the-shinyo-maru.pdf.

Ferguson, Max B. *Bats Outa Hell over Biak*. Charleston, IL: Self, 1991.

Gamble, Bruce. *Target Rabaul: The Allied Siege of Japan's Most Infamous Stronghold, March 1943–August 1945*. Beverley, MA: Voyageur Press, 2013.

General Staff. "Report on the Destruction of Manila and Japanese Atrocities." Philippines: Headquarters, South West Pacific Area, 1945.

Guillain, Robert. "I Thought My Last Hour Had Come." *The Atlantic*, August 1, 1980. https://www.theatlantic.com/magazine/archive/1980/08/-i-thought-my-last-hour-had-come/306349/.

Hara, Tameichi, Fred Saito, and Roger Pineau. *Japanese Destroyer Captain: Pearl Harbor, Guadalcanal, Midway—The Great Naval Battles as Seen through Japanese Eyes*. Annapolis, MD: Naval Institute Press, 2011.

Hickey, Lawrence J. *Warpath across the Pacific: The Illustrated History of the 345th Bombardment Group during World War II*. Boulder, CO: International Historical Research Associates, 2008.

Hillegas, Ann Marsh. *Help Is on the Way: The Santo Tomas Diary of Annette and Scotty Marsh*. Bennington, VT: Merriam Press, 2009.

Holland, Robert B. *100 Miles to Freedom: The Epic Story of the Rescue of Santo Tomas and the Liberation of Manila, 1943–1945*. New York, NY: Turner Pub. Co., 2011.

Huff, Sidney L. *My Fifteen Years with General MacArthur*. New York, NY: Paperback Library, 1964.

Kenney, George C. *General Kenney Reports: A Personal History of the Pacific War*. Washington, D.C.: Air Force History and Museums Program, 1997.

Kenney, George C. *The Saga of Pappy Gunn*. Los Angeles, CA: Enhanced Media Publishing, 2017.

La Forte, Robert S., Ronald E. Marcello, and Richard L. Himmel. *With Only the Will to Live: Accounts of Americans in Japanese Prison Camps, 1941–1945*. Wilmington, DE: SR Books, 1994.

Mazza, Eugene A. "The American Prisoners of War Rescued after the Sinking of the Japanese Transport, Shinyo Maru, by the USS Paddle, SS 263, on 1 September 1944." SubmarineSailor.com, February 15, 2004. http://www.submarinesailor.com/history/pow/paddlesinksshinyomaru/#Ref.

Middlebrook, Garrett. *Air Combat at 20 Feet: Selected Missions from a Strafer Pilot's Diary.* Bloomington, IN: Author House, 2004.

Miner, William D., and Lewis A. Miner. *Surrender on Cebu: a POWs Diary—WWII.* Paducah, KY: Turner Pub. Co., 2001.

PacificWrecks.com. "C-47A-30-DL 'The Amazon' Serial Number 42-23659." Pacific Wrecks, February 14, 2020. https://www.pacificwrecks.com/Aircraft/c-47/42-23659.html.

Pan Am Clipper Flying Boats. "Edwin Musick." Accessed April 1, 2020. https://www.clipperflyingboats.com/edwin-musick.

"Possibility of Reich-American Clash Mounts." *Nippon Jiji,* July 8, 1941. https://hojishinbun.hoover.org/?a=d&d=tnj19410708-01.1.8&l=ja.

Rhodes, Mick. "He Was Just a Kid in an Ugly War." *Claremont Courier,* October 19, 2017. https://www.claremont-courier.com/articles/news/t25369-jack.

Smith, Robert Ross. *Triumph in the Philippines.* Washington, D.C.: Center of Military History, United States Army, 1993.

"The Battle of Brisbane by Raymond Evans and Jacqui Donegan." Politics and Culture, August 10, 2010. https://politicsandculture.org/2010/08/10/the-battle-of-brisbane-by-raymond-evans-and-jacqui-donegan-2/.

The Philippine Diary Project. "Francis Burton Harrison." Accessed April 1, 2020. https://philippinediaryproject.wordpress.com/tag/francis-burton-harrison/.

Tiempo, Edilberto K., and Edith Tiempo. *College Writing and Reading.* Manila: Rex, 1980.

United States, Formal Relations of the United States. *Formal Relations of the United States, Diplomatic Papers, 1944, Volume V, The Near East, South Asia and Africa, the Far East, United States.* Washington, D.C.: Historical Office, Bureau of Public Affairs, 1965.

Wilkinson, Rupert. *Surviving a Japanese Internment Camp: Life and Liberation at Santo Tomás, Manila, in World War II.* Jefferson, NC: McFarland, 2014.

Wilkinson, Rupert. "Standoff at Santo Tomas." HistoryNet, May 17, 2017. https://www.historynet.com/standoff-santo-tomas.htm.

Williams, Nick, "Forest Ave—Century of Industry," *Ypsilanti Automotive Heritage Newsletter,* Vol. 1, No. 2, Spring 2014.

Zimmerman, Dwight. "Senator Harry S Truman and the Truman Committee." Defense Media Network, accessed April 1, 2020. https://www.defensemedianetwork.com/stories/senator-harry-s-truman-and-the-truman-committee/.

# Endnotes

*Jayhawk* is a biography of a living man and most of the material in the book came from many interviews with that living man, George L. Cooper. Also useful were the wartime segments from Cooper's abbreviated, self-written remembrances, as well as the letters between him and his wife from that period, and other letters from friends and family. George's mother and father also wrote various recollections of their wartime experiences which were valuable in writing this book.

None of these sources are publicly available and they are not footnoted.

## Chapter 1

1   "Francis Burton Harrison," The Philippine Diary Project, accessed April 1, 2020, https://philippinediaryproject.wordpress.com/tag/francis-burton-harrison/).
2   "Edwin Musick," Pan Am Clipper Flying Boats, accessed April 1, 2020, https://www.clipperflyingboats.com/edwin-musick).

## Chapter 2

1   Roedspaetten, Laura Maersk IDNo 5204027, Coasters Remembered, January 14, 2015, http://www.coasters-remembered.net/showthread.php?t=15210.

## Chapter 3

1   Nick Williams, "Forest Ave—Century of Industry," *Ypsilanti Automotive Heritage Newsletter*, 1, no. 2, (Spring 2014): 2.
2   "Possibility of Reich-American Clash Mounts," *Nippon Jiji*, July 8, 1941, https://hojishinbun.hoover.org/?a=d&d=tnj19410708-01.1.8&l=ja.

## Chapter 4

1   Wesley Frank Craven and James Lea Cate, *The Army Air Forces in World War II, Volume VI: Men and Planes* (Washington, DC: Office of Air Force History, 1984), 486.
2   "Boyd Wagner," Wikipedia, Wikimedia Foundation, November 30, 2019, https://en.wikipedia.org/wiki/Boyd_Wagner.

## Chapter 5

1    Edilberto K. Tiempo and Edith Tiempo, *College Writing and Reading* (Manila: Rex, 1980), 329.

## Chapter 6

1    Dwight Zimmerman, "Senator Harry S Truman and the Truman Committee," Defense Media Network, accessed December 19, 2012, https://www.defensemedianetwork.com/stories/senator-harry-s-truman-and-the-truman-committee/.

## Chapter 7

1    379th Bombardment Group (H) World War II Association, *379th Bombardment Group (H) Anthology, November 1942–July 1945: A Textual, Statistical, and Photographic History of the 379 Bombardment Group* (Paducah, KY: Turner, 2000), 264.

## Chapter 8

1    George C. Kenney, *The Saga of Pappy Gunn* (Los Angeles, CA: Enhanced Media Publishing, 2017).

2    Garrett Middlebrook, *Air Combat at 20 Feet: Selected Missions from a Strafer Pilot's Diary* (Bloomington, IN: Author House, 2004), 159.

3    "The Battle of Brisbane by Raymond Evans and Jacqui Donegan," Politics and Culture, August 10, 2010, https://politicsandculture.org/2010/08/10/the-battle-of-brisbane-by-raymond-evans-and-jacqui-donegan-2/.

4    Kate Darian-Smith, *On the Home Front: Melbourne in Wartime: 1939–1945* (Carlton, Vic.: Melbourne University Press, 2009), 183.

## Chapter 9

1    Thompson, MACR #15469.

2    Whipple, MACR #754.

3    George C. Kenney, *General Kenney Reports: A Personal History of the Pacific War* (Washington, D.C.: Air Force History and Museums Program, 1997) 136.

## Chapter 10

1    Bruce Gamble, *Target Rabaul: The Allied Siege of Japans Most Infamous Stronghold, March 1943–August 1945* (United States: Voyageur Press, 2013), 174.

2    Tameichi Hara, Fred Saito, and Roger Pineau, *Japanese Destroyer Captain: Pearl Harbor, Guadalcanal, Midway—The Great Naval Battles as Seen through Japanese Eyes* (Annapolis, MD: Naval Institute Press, 2011), 161.

3    USS *Drum*, Report of War Patrol EIGHT, 3–6.

4    Max B. Ferguson, *Bats Outa Hell over Biak* (Charleston, IL: Self, 1991), 94–95.

5    "C-47A-30-DL '*The Amazon*' Serial Number 42-23659," PacificWrecks.com, accessed February 14, 2020, https://www.pacificwrecks.com/Aircraft/c-47/42-23659.html.

## Chapter 11

1    Constable J. Althaus. "Police Report in Case of C-47 Crash near Canal Creek, 19 December, 1943," December 21, 1943, https://www.ozatwar.com/ozcrashes/qld56e.jpg.

## Chapter 12

1    Ferguson, *Bats Outa Hell over Biak*, 95.

## Chapter 14

1    William D. Miner and Lewis A. Miner, *Surrender on Cebu: a POWs Diary—WWII* (Paducah, KY: Turner Pub. Co., 2001), 121.

2    United States, Formal Relations of the United States, *Diplomatic Papers, 1944, Volume V, The Near East, South Asia and Africa, the Far East*, United States (Washington, D.C.: Historical Office, Bureau of Public Affairs, 1965), 932.

3    Gary Dielman, "The WWII Sinking of the 'Shinyo Maru': A Story of Loss and Survival of Two Baker POW's," Baker Library, 2015, https://www.bakerlib.org/files/archive/dielman-essays/2015-sinking-of-the-shinyo-maru.pdf

4    USS *Paddle*, Report of War Patrol FIVE, 7–11.

5    La Forte Robert S., Ronald E. Marcello, and Richard L. Himmel, *With Only the Will to Live: Accounts of Americans in Japanese Prison Camps, 1941–1945* (Wilmington, DE: SR Books, 1994), 264-265.

6    Eugene A. Mazza, "The American Prisoners of War Rescued after the Sinking of the Japanese Transport, *Shinyo Maru*, by the USS *Paddle*, SS 263, on 7 September 1944.," SubmarineSailor.com, February 15, 2004, http://www.submarinesailor.com/history/pow/paddlesinksshinyomaru/#Ref.

## Chapter 15

1    Robert Ross Smith, *Triumph in the Philippines* (Washington, D.C.: Center of Military History, United States Army, 1993), 220–241.

2    Robert B. Holland, *100 Miles to Freedom: The Epic Story of the Rescue of Santo Tomas and the Liberation of Manila, 1943-1945* (New York, NY: Turner Pub. Co., 2011), 58.

3    Mick Rhodes, "He Was Just a Kid in an Ugly War," *Claremont Courier,* October 19, 2017, https://www.claremont-courier.com/articles/news/t25369-jack.

4    Smith, *Triumph in the Philippines*, 220.

5    Rupert Wilkinson, *Surviving a Japanese Internment Camp Life and Liberation at Santo Tomás, Manila, in World War II* (Jefferson, NC: McFarland, 2014), 150.

6    Rupert Wilkinson, "Standoff at Santo Tomas," HistoryNet, May 17, 2017, https://www.historynet.com/standoff-santo-tomas.htm.

7   Holland, *100 Miles to Freedom*, 193.

8   Ann Marsh Hillegas, *Help Is on the Way: The Santo Tomas Diary of Annette and Scotty Marsh* (Bennington, VT: Merriam Press, 2009), 64.

9   Sidney L. Huff, *My Fifteen Years with General MacArthur* (New York, NY: Paperback Library, 1964), 92.

10  Marsh, *Help is on the Way*, 65.

## Chapter 16

1   Stephen Badsey, *The Hutchinson Atlas of World War II Battle Plans* (London: Routledge, 2016), 238.

2   Staff General, "Report on the Destruction of Manila and Japanese Atrocities" (Philippines: Headquarters, South West Pacific Area, February 1945), 8.

3   Ibid., 11–13.

4   Ibid., 38–40.

5   Ibid., 34.

6   Ibid., 64.

7   Ibid., 15–17.

## Chapter 18

1   Directive from Headquarters, Fifth Air Force, "Strafing of Friendly Forces," March 10, 1945.

2   Letter of Commendation, Headquarters, V Bomber Command, Office of the Commanding General, April 25, 1945.

3   Message to Commanding Officer, 3rd Bomb Group, from Colonel L.E. Lahti, Commanding Officer, 511th Parachute Infantry Regiment, May 4, 1945.

## Chapter 20

1   Robert Guillain, "I Thought My Last Hour Had Come," *The Atlantic*, August 1, 1980, https://www.theatlantic.com/magazine/archive/1980/08/-i-thought-my-last-hour-had-come/306349/.